OOMS FOR LIVING

126 Home Plans with Fabulous Great Rooms, Kitchens and Master Suites

Simple Design Tips for Creating a Comfortable Home

ROOMS FOR LIVING

Published by Home Planners, LLC
Wholly Owned by Hanley-Wood, LLC
One Thomas Circle, NW, Suite 600
Washington, DC 20005

Distribution Center
29333 Lorie Lane
Wixom, Michigan 48393

Group Vice President, General Manager, Andrew Schultz
Vice President, Publishing, Jennifer Pearce
Executive Editor, Linda Bellamy
Managing Editor, Jason D. Vaughan
Editor, Nate Ewell
Associate Editor, Simon Hyoun
Lead Plan Merchandiser, Morenci C. Clark
Plan Merchandiser, Nicole Phipps
Proofreader/Copywriter, Dyana Weis
Graphic Artist, Joong Min
Plan Data Team Leader, Ryan Emge
Production Manager, Brenda McClary

Vice President, Retail Sales, Scott Hill
National Sales Manager, Bruce Holmes
Director, Plan Products, Matt Higgins

For direct sales, contact Retail Vision at (800) 381-1288 ext 6053

BIG DESIGNS, INC.

President, Creative Director, Anthony D'Elia
Vice President, Business Manager, Megan D'Elia
Vice President, Design Director, Chris Bonavita
Editorial Director, John Roach
Assistant Editor, Tricia Starkey
Senior Art Director, Stephen Reinfurt
Production Director, David Barbella
Photo Editor, Christine DiVuolo
Art Director, Jessica Hagenbuch
Graphic Designer, Mary Ellen Mulshine
Graphic Designer, Lindsey O'Neill-Myers
Graphic Designer, Jacque Young
Assistant Photo Editor, Brian Wilson
Assistant Production Manager, Rich Fuentes

PHOTO CREDITS
Front Cover and Page 1, clockwise from left: Peter Loppacher;
Ivy D. Moriber; Alex Hayden; Mark Samu
Back Cover, top to bottom: Peter Loppacher; Mark Samu; Sam Gray

10 9 8 7 6 5 4 3 2 1

All floor plans and elevations copyright by the individual designers and may not be reproduced by any means without permission. All text, designs, and illustrative material copyright ©2004 by Home Planners, LLC, wholly owned by Hanley-Wood, LLC. All rights reserved. No part of this publication may be reproduced in any form or by any means — electronic, mechanical, photomechanical, recorded, or otherwise — without the prior written permission of the publisher.

Printed in the United States of America
Library of Congress Control Number: 2004106184

ISBN #: 1-931131-29-5

NIAGARA FALLS PUBLIC LIBRARY

COMMUNITY CENTRE BRANCH LIBRARY
MAY -- 2005

ROOMS FOR LIVING

Chapter One
GREAT ROOMS
4

Chapter Two
KITCHENS
54

Chapter Three
MASTER SUITES
102

153 APPENDIX: How to Order Blueprints

Rooms For Living

GREAT ROOMS

By virtue of their size and function, great rooms can do more to define the interior of our homes than any other room in the house. They are our natural gathering areas, usually connecting seamlessly with other rooms and offering plenty of space for family and friends to get together. There's also a warm, comfortable feeling in the very best great rooms, something that was missing in so many of the traditional living room designs of the past. Creating this welcoming atmosphere begins with the design and décor of your great room— start there, and you'll be able to boast a great room that truly lives up to its name.

window seats offer
the best view in the house
plus added space when entertaining

GREAT ROOMS

Above: The thoughtful addition of a bar makes the great room a perfect spot for entertaining. While an open floor plan connects the room the dining room, breakfast area, and kitchen, the built-in bar saves steps for guests and gives the room an all-inclusive feel.

Left: A distinctive granite fireplace and soft leather furnishings create a wonderful rustic atmosphere in this room. The soaring windows fit well, highlighting the spectacular view. The drapes on the lower windows can be drawn for privacy while still allowing natural light to stream in from above.

ROOMS FOR LIVING   7

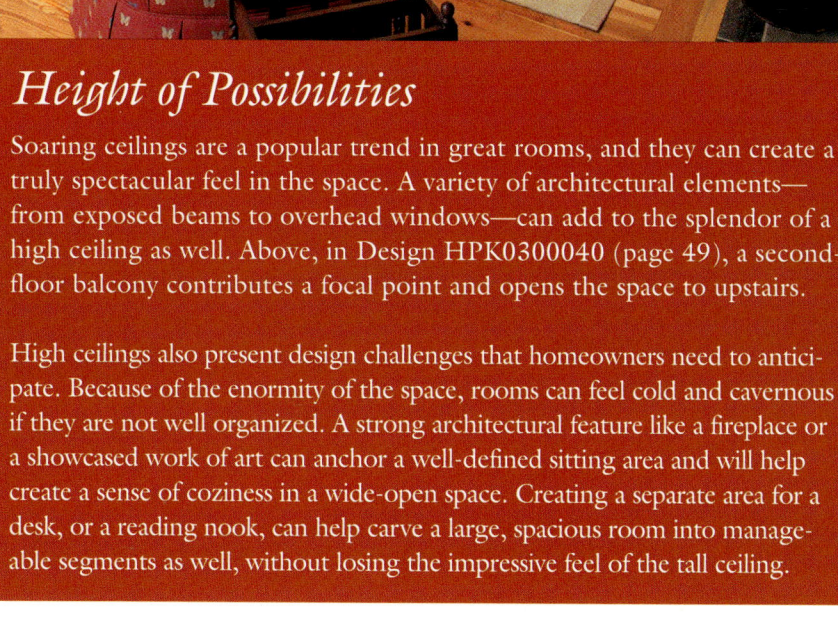

GREAT ROOMS

Height of Possibilities

Soaring ceilings are a popular trend in great rooms, and they can create a truly spectacular feel in the space. A variety of architectural elements—from exposed beams to overhead windows—can add to the splendor of a high ceiling as well. Above, in Design HPK0300040 (page 49), a second-floor balcony contributes a focal point and opens the space to upstairs.

High ceilings also present design challenges that homeowners need to anticipate. Because of the enormity of the space, rooms can feel cold and cavernous if they are not well organized. A strong architectural feature like a fireplace or a showcased work of art can anchor a well-defined sitting area and will help create a sense of coziness in a wide-open space. Creating a separate area for a desk, or a reading nook, can help carve a large, spacious room into manageable segments as well, without losing the impressive feel of the tall ceiling.

Great rooms provide space for everyone in the family, even if they are engaged in different activities. Here, the focus of the room is a charming sitting area, but a corner desk provides a spot to write correspondence or pay bills.

Welcome Home

This beautiful farmhouse, with its prominent twin gables and bays, adds just the right amount of country style. The master suite is quietly tucked away downstairs with no rooms directly above. The family cook will love the spacious U-shaped kitchen and adjoining bayed breakfast nook. A bonus room awaits expansion on the second floor, where three large bedrooms share two full baths. Just steps away from any spot in the home, the stunning two-story family room anchors the plan. Its stone hearth and second-floor balcony add unique touches to a room family and friends will never want to leave.

Clockwise from top right: A grand stone hearth highlights the soaring ceiling in the spacious family room. The dining room enjoys access to the outdoors, perfect for summer gatherings. The large front porch sets the tone for this charming farmhouse, which features large bay windows and expansive outdoor living spaces.

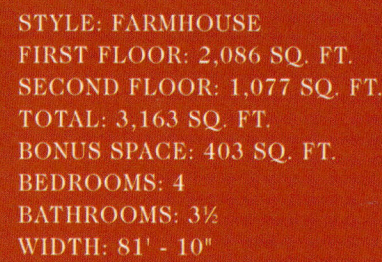

GREAT ROOMS

the balcony and windows above
accentuate the height
of the impressive two-story family room

plan# HPK0300007

STYLE: FARMHOUSE
FIRST FLOOR: 2,086 SQ. FT.
SECOND FLOOR: 1,077 SQ. FT.
TOTAL: 3,163 SQ. FT.
BONUS SPACE: 403 SQ. FT.
BEDROOMS: 4
BATHROOMS: 3½
WIDTH: 81' - 10"
DEPTH: 51' - 8"

SEARCH ONLINE @ EPLANS.COM

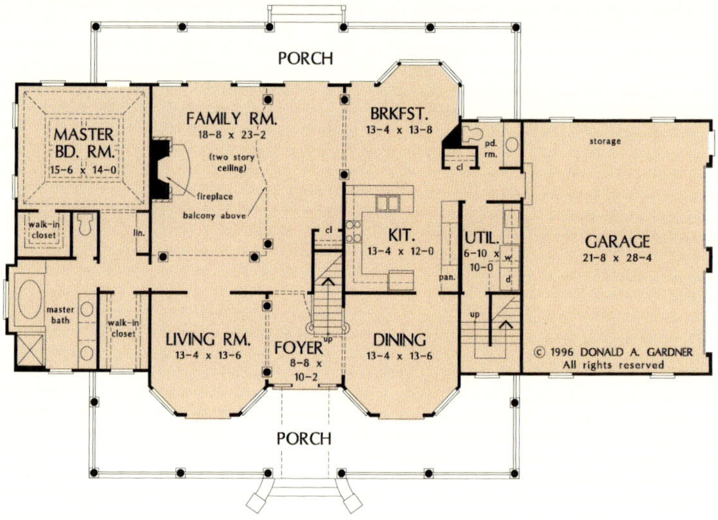

FOR MORE DETAILED INFORMATION, PLEASE CHECK THE FLOOR PLANS CAREFULLY.

FIRST FLOOR

PORCH

MASTER BD. RM. 15-6 x 14-0

FAMILY RM. 18-8 x 23-2 (two story ceiling) fireplace balcony above

BRKFST. 13-4 x 13-8

storage

walk-in closet

lin.

pd. rm.

cl

KIT. 13-4 x 12-0

UTIL. 6-10 x 10-0

GARAGE 21-8 x 28-4

pan.

master bath

walk-in closet

LIVING RM. 13-4 x 13-6

FOYER 8-8 x 10-2 up

DINING 13-4 x 13-6

up

© 1996 DONALD A. GARDNER
All rights reserved

PORCH

SECOND FLOOR

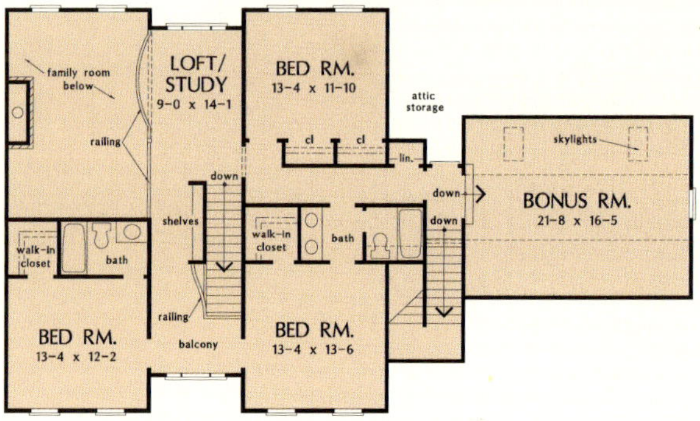

family room below

LOFT/ STUDY 9-0 x 14-1

BED RM. 13-4 x 11-10

attic storage

railing

cl cl

lin.

skylights

down

down

BONUS RM. 21-8 x 16-5

walk-in closet

bath

shelves

walk-in closet

bath

down

BED RM. 13-4 x 12-2

railing

balcony

BED RM. 13-4 x 13-6

ORDER BLUEPRINTS 24 HOURS, 7 DAYS A WEEK, AT 1-800-521-6797

ROOMS FOR LIVING   11

Poolside Retreat

Three dormers top a very welcoming covered wraparound porch on this attractive country home. The entrance enjoys a Palladian clerestory window, lending an abundance of natural light to the foyer. The great room furthers this feeling of airiness with a balcony above and two sets of sliding glass doors leading to the back porch. For privacy, the master suite occupies the right side of the first floor. With a sitting bay and all the amenities of a modern master bath, this lavish retreat will be a welcome haven for the homeowner. Two family bedrooms reside upstairs, sharing a balcony overlook into the great room.

With porches in the front (below) and back (right), this country home embraces outdoor living.

GREAT ROOMS

an open design
connects this room
with the kitchen and outdoors

---

plan# HPK0300008

STYLE: FARMHOUSE
FIRST FLOOR: 2,316 SQ. FT.
SECOND FLOOR: 721 SQ. FT.
TOTAL: 3,037 SQ. FT.
BONUS SPACE: 545 SQ. FT.
BEDROOMS: 4
BATHROOMS: 3½
WIDTH: 95' - 4"
DEPTH: 54' - 10"

SEARCH ONLINE @ EPLANS.COM

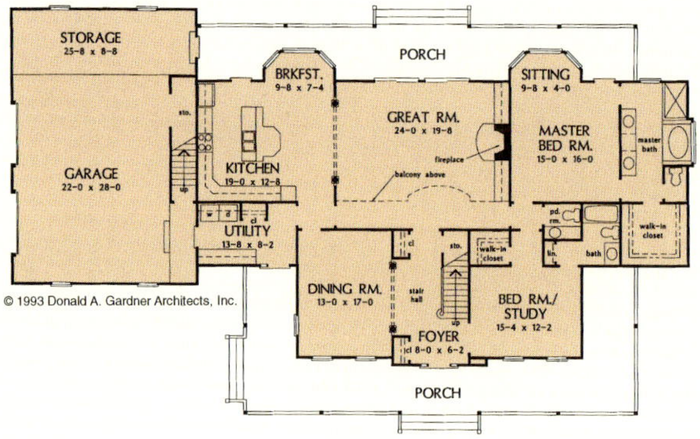

FIRST FLOOR

SECOND FLOOR

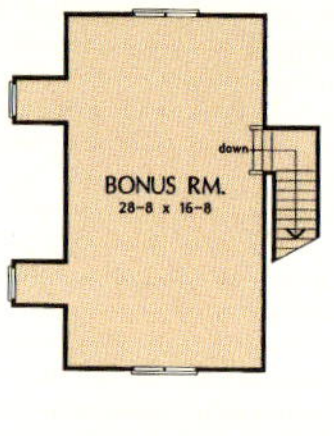

BONUS RM.
28-8 x 16-8

© 1993 Donald A. Gardner Architects, Inc.

ORDER BLUEPRINTS 24 HOURS, 7 DAYS A WEEK, AT 1-800-521-6797   ROOMS FOR LIVING   13

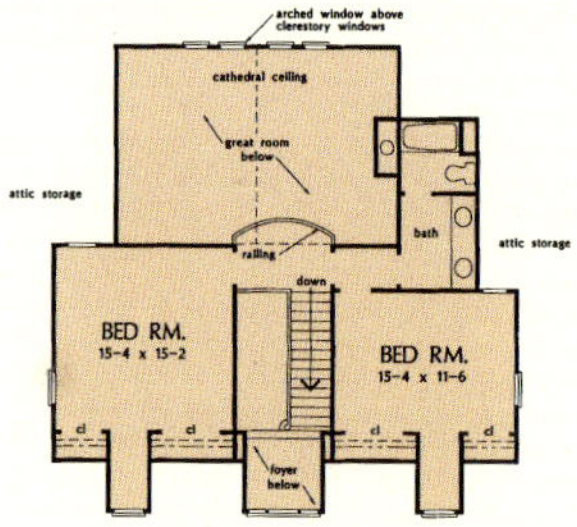

GREAT ROOMS

GABLE-ON-GABLE DETAILS AND AN ENTRY ADORNED with

thick columns creates a distinctly interesting exterior for this four-bedroom home. The den and formal dining rooms take their traditional position near the entry for this design. At the center of the plan, the family room enjoys a warming fireplace. To the left are two family bedrooms and a den/study and to the right are the gourmet kitchen and breakfast nook. The luxurious master suite contains many amenities, including a tray ceiling, a walk-in closet, French-door access to the rear patio, and a sumptuous bathroom with a corner oval soaking tub. Bedroom 4 features a full bath and a sitting room on the second floor.

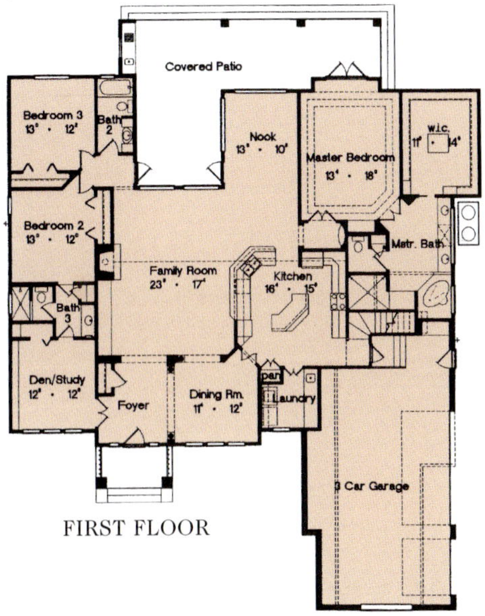

plan # HPK0300006

STYLE: FARMHOUSE
FIRST FLOOR: 2,837 SQ. FT.
SECOND FLOOR: 609 SQ. FT.
TOTAL: 3,446 SQ. FT.
BEDROOMS: 4
BATHROOMS: 4
WIDTH: 68' - 0"
DEPTH: 83' - 4"
FOUNDATION: SLAB

SEARCH ONLINE @ EPLANS.COM

FIRST FLOOR

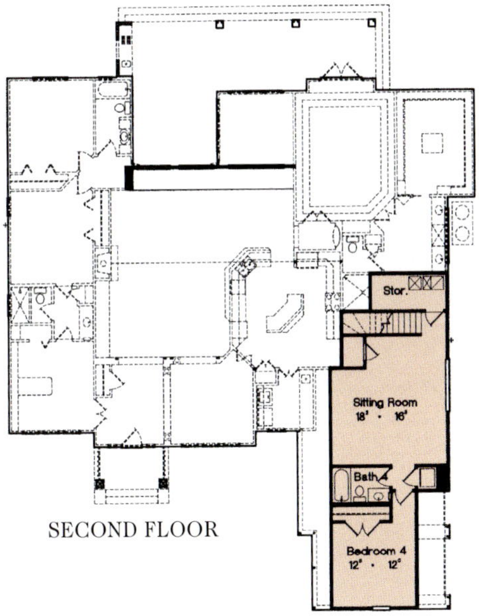

SECOND FLOOR

GREAT ROOMS

plan# HPK0300009

STYLE: CRAFTSMAN
FIRST FLOOR: 2,782 SQ. FT.
SECOND FLOOR: 1,027 SQ. FT.
TOTAL: 3,809 SQ. FT.
BEDROOMS: 4
BATHROOMS: 4½
WIDTH: 78' - 2"
DEPTH: 74' - 6"
FOUNDATION: BASEMENT

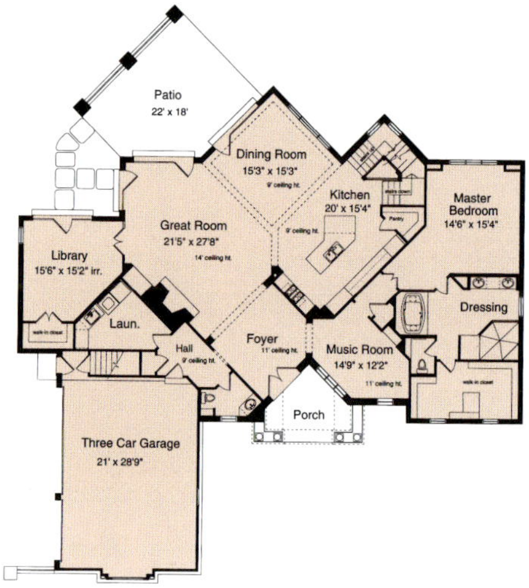

SEARCH ONLINE @ EPLANS.COM

FILLED WITH SPECIALTY ROOMS AND ABUNDANT amenities, this countryside house is the perfect dream home. Double doors open into an angled foyer, flanked by a music room and a formal great room warmed by a fireplace. The music room leads to the master wing of the home, which includes a spacious bath with a dressing area and double walk-in closet. The great room is the heart of the home—its central position allows access to the island kitchen, formal dining room, and library. Stairs behind the kitchen lead upstairs to a balcony, accessing three family bedrooms. The lower level features a billiard room, hobby room, media room, and future possibilities.

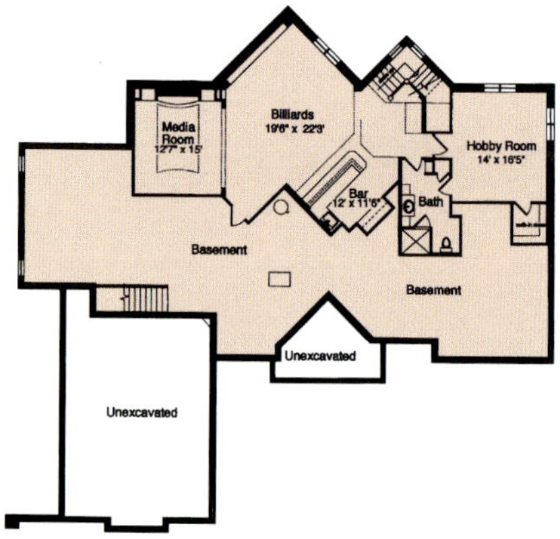

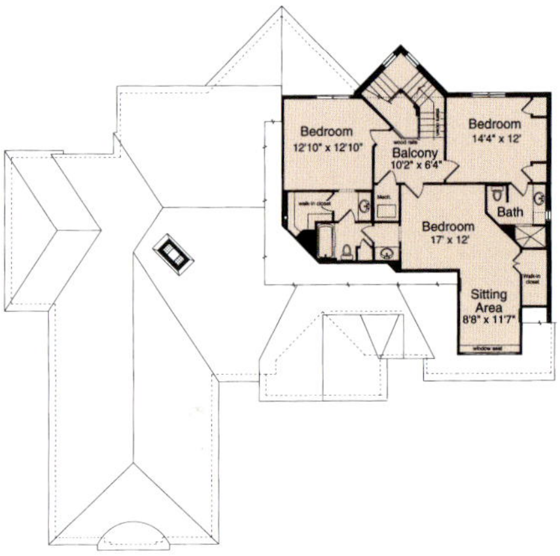

SECOND FLOOR

FIRST FLOOR

BASEMENT

GREAT ROOMS

PERHAPS THE MOST NOTABLE CHARACTERISTIC OF this traditional house is its masterful use of space. The glorious great room, open dining room, and handsome den serve as the heart of the home. A cozy hearth room with a fireplace rounds out the kitchen and breakfast area. The master bedroom opens up to a private sitting room with a fireplace. Three family bedrooms occupy the second floor, each with private baths. Other special features include a four-car garage, a corner whirlpool tub in the master bath, a walk-in pantry and snack bar in the kitchen, and transom windows in the dining room.

plan # HPK03000010

STYLE: TRADITIONAL
FIRST FLOOR: 2,603 SQ. FT.
SECOND FLOOR: 1,020 SQ. FT.
TOTAL: 3,623 SQ. FT.
BEDROOMS: 4
BATHROOMS: 4½
WIDTH: 76' - 8"
DEPTH: 68' - 0"

SEARCH ONLINE @ EPLANS.COM

GREAT ROOMS

plan# HPK0300001

STYLE: TRADITIONAL
FIRST FLOOR: 3,218 SQ. FT.
SECOND FLOOR: 1,240 SQ. FT.
TOTAL: 4,458 SQ. FT.
BONUS SPACE: 656 SQ. FT.
BEDROOMS: 4
BATHROOMS: 3½
WIDTH: 76' - 0"
DEPTH: 73' - 10"
FOUNDATION: BASEMENT

SEARCH ONLINE @ EPLANS.COM

THIS DESIGN FEATURES A BREATHTAKING FACADE WITH

an upper rear balcony, four covered porches, and an inconspicuous side garage. The foyer is flanked by the dining room and the two-story library, which includes a fireplace and built-in bookcases. The elegant master bath provides dual vanities, a bright radius window, and a separate leaded-glass shower. A unique double-decker walk-in closet provides plenty of storage. Nearby, a home office offers stunning views of the backyard. Upstairs, two family bedrooms share a compartmented bath and a covered porch; a third offers a private bath. A bonus room is included for future expansion.

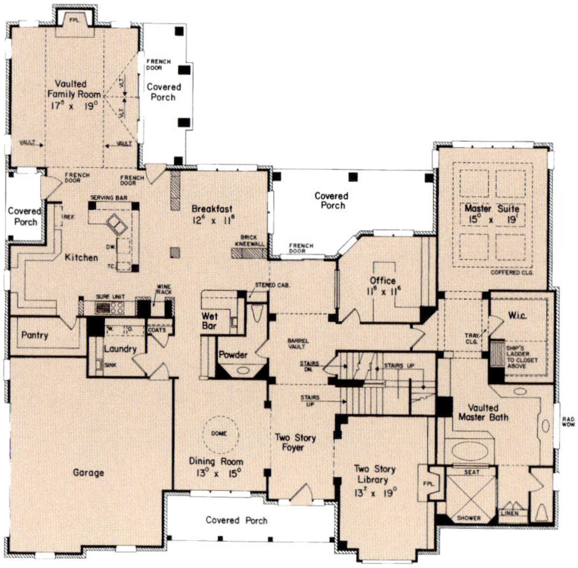

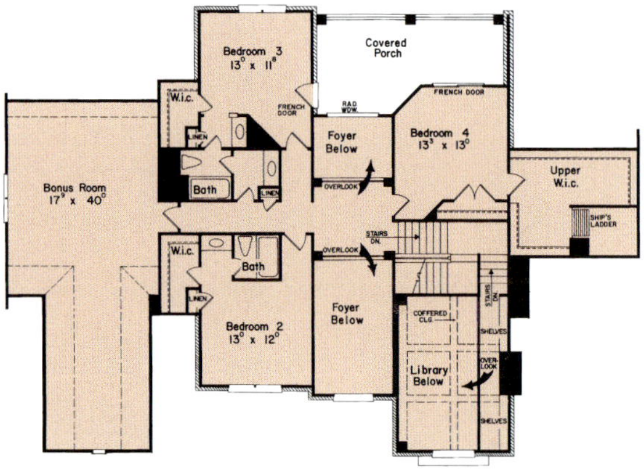

ORDER BLUEPRINTS 24 HOURS, 7 DAYS A WEEK, AT 1-800-521-6797

GREAT ROOMS

MAKE DREAMS COME TRUE

with this fine sunny design. An octagonal study provides a nice focal point both inside and out. The living areas remain open to each other and access outdoor areas. A wet bar makes entertaining a breeze, especially with a window pass-through to a grill area on the lanai. The kitchen enjoys shared space with a lovely breakfast nook and a bright leisure room. Two bedrooms are located near the family living center. In the master bedroom suite, luxury abounds with a two-way fireplace, a morning kitchen, two walk-in closets, and a compartmented bath. Another full bath accommodates a pool area.

plan # HPK0300011

STYLE: FLORIDIAN
SQUARE FOOTAGE: 3,477
BEDROOMS: 3
BATHROOMS: 3½
WIDTH: 95' - 0"
DEPTH: 88' - 8"
FOUNDATION: SLAB

SEARCH ONLINE @ EPLANS.COM

GREAT ROOMS

plan# HPK0300012

STYLE: FLORIDIAN
SQUARE FOOTAGE: 4,187
BEDROOMS: 3
BATHROOMS: 3½
WIDTH: 84' - 8"
DEPTH: 114' - 0"
FOUNDATION: SLAB

SEARCH ONLINE @ EPLANS.COM

THIS CONTEMPORARY

masterpiece features many trendsetting details. The exterior lines are clean, but exciting. At the covered entry, a Palladian-style metal grille adds interest. Beyond the foyer, the living room opens up to the lanai through corner glass doors. The doors pocket into the wall, giving the feeling that the outdoors become one with the living area. The informal leisure area is perfect for family gatherings. Full guest suites and an exercise or hobby room are located in the guest wing. The master wing features a study with curved glass, a luxurious bath with His and Hers vanities, a large walk-in closet, and a large sleeping area and sitting bay.

GREAT ROOMS

plan # HPK0300013

STYLE: FRENCH
FIRST FLOOR: 2,899 SQ. FT.
SECOND FLOOR: 1,472 SQ. FT.
TOTAL: 4,371 SQ. FT.
BEDROOMS: 4
BATHROOMS: 3½
WIDTH: 69' - 4"
DEPTH: 76' - 8"
FOUNDATION: SLAB

SEARCH ONLINE @ EPLANS.COM

FINISHED WITH FRENCH COUNTRY ADORNMENTS, THIS estate home is comfortable in just about any setting. Main living areas are sunk down just a bit from the entry foyer, providing them with soaring ceilings and sweeping views. The family room features a focal fireplace. A columned entry gains access to the master suite where separate sitting and sleeping areas are defined by a three-sided fireplace. There are three bedrooms upstairs; one has a private bath. The sunken media room on this level includes storage space. Look for the decks on the second level.

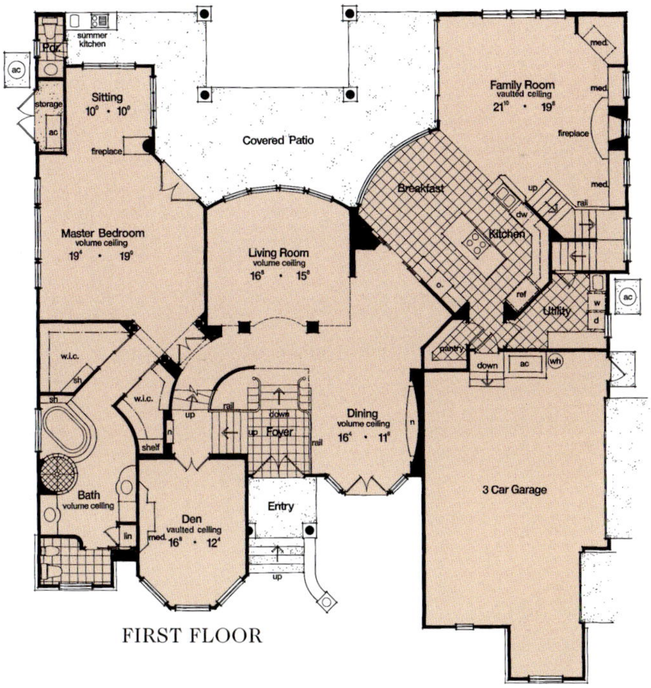

FIRST FLOOR

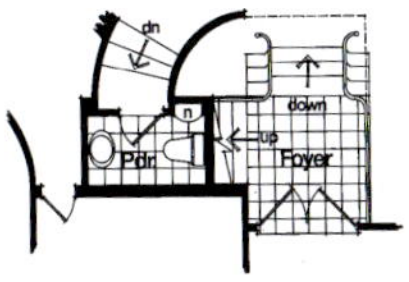

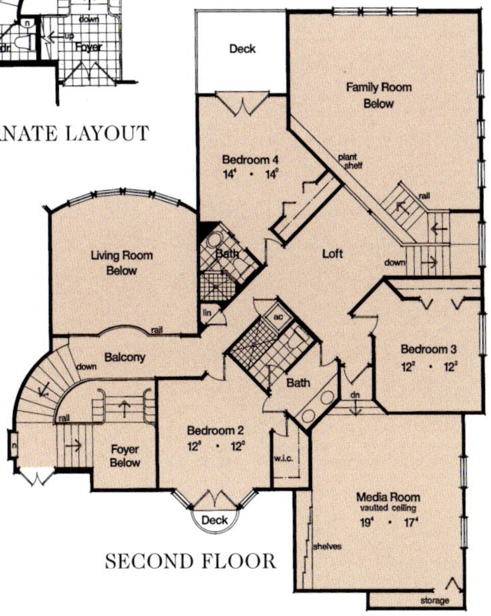

SECOND FLOOR

ALTERNATE LAYOUT

GREAT ROOMS

plan # HPK03000014

STYLE: MEDITERRANEAN
SQUARE FOOTAGE: 3,424
BONUS SPACE: 507 SQ. FT.
BEDROOMS: 5
BATHROOMS: 4
WIDTH: 82' - 4"
DEPTH: 83' - 8"
FOUNDATION: SLAB

SEARCH ONLINE @ EPLANS.COM

THIS LOVELY FIVE-BEDROOM home exudes the beauty and warmth of a Mediterranean villa. The foyer views explode in all directions with the dominant use of octagonal shapes throughout. Double doors lead to the master wing, which abounds with niches. The sitting area of the master bedroom has a commanding view of the rear gardens. A bedroom just off the master suite is perfect for a guest room or office. The formal living and dining rooms share expansive glass walls and marble or tile pathways. The mitered glass wall of the breakfast nook can be viewed from the huge island kitchen. Two secondary bedrooms share the convenience of a Pullman-style bath. An additional rear bedroom completes this design.

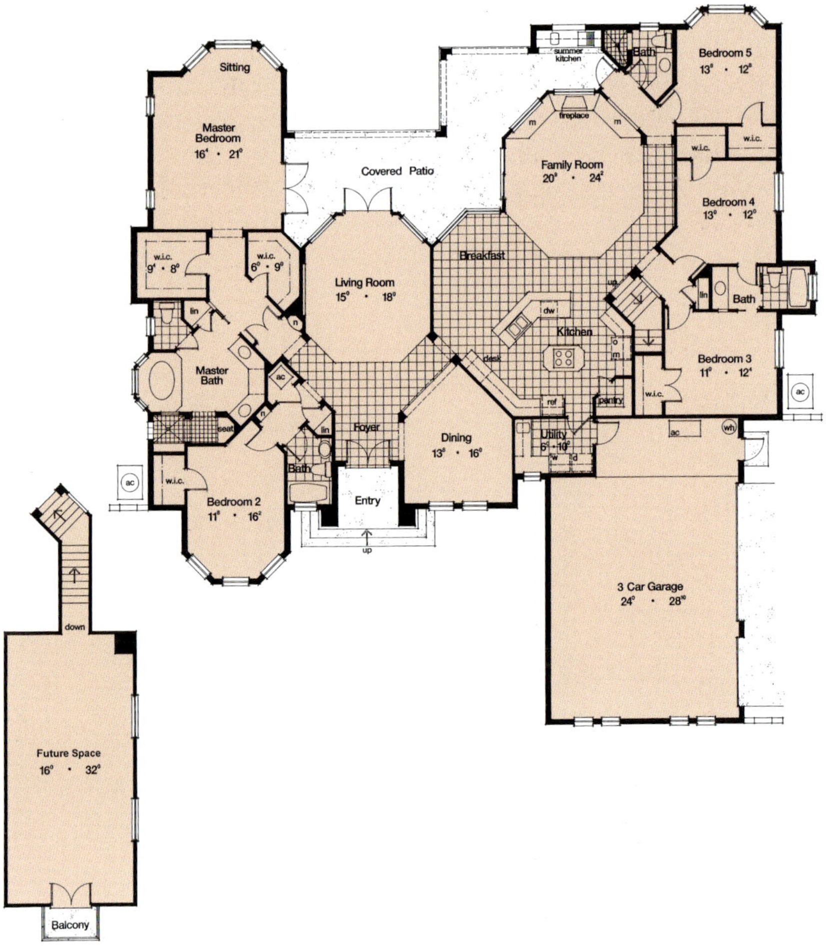

GREAT ROOMS

plan # HPK0300015

STYLE: FLORIDIAN
FIRST FLOOR: 1,684 SQ. FT.
SECOND FLOOR: 1,195 SQ. FT.
TOTAL: 2,879 SQ. FT.
BONUS SPACE: 674 SQ. FT.
BEDROOMS: 3
BATHROOMS: 3
WIDTH: 45' - 0"
DEPTH: 52' - 0"
FOUNDATION: PIER

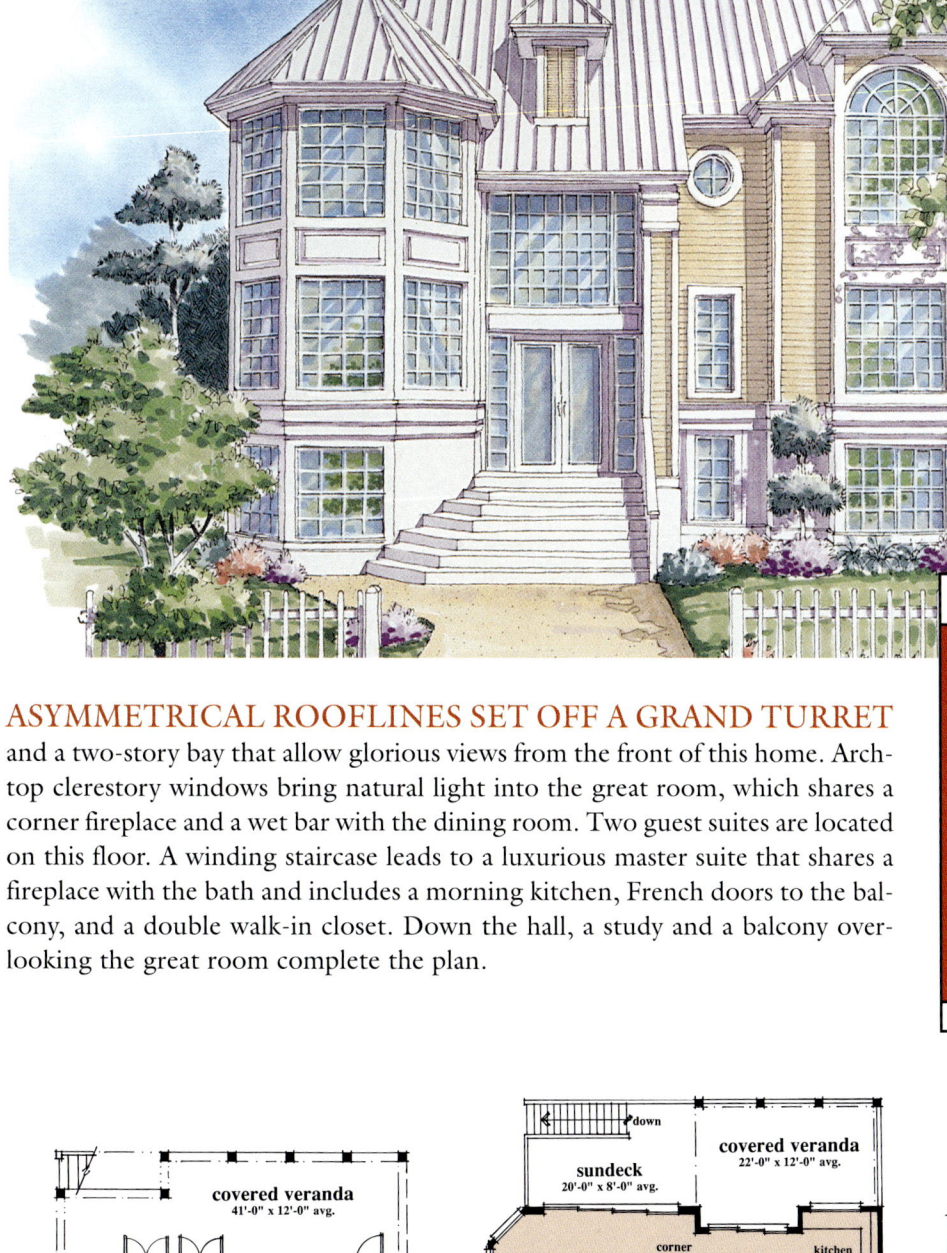

SEARCH ONLINE @ EPLANS.COM

ASYMMETRICAL ROOFLINES SET OFF A GRAND TURRET

and a two-story bay that allow glorious views from the front of this home. Arch-top clerestory windows bring natural light into the great room, which shares a corner fireplace and a wet bar with the dining room. Two guest suites are located on this floor. A winding staircase leads to a luxurious master suite that shares a fireplace with the bath and includes a morning kitchen, French doors to the balcony, and a double walk-in closet. Down the hall, a study and a balcony overlooking the great room complete the plan.

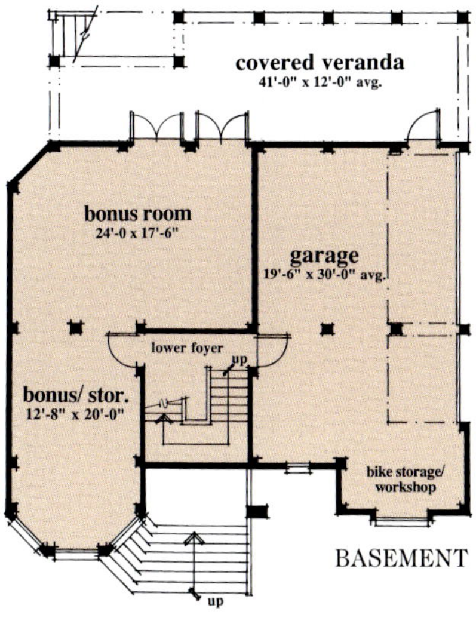

BASEMENT

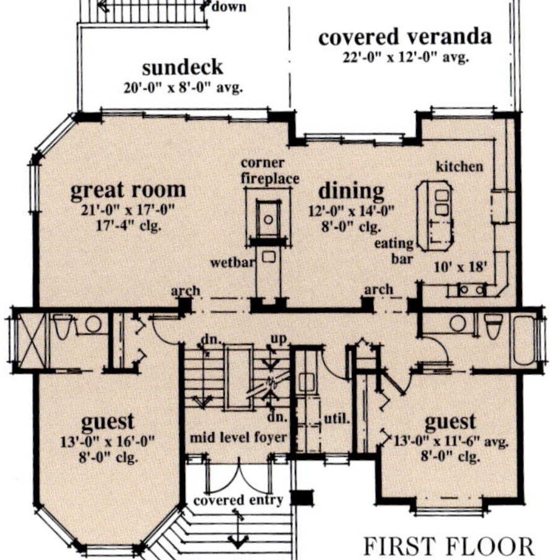

FIRST FLOOR

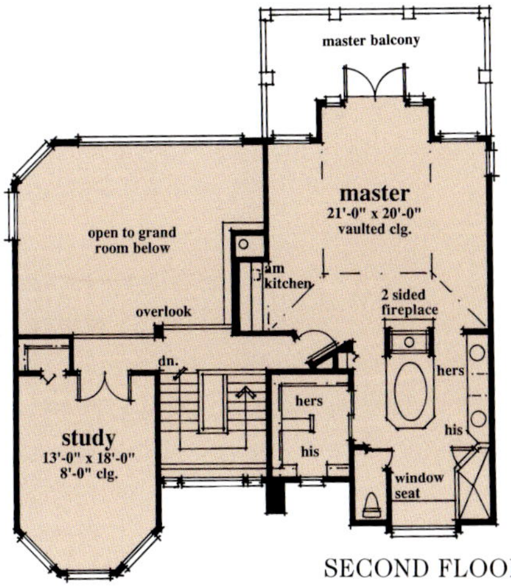

SECOND FLOOR

22   ROOMS FOR LIVING

ORDER BLUEPRINTS 24 HOURS, 7 DAYS A WEEK, AT 1-800-521-6797

GREAT ROOMS

IF ENTERTAINING IS YOUR PASSION, THEN THIS IS THE

design for you. With a large, open floor plan and an array of amenities, every gathering will be a success. The foyer embraces living areas accented by a glass fireplace and a wet bar. The grand room and dining room each access a screened veranda for outside enjoyment. The gourmet kitchen delights with its openness to the rest of the house. A morning nook here also adds a nice touch. Two bedrooms and a study radiate from the first-floor living areas. Upstairs—or use the elevator—is a masterful master suite. It contains a huge walk-in closet, a whirlpool tub, and a private sundeck with a spa.

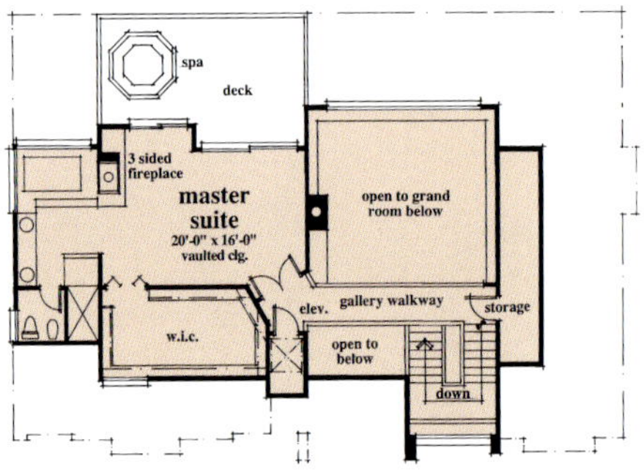

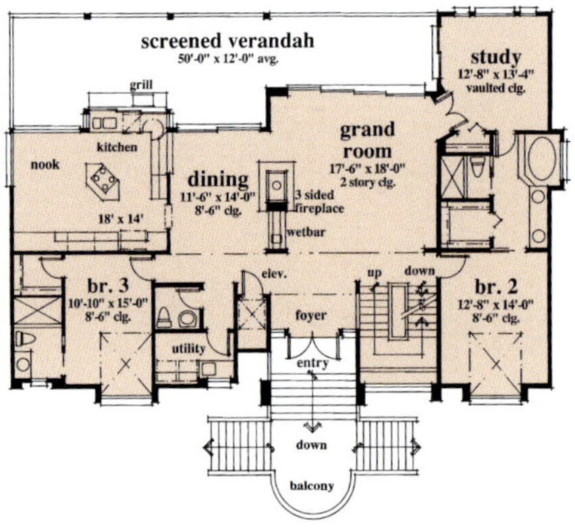

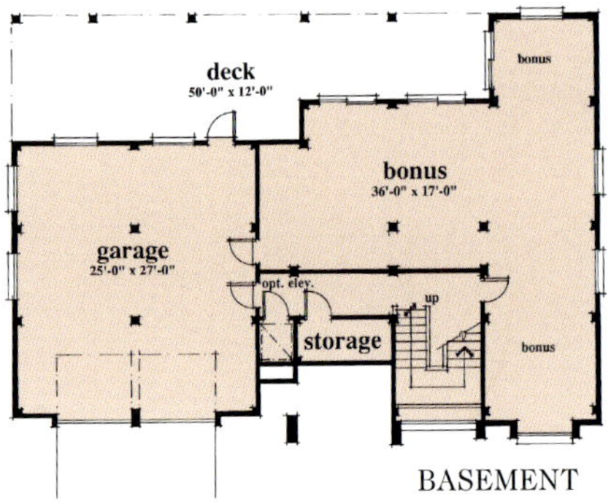

plan # HPK0300016

STYLE: FLORIDIAN
FIRST FLOOR: 2,066 SQ. FT.
SECOND FLOOR: 809 SQ. FT.
TOTAL: 2,875 SQ. FT.
BONUS SPACE: 1,260 SQ. FT.
BEDROOMS: 3
BATHROOMS: 3½
WIDTH: 64' - 0"
DEPTH: 45' - 0"
FOUNDATION: PIER

SEARCH ONLINE @ EPLANS.COM

ROOMS FOR LIVING 23

ORDER BLUEPRINTS 24 HOURS, 7 DAYS A WEEK, AT 1-800-521-6797

GREAT ROOMS

THIS ITALIAN RENAISSANCE MARVEL HAS IT ALL—FIVE

bedrooms, a game room, a theater, and expansive areas for formal parties and relaxed barbecues. A covered patio winds around the entire rear of the home, and a sundeck is located on the second level. A wet bar and circular balcony, with an outside spiral stairway, make the upstairs game room a great party site. The lavish master suite features a circular sitting area with windows drawing in natural light from many directions. A spiral stairway winds gracefully upstairs from the impressive main-floor entry, or, if you prefer, take the elevator. A semicircular turret on the corner of the three-car garage is not only flashy, it is a handy storage area.

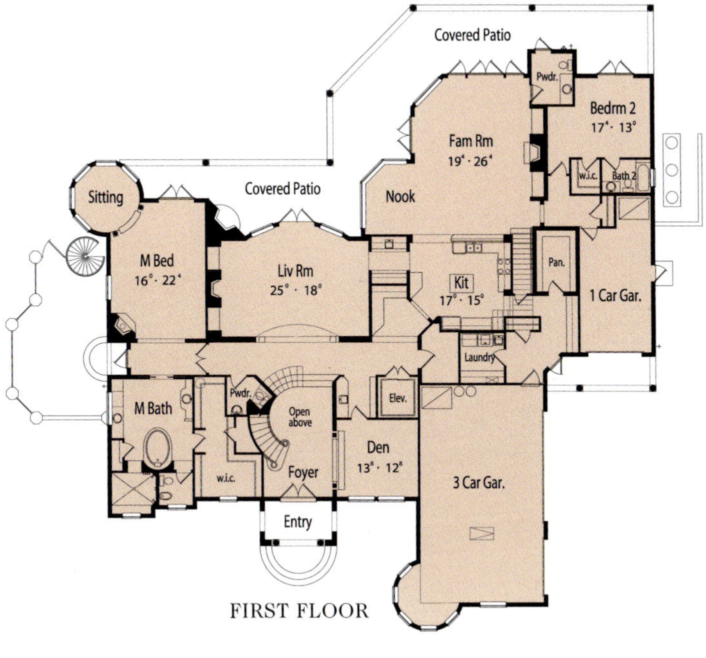

plan# HPK0300017

STYLE: MEDITERRANEAN
FIRST FLOOR: 4,323 SQ. FT.
SECOND FLOOR: 2,226 SQ. FT.
TOTAL: 6,549 SQ. FT.
BONUS SPACE: 453 SQ. FT.
BEDROOMS: 5
BATHROOMS: 5½ + ½
WIDTH: 98' - 8"
DEPTH: 102' - 8"
FOUNDATION: SLAB

SEARCH ONLINE @ EPLANS.COM

FIRST FLOOR

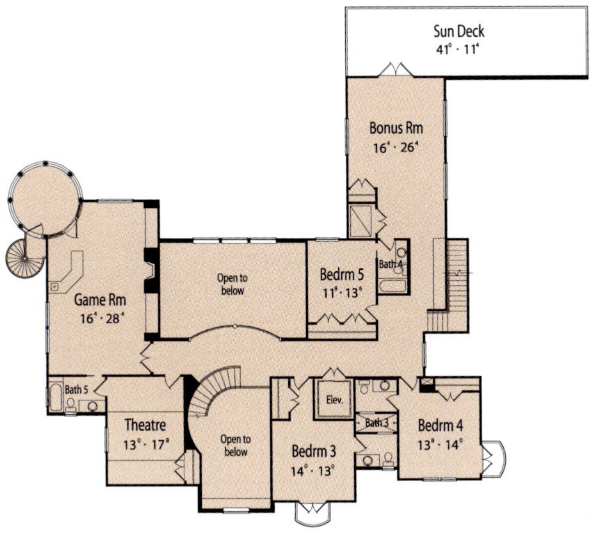

SECOND FLOOR

24   ROOMS FOR LIVING   ORDER BLUEPRINTS 24 HOURS, 7 DAYS A WEEK, AT 1-800-521-6797

GREAT ROOMS

plan # HPK0300018

STYLE: ITALIANATE
FIRST FLOOR: 3,745 SQ. FT.
SECOND FLOOR: 1,250 SQ. FT.
TOTAL: 4,995 SQ. FT.
BEDROOMS: 4
BATHROOMS: 4½
WIDTH: 95' - 4"
DEPTH: 89' - 10"
FOUNDATION: SLAB

SEARCH ONLINE @ EPLANS.COM

GIVING THE IMPRESSION OF A LUXURIOUS VILLA resort, this Italian country home is a study in fine living. Arched windows mark the grand entry, where a formal foyer reveals an elegant dining room on the right and a light-filled great room just ahead. An inglenook, characterized by its cozy fireplace, is a wonderful place to relax or enjoy a casual meal. Three family suites are located on the left, graced by a curved-window hallway. The master suite enjoys solitude on the upper level and hosts a private sitting room and lavish bath with a separate vanity and Roman tub. Other extras not to be missed: a cabana bath, eight pairs of French doors to the rear lanai, and ample garage storage.

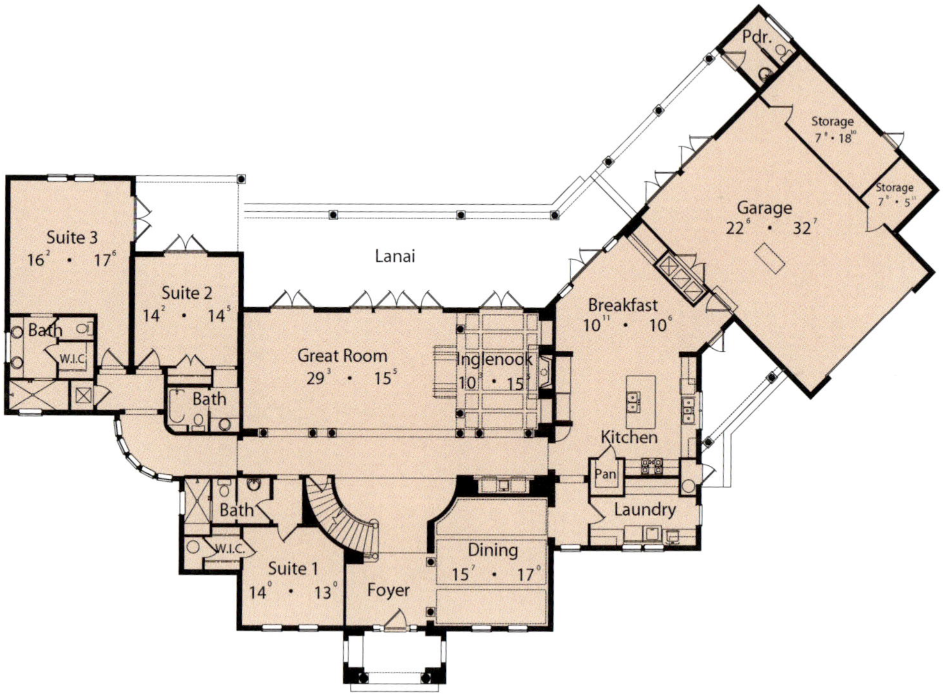

FIRST FLOOR

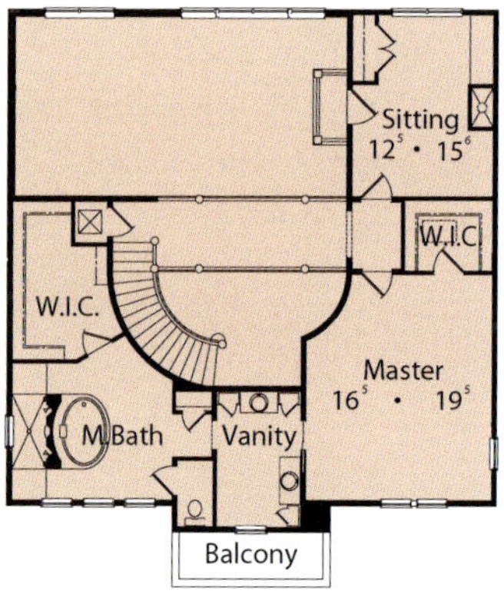

SECOND FLOOR

GREAT ROOMS

plan # HPK0300019

STYLE: MEDITERRANEAN
FIRST FLOOR: 4,760 SQ. FT.
SECOND FLOOR: 1,552 SQ. FT.
TOTAL: 6,312 SQ. FT.
BEDROOMS: 5
BATHROOMS: 6½
WIDTH: 98' - 0"
DEPTH: 103' - 8"
FOUNDATION: SLAB

SEARCH ONLINE @ EPLANS.COM

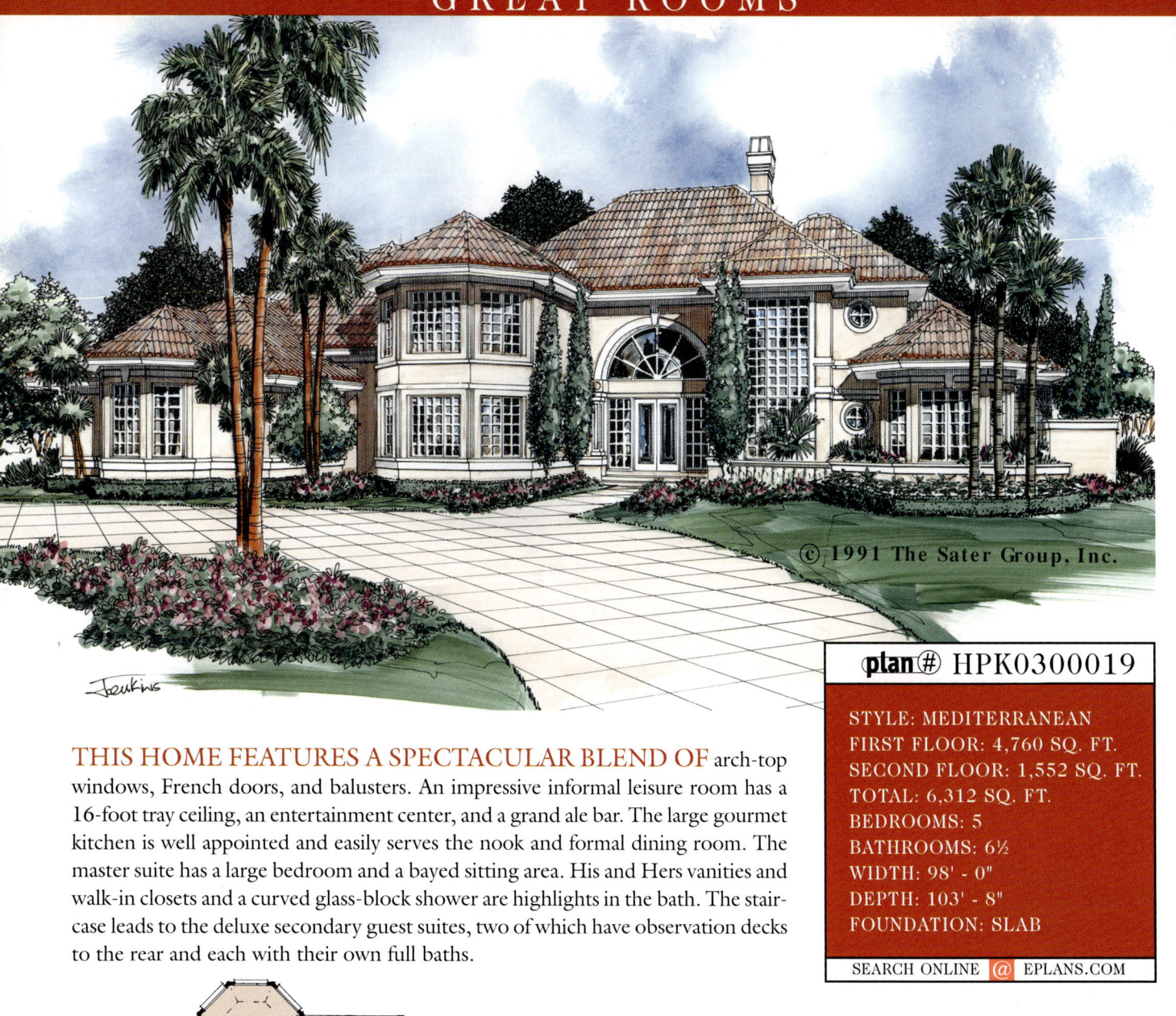

THIS HOME FEATURES A SPECTACULAR BLEND OF arch-top windows, French doors, and balusters. An impressive informal leisure room has a 16-foot tray ceiling, an entertainment center, and a grand ale bar. The large gourmet kitchen is well appointed and easily serves the nook and formal dining room. The master suite has a large bedroom and a bayed sitting area. His and Hers vanities and walk-in closets and a curved glass-block shower are highlights in the bath. The staircase leads to the deluxe secondary guest suites, two of which have observation decks to the rear and each with their own full baths.

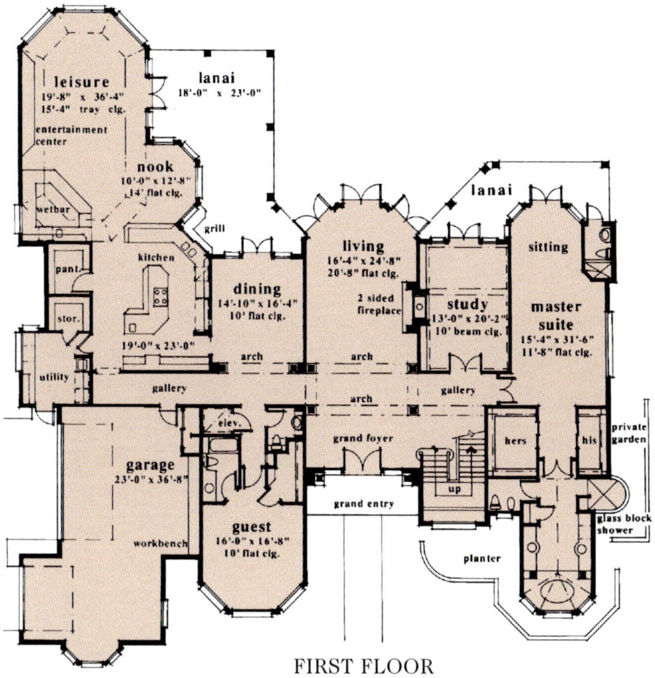

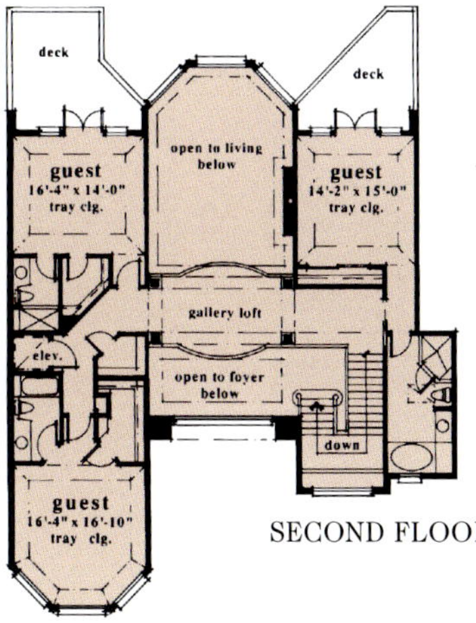

© 1991 The Sater Group, Inc.

GREAT ROOMS

plan # HPK0300020

STYLE: ITALIANATE
FIRST FLOOR: 2,841 SQ. FT.
SECOND FLOOR: 1,052 SQ. FT.
TOTAL: 3,893 SQ. FT.
BEDROOMS: 4
BATHROOMS: 3½
WIDTH: 85' - 0"
DEPTH: 76' - 8"
FOUNDATION: SLAB, BASEMENT

SEARCH ONLINE @ EPLANS.COM

ENSURE AN ELEGANT LIFESTYLE WITH THIS LUXURIOUS

plan. A turret, two-story bay windows, and plenty of arched glass impart a graceful style to the exterior, and rich amenities inside furnish contentment. A grand foyer decked with columns introduces the living room with curved-glass windows viewing the rear gardens. The study and living room share a through-fireplace. The master suite enjoys a tray ceiling, two walk-in closets, a separate shower, and a garden tub set in a bay window. Informal entertainment will be a breeze with a rich leisure room adjoining the kitchen and breakfast nook and opening to a rear veranda. Upstairs, two family bedrooms and a guest suite complete with a private deck complete the plan.

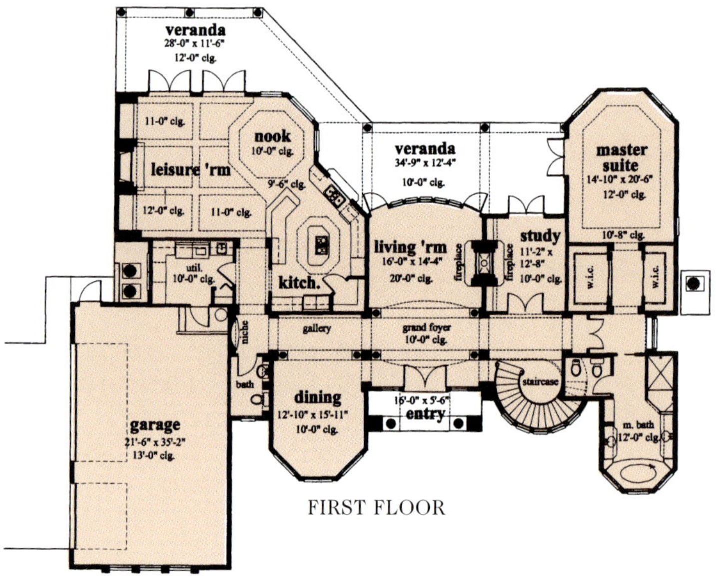

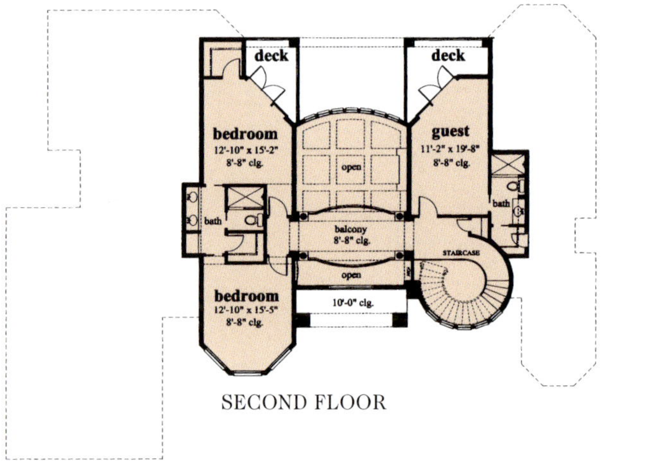

GREAT ROOMS

plan# HPK0300021

STYLE: MEDITERRANEAN
SQUARE FOOTAGE: 4,222
BONUS SPACE: 590 SQ. FT.
BEDROOMS: 4
BATHROOMS: 5
WIDTH: 83' - 10"
DEPTH: 112' - 0"
FOUNDATION: SLAB

SEARCH ONLINE @ EPLANS.COM

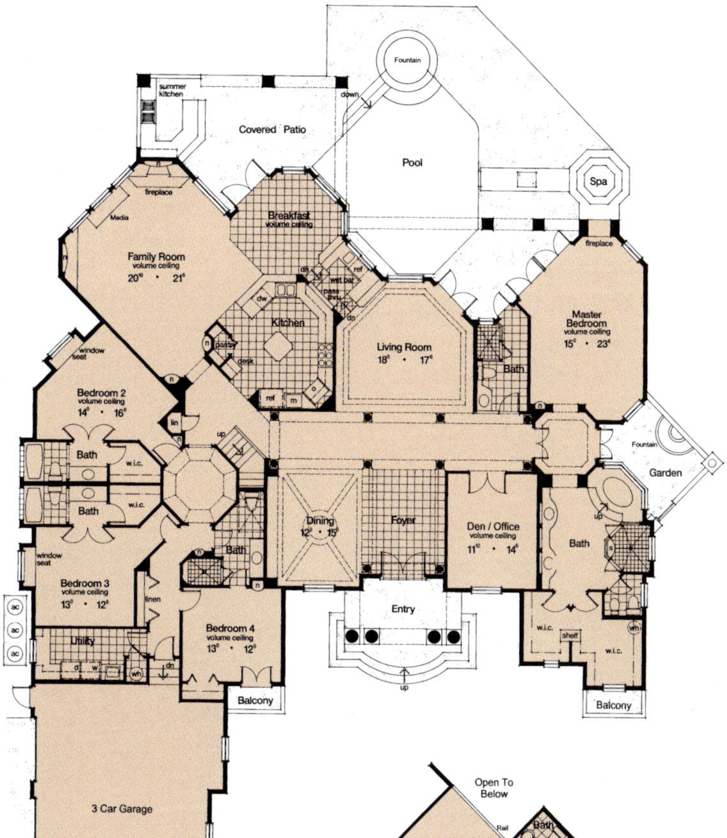

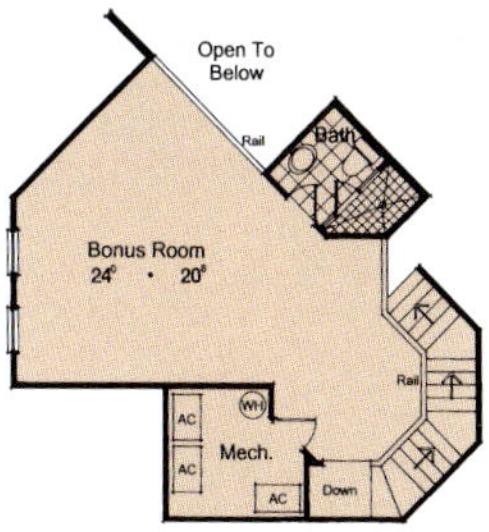

THE STRIKING FACADE of this magnificent estate is just the beginning of the excitement you will encounter inside. The foyer passes the formal dining room on the way to the columned gallery. The formal living room opens to the rear patio and has easy access to a wet bar. The contemporary kitchen has a work island and all the amenities for gourmet preparation. The family room will be a favorite for casual entertainment. The family sleeping wing begins with an octagonal vestibule and has three bedrooms with private baths. The master wing features a private garden and an opulent bath.

28   ROOMS FOR LIVING   ORDER BLUEPRINTS 24 HOURS, 7 DAYS A WEEK, AT 1-800-521-6797

GREAT ROOMS

plan # HPK0300022

STYLE: MEDITERRANEAN
SQUARE FOOTAGE: 2,456
BEDROOMS: 3
BATHROOMS: 3
WIDTH: 63' - 8"
DEPTH: 58' - 0"
FOUNDATION: SLAB

SEARCH ONLINE @ EPLANS.COM

THE IMPRESSIVE FAÇADE of this home—brick quoins, sunburst and muntin windows, and stately pillars—is complemented by the beauty and elegance found within. A raised foyer and living room are unique features of this plan. The huge family gathering space boasts a magnificent media/fireplace wall. There is a mitered glass nook off the kitchen, which has a walk-in pantry. The master suite is remarkable with its arched entry, windowed wall in the trayed sleeping chamber, His and Hers vanities, compartmented toilet, and huge walk-in dressing salon. Two additional bedrooms share a full bath.

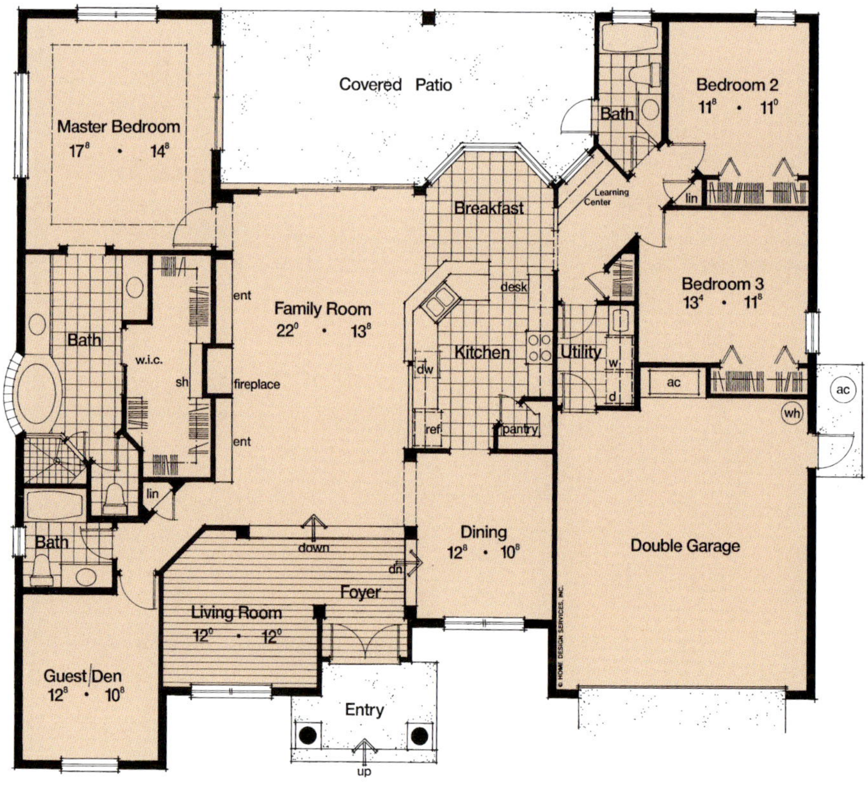

GREAT ROOMS

plan# HPK03000023

STYLE: CONTEMPORARY
SQUARE FOOTAGE: 3,556
BEDROOMS: 4
BATHROOMS: 3½
WIDTH: 85' - 0"
DEPTH: 85' - 0"
FOUNDATION: SLAB

SEARCH ONLINE @ EPLANS.COM

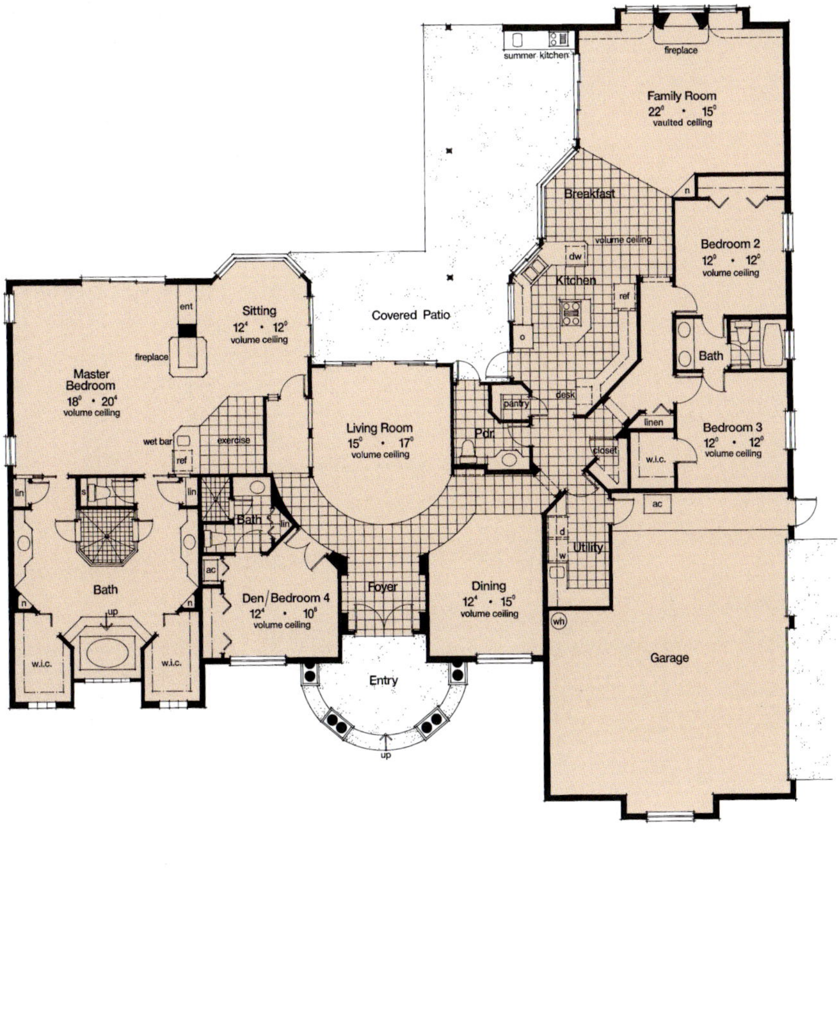

A BEAUTIFUL CURVED portico provides a majestic entrance to this one-story home. To the left of the foyer is a den/bedroom with a private bath, ideal for use as a guest suite. The exquisite master suite features a see-through fireplace and an exercise area with a wet bar. The family wing is geared for casual living with a powder room/patio bath, a huge island kitchen with a walk-in pantry, a glass-walled breakfast nook, and a grand family room with a fireplace and media wall. Two family bedrooms share a private bath.

GREAT ROOMS

FOR MORE DETAILED INFORMATION, PLEASE CHECK THE FLOOR PLANS CAREFULLY.

plan# HPK0300024

STYLE: FRENCH COUNTRY
FIRST FLOOR: 2,734 SQ. FT.
SECOND FLOOR: 1,605 SQ. FT.
TOTAL: 4,339 SQ. FT.
BONUS SPACE: 391 SQ. FT.
BEDROOMS: 4
BATHROOMS: 4½
WIDTH: 88' - 0"
DEPTH: 92' - 8"
FOUNDATION: BASEMENT

SEARCH ONLINE @ EPLANS.COM

ATTRACTIVE STONE, CURVED DORMERS, AND VARIED

rooflines give this fine European manor a graceful dose of class. Inside, the foyer introduces a formal dining room defined by columns and a spacious gathering room with a fireplace. The nearby kitchen features a walk-in pantry, beamed ceiling, adjacent breakfast nook, and a screened porch. The first-floor master suite features two walk-in closets, a lavish bath, a corner fireplace, and a sitting room with access to the rear veranda. Upstairs, three suites offer walk-in closets and surround a study loft. On the lower level, a huge recreation room awaits to entertain with a bar, a fireplace, and outdoor access. A secluded office provides a private entrance—perfect for a home business.

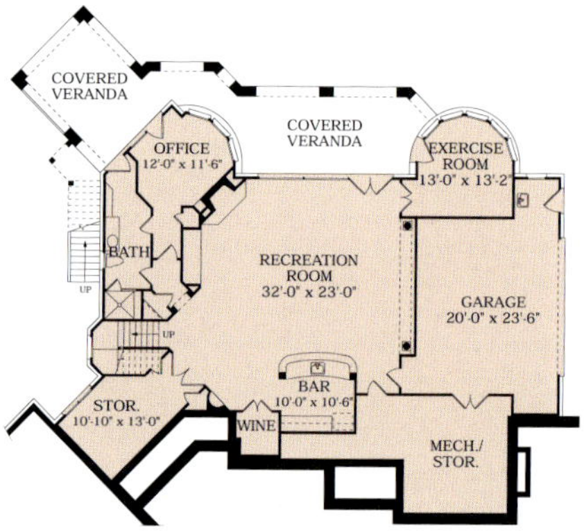

BASEMENT

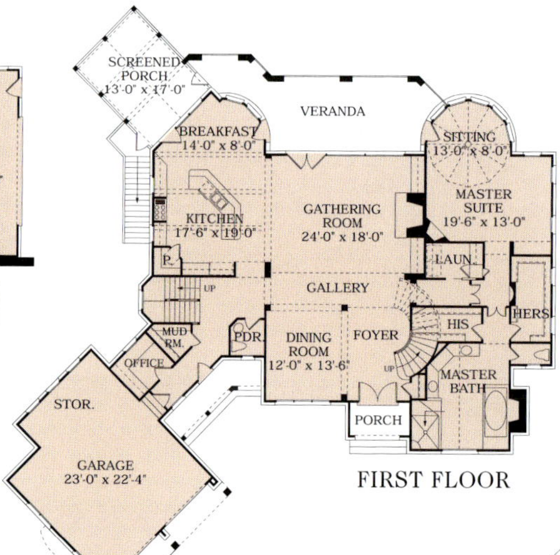

FIRST FLOOR

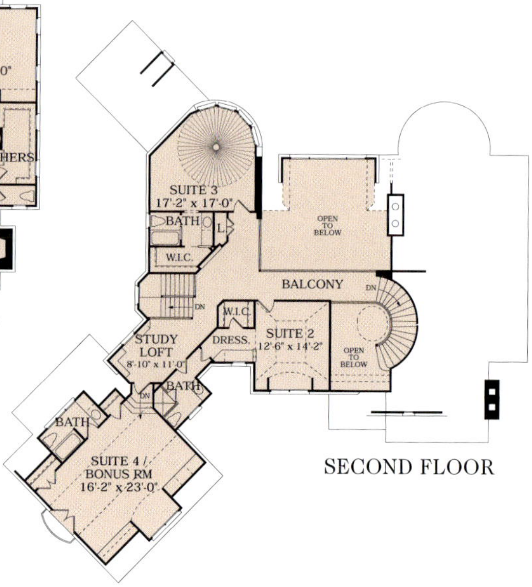

SECOND FLOOR

ORDER BLUEPRINTS 24 HOURS, 7 DAYS A WEEK, AT 1-800-521-6797

ROOMS FOR LIVING   31

GREAT ROOMS

plan# HPK0300025

STYLE: TRADITIONAL
SQUARE FOOTAGE: 2,456
BEDROOMS: 3
BATHROOMS: 2½
WIDTH: 66' - 0"
DEPTH: 68' - 0"

SEARCH ONLINE @ EPLANS.COM

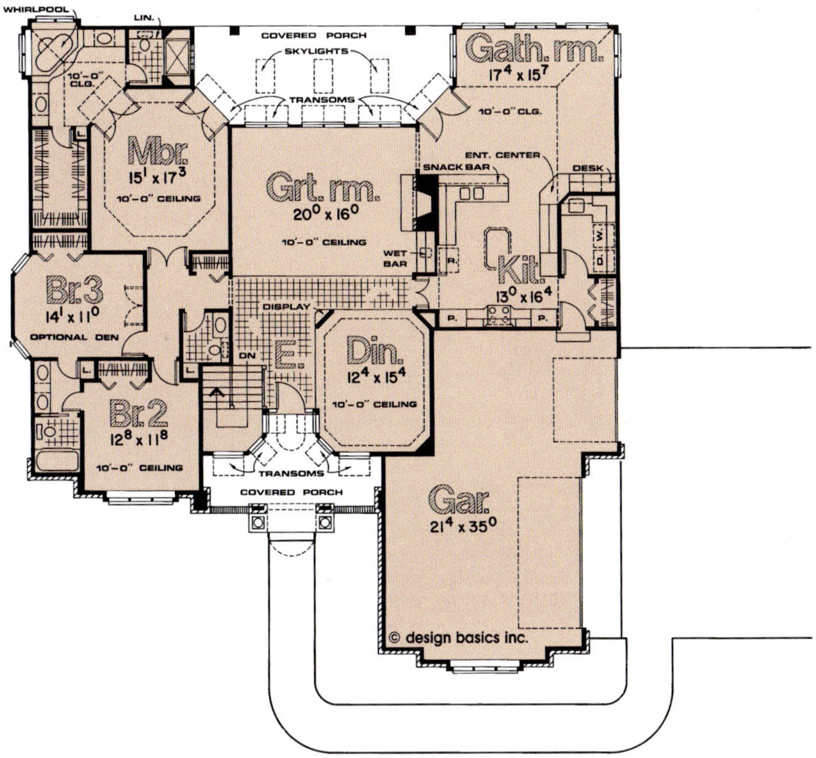

GENTLY TAPERED COLUMNS set off an elegant arched entry framed by multi-pane windows. Inside, an open great room features a wet bar, fireplace, tall transom windows, and access to a covered porch with skylights. The gourmet kitchen boasts a food-preparation island and a snack bar and overlooks the gathering room. Double doors open to the master suite, where French doors lead to a private bath with an angled whirlpool tub and a sizable walk-in closet. One of two nearby family bedrooms could serve as a den, with optional French doors opening from a hall central to the sleeping wing.

32   ROOMS FOR LIVING   ORDER BLUEPRINTS 24 HOURS, 7 DAYS A WEEK, AT 1-800-521-6797

GREAT ROOMS

plan# HPK0300026

STYLE: EUROPEAN COTTAGE
SQUARE FOOTAGE: 2,553
BEDROOMS: 3
BATHROOMS: 2½
WIDTH: 80' - 0"
DEPTH: 56' - 10"
FOUNDATION: SLAB

SEARCH ONLINE @ EPLANS.COM

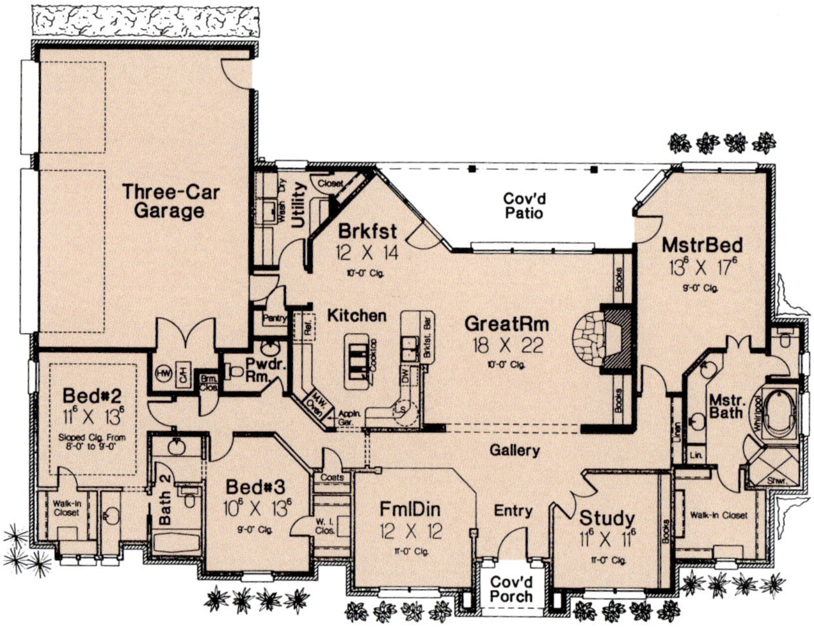

CONTRASTING BRICK LENDS itself to the ornate shapes of Old World arches and angles, creating a compelling example of European architecture, right in your own neighborhood. An arched window and sidelights brighten the entry, which opens on either side to the dining room and study. The great room emphasizes a grand stone hearth and clear views of the rear property. The island-cooktop kitchen is truly a chef's delight, opening to the uniquely angled breakfast nook. Bedrooms are designed to value peace and quiet; the master suite—remarkable with patio access and a magnificent bath—resides to the right, as two additional bedrooms occupy the left wing. The three-car garage is large enough to hold cars, garden equipment... even a small boat!

ORDER BLUEPRINTS 24 HOURS, 7 DAYS A WEEK, AT 1-800-521-6797

ROOMS FOR LIVING   33

GREAT ROOMS

plan # HPK0300027

STYLE: COUNTRY COTTAGE
SQUARE FOOTAGE: 3,418
BEDROOMS: 4
BATHROOMS: 3½
WIDTH: 70' - 7"
DEPTH: 81' - 10"
FOUNDATION:
CRAWLSPACE, BASEMENT

SEARCH ONLINE @ EPLANS.COM

THIS COUNTRY COTTAGE OFFERS THE BEST OF LUXURY

living...all on one level! Enter to find heightened ceilings in most living areas. The foyer opens to the dining room, defined by columns. Double doors access a vaulted hearth-warmed study. In the family room, a coffered ceiling and radius windows give a grand appearance as the fireplace lends a cozy touch. An octagonal tray ceiling in the breakfast nook adds architectural interest; the island kitchen features tons of counter space. A bedroom tucked near the keeping room makes an ideal guest room. Located for ultimate privacy, the master suite delights in a bayed sitting room and vaulted bath. An optional upper level would include a fifth bedroom and a full bath.

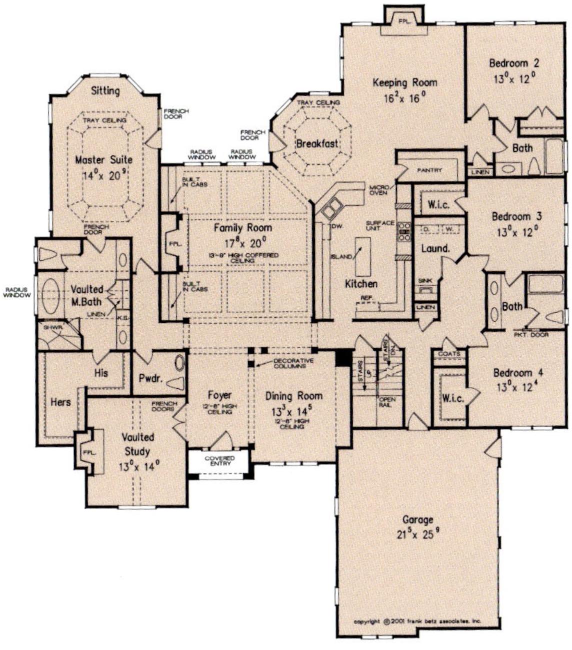

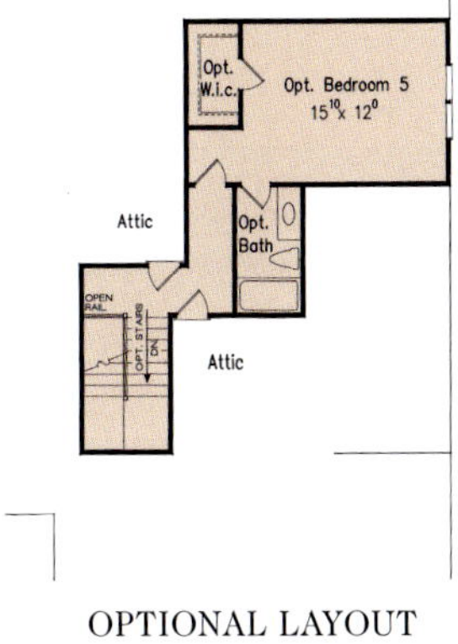

OPTIONAL LAYOUT

34   ROOMS FOR LIVING   ORDER BLUEPRINTS 24 HOURS, 7 DAYS A WEEK, AT 1-800-521-6797

GREAT ROOMS

plan# HPK0300028

STYLE: FRENCH
FIRST FLOOR: 1,685 SQ. FT.
SECOND FLOOR: 1,596 SQ. FT.
TOTAL: 3,281 SQ. FT.
BEDROOMS: 5
BATHROOMS: 4½
WIDTH: 51' - 0"
DEPTH: 66' - 10"
FOUNDATION: CRAWLSPACE,
BASEMENT

SEARCH ONLINE @ EPLANS.COM

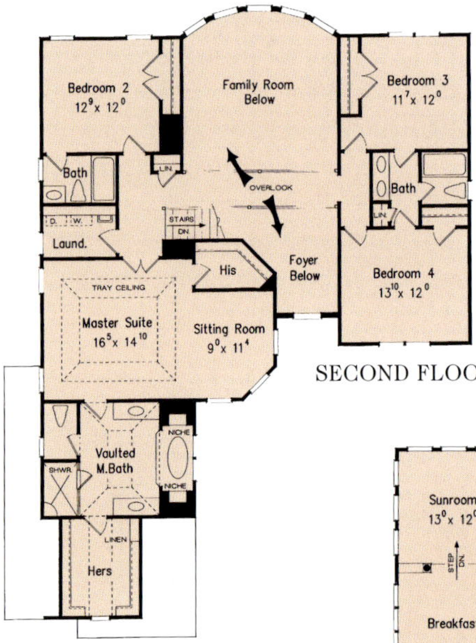

STRONG LINES LEAD the eye upwards toward this home's varied roofline. The formal dining room enjoys views from the two-story turret. The breakfast room opens to a glorious sunroom with access to the rear property. The two-story family room enjoys a curved wall of windows and a double-sided fireplace. At the right of the plan, a study and powder room share space with a comfortable guest suite. Upstairs, three family bedrooms with ample closet space share two baths. The sumptuous master suite boasts a sitting room, vaulted bath, and His and Hers walk-in closets.

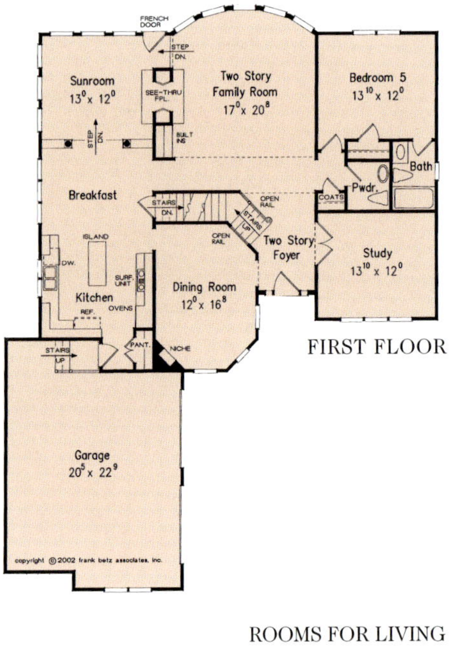

SECOND FLOOR

FIRST FLOOR

ORDER BLUEPRINTS 24 HOURS, 7 DAYS A WEEK, AT 1-800-521-6797   ROOMS FOR LIVING   35

GREAT ROOMS

PHOTO COURTESY OF LIVING CONCEPTS HOME PLANNING

plan# HPK0300029

STYLE: TRANSITIONAL
SQUARE FOOTAGE: 2,677
BONUS SPACE: 319 SQ. FT.
BEDROOMS: 3
BATHROOMS: 3½
WIDTH: 63' - 10"
DEPTH: 80' - 4"
FOUNDATION: CRAWLSPACE

SEARCH ONLINE @ EPLANS.COM

A BEAUTIFUL COVE ENTRY WITH DOUBLE DOORS OPENS

to a foyer with unobstructed views to the grand room. A formal dining room with a tray ceiling is to the right and the master suite fills the wing to the left. A sitting area with a bay window and entrance to the deck highlight the master bedroom. A garden tub in its own bay window and a large walk-in closet enhance this area. A breakfast nook occupies a third bay window just off the U-shaped kitchen with a pass-through window to the deck. The island cooktop borders the keeping den, which includes a sloped ceiling and a fireplace. Two additional bedrooms have their own baths.

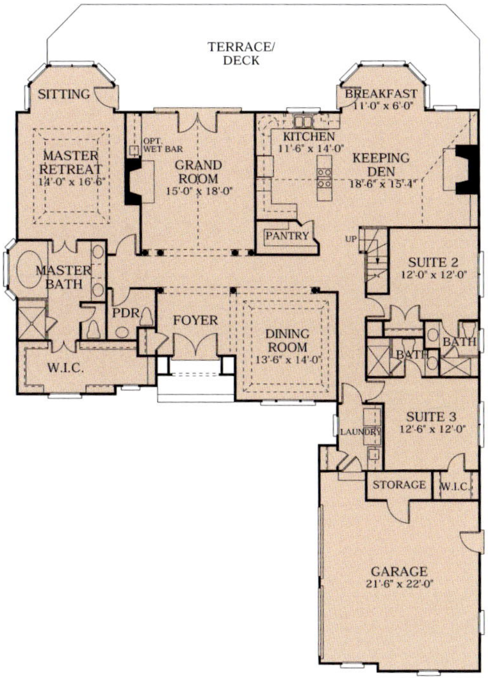

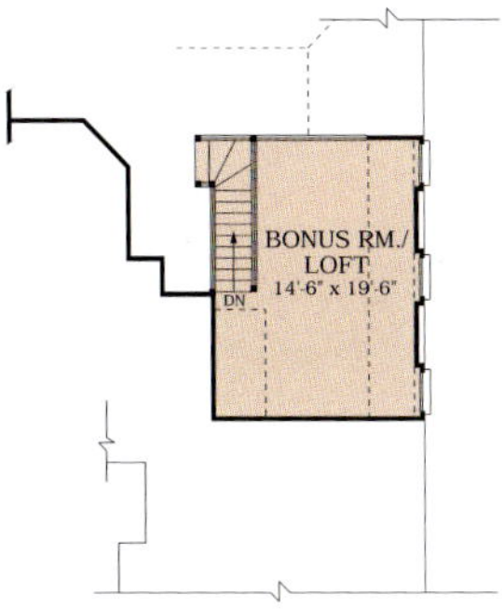

36   ROOMS FOR LIVING

ORDER BLUEPRINTS 24 HOURS, 7 DAYS A WEEK, AT 1-800-521-6797

GREAT ROOMS

plan# HPK0300003

STYLE: NORMAN
FIRST FLOOR: 2,461 SQ. FT.
SECOND FLOOR: 1,114 SQ. FT.
TOTAL: 3,575 SQ. FT.
BEDROOMS: 4
BATHROOMS: 3½
WIDTH: 84' - 4"
DEPTH: 63' - 0"
FOUNDATION: WALKOUT
BASEMENT

SEARCH ONLINE @ EPLANS.COM

A MYRIAD OF GLASS AND ORNAMENTAL STUCCO detailing complements the asymmetrical facade of this two-story home. Inside, the striking, two-story foyer provides a dramatic entrance. To the right is the formal dining room. An efficient L-shaped kitchen and bayed breakfast nook are conveniently located near the dining area. The living room, with its welcoming fireplace, opens through double doors to the rear terrace. The private master suite provides access to the rear terrace and adjacent study. The master bath is sure to please with its relaxing garden tub, separate shower, grand His and Hers walk-in closets, and a compartmented toilet. The second floor contains three large bedrooms, one with a private bath; the others share a bath.

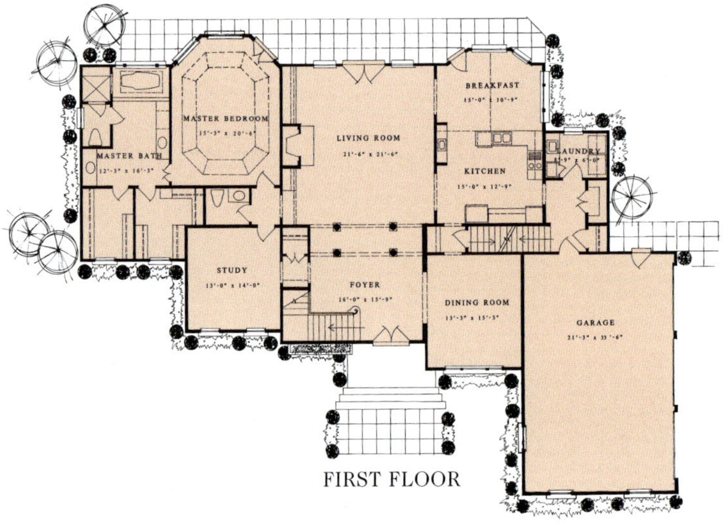

FIRST FLOOR

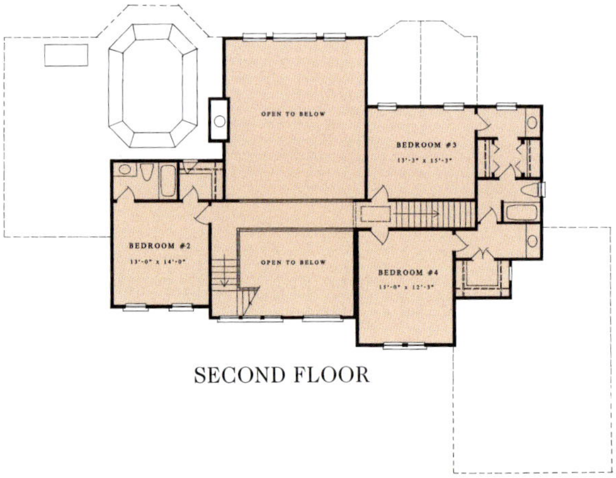

SECOND FLOOR

ORDER BLUEPRINTS 24 HOURS, 7 DAYS A WEEK, AT 1-800-521-6797

ROOMS FOR LIVING 37

GREAT ROOMS

plan # HPK0300030

STYLE: FARMHOUSE
FIRST FLOOR: 2,073 SQ. FT.
SECOND FLOOR: 2,079 SQ. FT.
TOTAL: 4,152 SQ. FT.
BEDROOMS: 5
BATHROOMS: 4½
WIDTH: 72' - 3"
DEPTH: 78' - 6"
FOUNDATION: BASEMENT,
CRAWLSPACE

SEARCH ONLINE @ EPLANS.COM

BUILD THE HOME OF YOUR DREAMS WITH THIS spectacular country manor. A wide two-story foyer opens on either side to reveal the formal living room and dining room. Just ahead, a fantastic two-story bowed window affords floods of natural light and grand views of the rear property. The gourmet kitchen is appointed with an island, walk-in pantry, dual ovens, and convenient serving bar, making any meal a snap. The sunny breakfast nook and hearth-warmed keeping room are perfect for casual get-togethers with friends. Upstairs, the master suite steals the show, with a full sitting room, outstanding Roman bath, immense His and Hers closets, and a romantic fireplace.

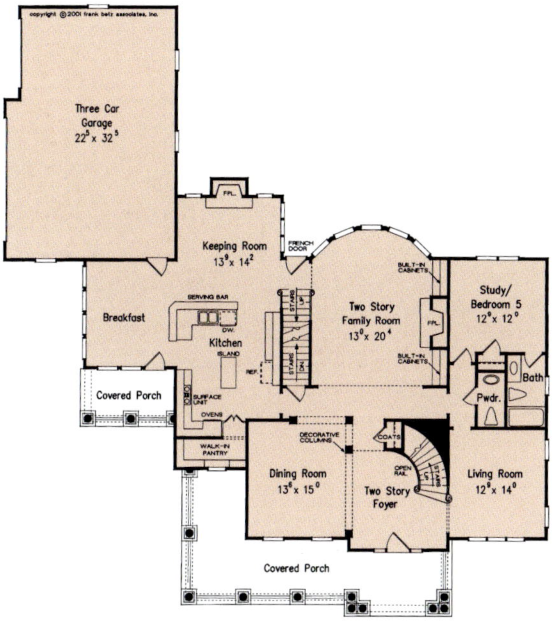

FIRST FLOOR

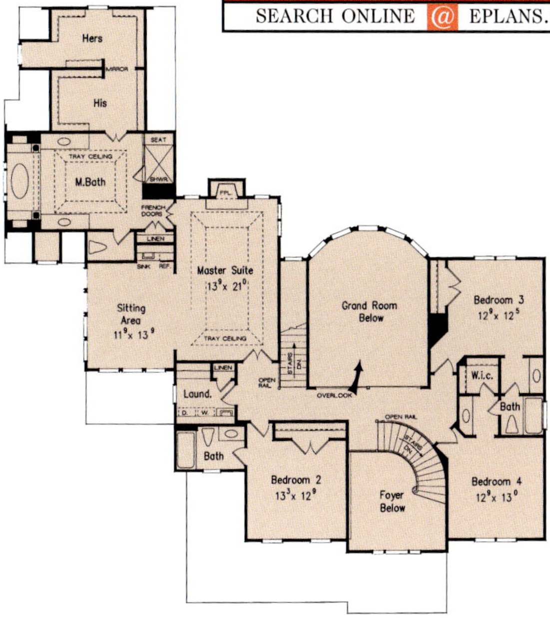

SECOND FLOOR

38   ROOMS FOR LIVING

ORDER BLUEPRINTS 24 HOURS, 7 DAYS A WEEK, AT 1-800-521-6797

GREAT ROOMS

plan # HPK0300031

STYLE: COUNTRY COTTAGE
FIRST FLOOR: 2,225 SQ. FT.
SECOND FLOOR: 1,360 SQ. FT.
TOTAL: 3,585 SQ. FT.
BONUS SPACE: 277 SQ. FT.
BEDROOMS: 4
BATHROOMS: 3½
WIDTH: 68' - 10"
DEPTH: 60' - 0"
FOUNDATION: CRAWLSPACE, BASEMENT

SEARCH ONLINE @ EPLANS.COM

THIS BREATHTAKING STONE-AND-SHINGLE EUROPEAN

cottage will turn the home of your dreams into a reality. Enter to a formal foyer with an elegant box-bay dining room on the left and vast vaulted family room ahead. A fireplace here gives the room a definite focus; tall windows bring in floods of natural light. An expansive kitchen makes it easy for multiple cooks to share space and effortlessly serve the bayed breakfast nook. A vaulted keeping room at the rear is a cozy hideaway. The master suite shines with a bayed sitting area and majestic vaulted bath with a corner garden tub.

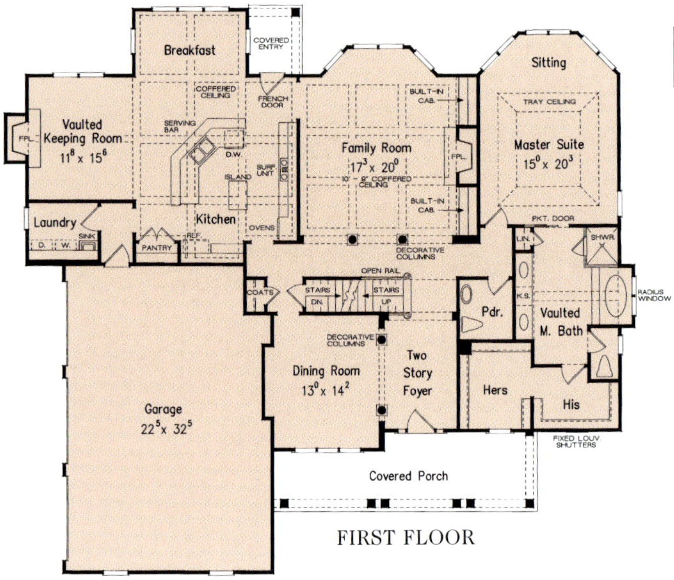

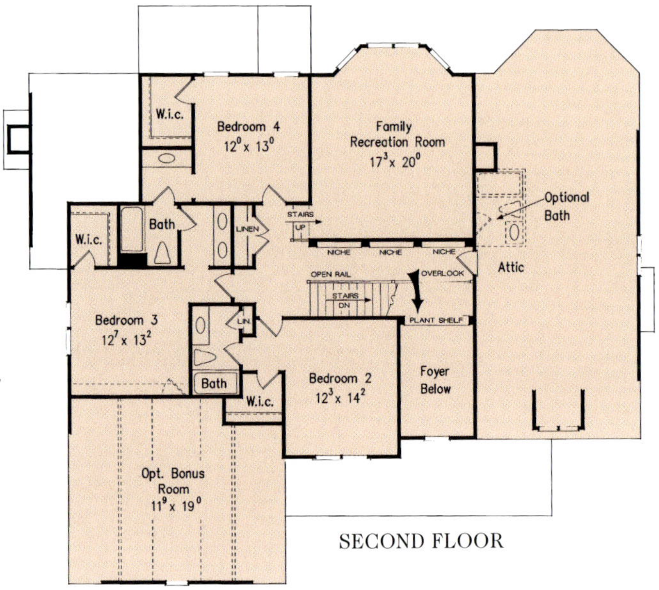

SECOND FLOOR

FIRST FLOOR

ORDER BLUEPRINTS 24 HOURS, 7 DAYS A WEEK, AT 1-800-521-6797

ROOMS FOR LIVING   39

GREAT ROOMS

plan# HPK0300032

STYLE: COUNTRY COTTAGE
FIRST FLOOR: 1,943 SQ. FT.
SECOND FLOOR: 950 SQ. FT.
TOTAL: 2,893 SQ. FT.
BONUS SPACE: 215 SQ. FT.
BEDROOMS: 4
BATHROOMS: 3½
WIDTH: 59' - 0"
DEPTH: 52' - 6"
FOUNDATION: BASEMENT,
CRAWLSPACE

SEARCH ONLINE @ EPLANS.COM

GRADUATED ROOFLINES LEND ARCHITECTURAL interest to this traditional siding home. Stone accents and box-bay windows embellish the exterior; inside, window seats and thoughtful touches are engaging. Enter to the two-story foyer: on the right resides a handsome home office. Columns define the formal dining room, which flows directly into an open kitchen. The vaulted family room is crowned with beam adornments—leave them unfinished for a vintage look—and made cozy with a fireplace framed by built-ins. In the private master suite, a luxurious garden tub and compartmented bath will pamper any homeowner. Upstairs, three bedrooms enjoy semiprivate baths and access an optional bonus room. The side-loading two-car garage allows space for storage.

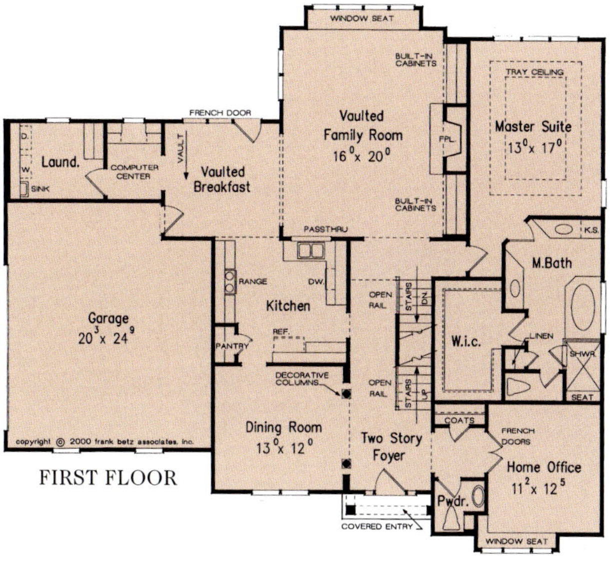

FIRST FLOOR

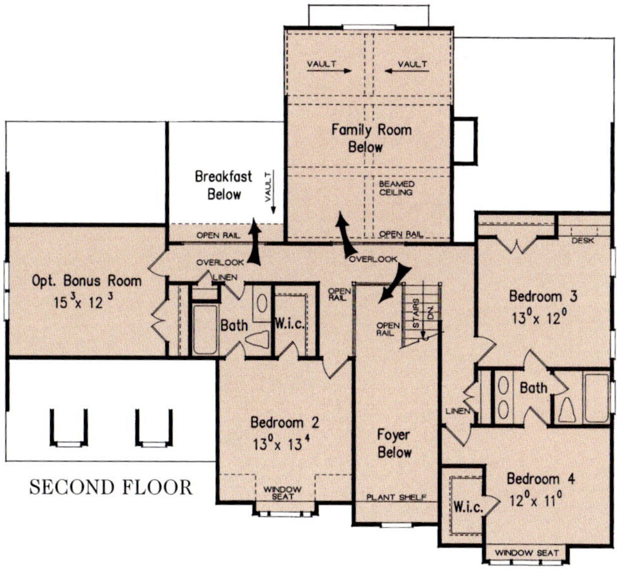

Laund.
Garage 20³ x 24⁹
Vaulted Breakfast
Vaulted Family Room 16⁰ x 20⁰
Master Suite 13⁰ x 17⁰
Kitchen
Dining Room 13⁰ x 12⁰
Two Story Foyer
Home Office 11² x 12⁵
M.Bath
W.i.c.
copyright © 2000 frank betz associates, inc.

SECOND FLOOR

Opt. Bonus Room 15³ x 12³
Breakfast Below
Family Room Below
Bedroom 2 13⁰ x 13⁴
Foyer Below
Bedroom 3 13⁰ x 12⁰
Bedroom 4 12⁰ x 11⁰
Bath
W.i.c.

40   ROOMS FOR LIVING

ORDER BLUEPRINTS 24 HOURS, 7 DAYS A WEEK, AT 1-800-521-6797

GREAT ROOMS

plan# HPK0300033

STYLE: GEORGIAN
FIRST FLOOR: 1,679 SQ. FT.
SECOND FLOOR: 1,605 SQ. FT.
TOTAL: 3,284 SQ. FT.
BEDROOMS: 5
BATHROOMS: 4
WIDTH: 57' - 0"
DEPTH: 45' - 4"
FOUNDATION: BASEMENT,
CRAWLSPACE

SEARCH ONLINE @ EPLANS.COM

THIS STATELY GEORGIAN HOME COMBINES VARIED

rooflines, a grand pediment entry, and eye-catching brick to create a place your family will delight in for generations. Inside, an intriguing floor plan directs traffic for increased flow and maximizes natural light. The foyer opens on the right to a formal dining room with a box-bay window and reveals a study on the left. An expansive kitchen features an island and a serving bar that views the bayed breakfast nook. Stunning vistas grace the two-story family room, courtesy of a rear bowed window wall. A see-through fireplace is shared with the sunroom. Three upstairs bedrooms are generously appointed. The master suite is a romantic retreat with a bayed sitting area and sumptuous bath with a window seat.

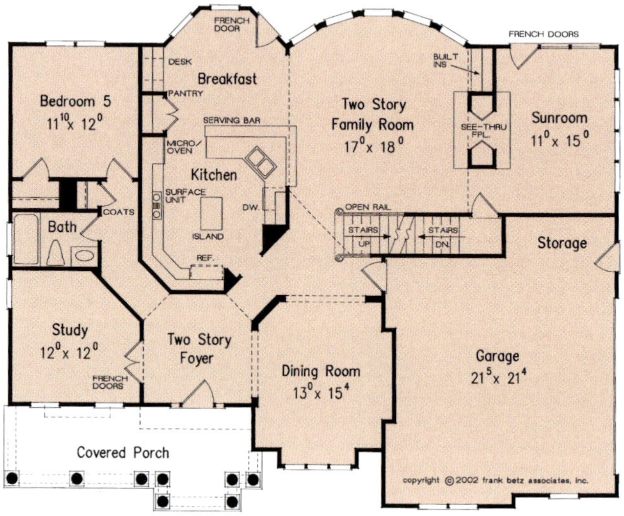

FIRST FLOOR

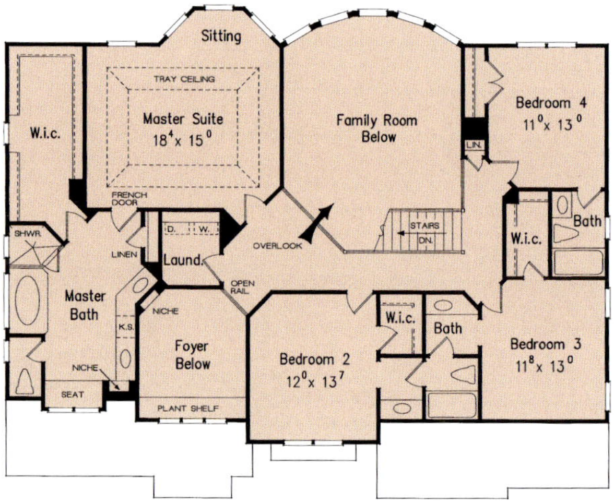

SECOND FLOOR

ORDER BLUEPRINTS 24 HOURS, 7 DAYS A WEEK, AT 1-800-521-6797

GREAT ROOMS

plan # HPK0300034

STYLE: SOUTHERN COLONIAL
FIRST FLOOR: 2,670 SQ. FT.
SECOND FLOOR: 1,795 SQ. FT.
TOTAL: 4,465 SQ. FT.
BONUS SPACE: 744 SQ. FT.
BEDROOMS: 5
BATHROOMS: 4½ + ½
WIDTH: 74' - 8"
DEPTH: 93' - 10"
FOUNDATION: CRAWLSPACE,
BASEMENT

SEARCH ONLINE @ EPLANS.COM

FIRST FLOOR

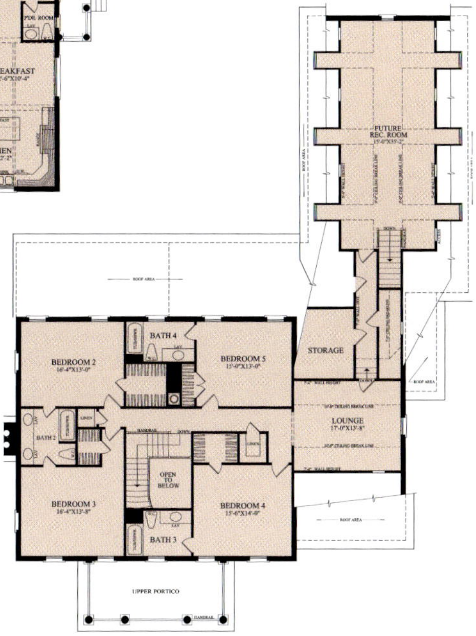

SECOND FLOOR

A STATELY BRICK PLANTATION

home, this plan presents all the luxuries that are so desired by today's homeowner. Enter past the columned portico to the formal two-story foyer. To the left is a library with a corner fireplace; to the right, the dining room flows into an enormous kitchen, outfitted with an island serving bar. Exposed wood-beam ceilings in the kitchen, breakfast area, and family room add a vintage element. The master suite is a romantic hideaway, with a corner fireplace, whirlpool tub, and seated shower. Upstairs, four well-appointed bedrooms join a lounge area to finish the plan. Future space above the three-car garage is limited only by your imagination.

42   ROOMS FOR LIVING   ORDER BLUEPRINTS 24 HOURS, 7 DAYS A WEEK, AT 1-800-521-6797

GREAT ROOMS

THE ELEGANT ENTRY of this Colonial home gives it a stately appearance with its columns and pediment. Inside, the entry opens to the living room where the first of two fireplaces is found. The formal dining room adjoins both the living room and the kitchen. The spacious breakfast area looks out onto the patio. The master suite is found on the right with two additional bedrooms and a fourth bedroom is on the left giving privacy for overnight guests.

plan# HPK0300035

STYLE: GEORGIAN
SQUARE FOOTAGE: 3,136
BEDROOMS: 4
BATHROOMS: 3½
WIDTH: 80' - 6"
DEPTH: 72' - 4"
FOUNDATION: CRAWLSPACE

SEARCH ONLINE @ EPLANS.COM

GREAT ROOMS

A WRAPAROUND COVERED PORCH ADDS PLENTY OF outdoor space to this already impressive home. Built-in cabinets flank the fireplace in the grand room; a fireplace also warms the hearth room. The gourmet kitchen includes an island counter, large walk-in pantry, and serving bar. A secluded home office, with a separate entrance nearby, provides a quiet work place. A front parlor provides even more room for entertaining or relaxing. The master suite dominates the second floor, offering a spacious sitting area with an elegant tray ceiling, a dressing area, and a luxurious bath with two walk-in closets, double vanities, and a raised garden tub. The second floor is also home to an enormous exercise room and three additional bedrooms.

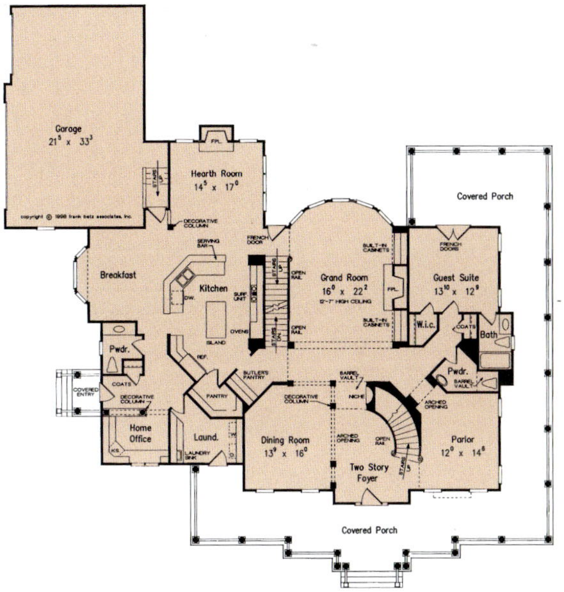

plan# HPK0300002

STYLE: PLANTATION
FIRST FLOOR: 2,732 SQ. FT.
SECOND FLOOR: 2,734 SQ. FT.
TOTAL: 5,466 SQ. FT.
BEDROOMS: 5
BATHROOMS: 5½ + ½
WIDTH: 85' - 0"
DEPTH: 85' - 6"
FOUNDATION: CRAWLSPACE, BASEMENT, SLAB

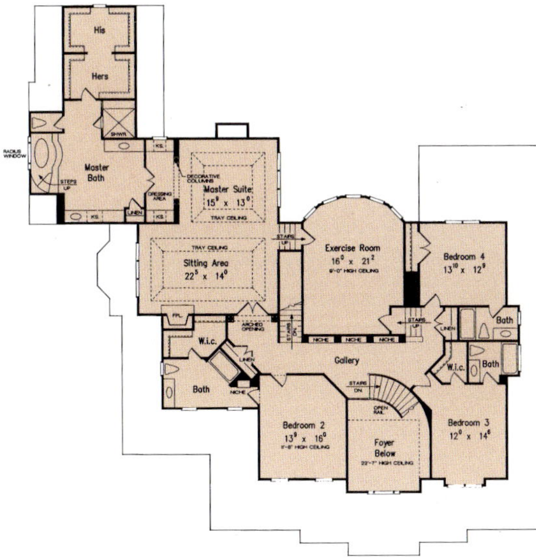

SEARCH ONLINE @ EPLANS.COM

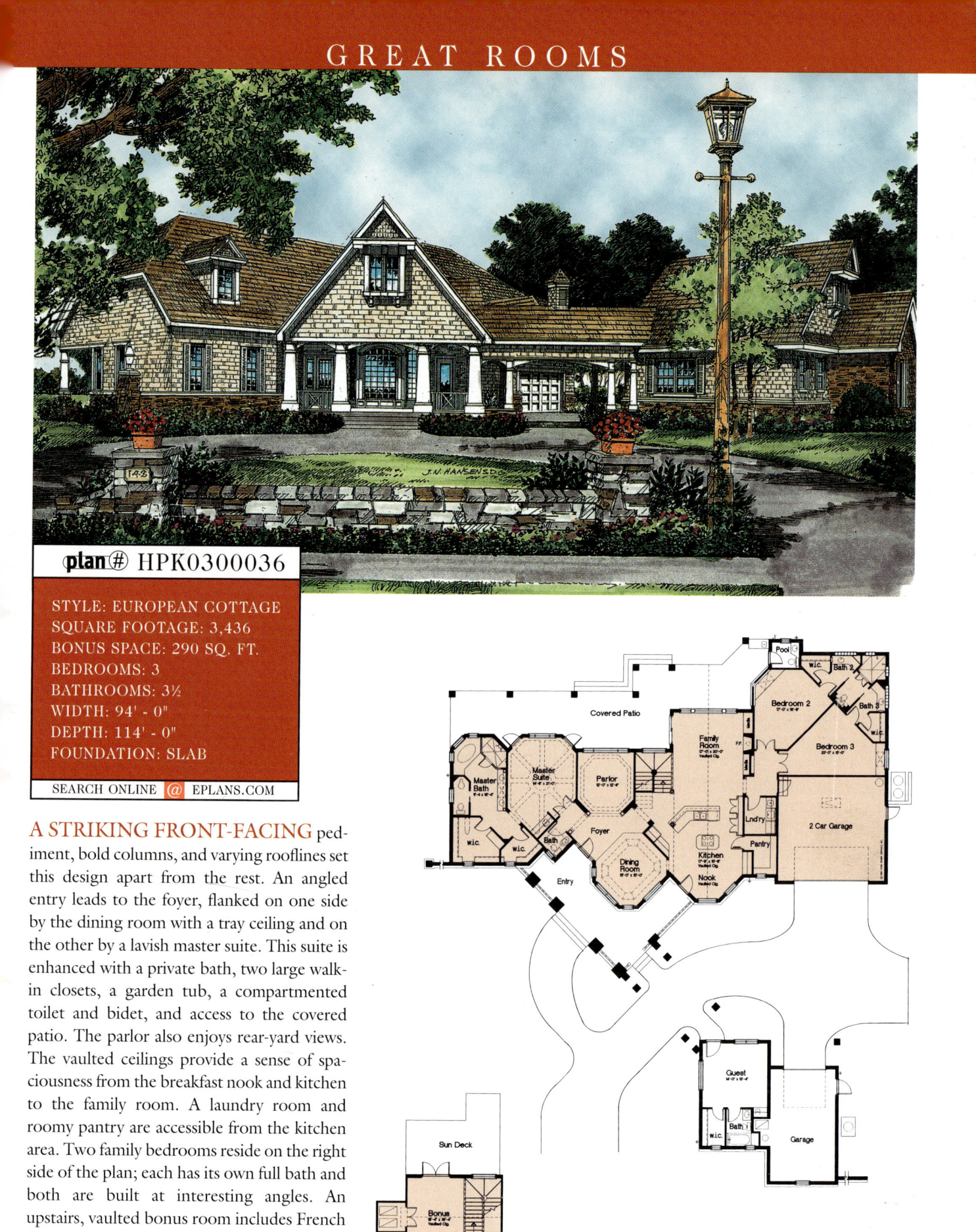

GREAT ROOMS

plan# HPK03000036

STYLE: EUROPEAN COTTAGE
SQUARE FOOTAGE: 3,436
BONUS SPACE: 290 SQ. FT.
BEDROOMS: 3
BATHROOMS: 3½
WIDTH: 94' - 0"
DEPTH: 114' - 0"
FOUNDATION: SLAB

SEARCH ONLINE @ EPLANS.COM

A STRIKING FRONT-FACING pediment, bold columns, and varying rooflines set this design apart from the rest. An angled entry leads to the foyer, flanked on one side by the dining room with a tray ceiling and on the other by a lavish master suite. This suite is enhanced with a private bath, two large walk-in closets, a garden tub, a compartmented toilet and bidet, and access to the covered patio. The parlor also enjoys rear-yard views. The vaulted ceilings provide a sense of spaciousness from the breakfast nook and kitchen to the family room. A laundry room and roomy pantry are accessible from the kitchen area. Two family bedrooms reside on the right side of the plan; each has its own full bath and both are built at interesting angles. An upstairs, vaulted bonus room includes French doors opening to a second-floor sundeck.

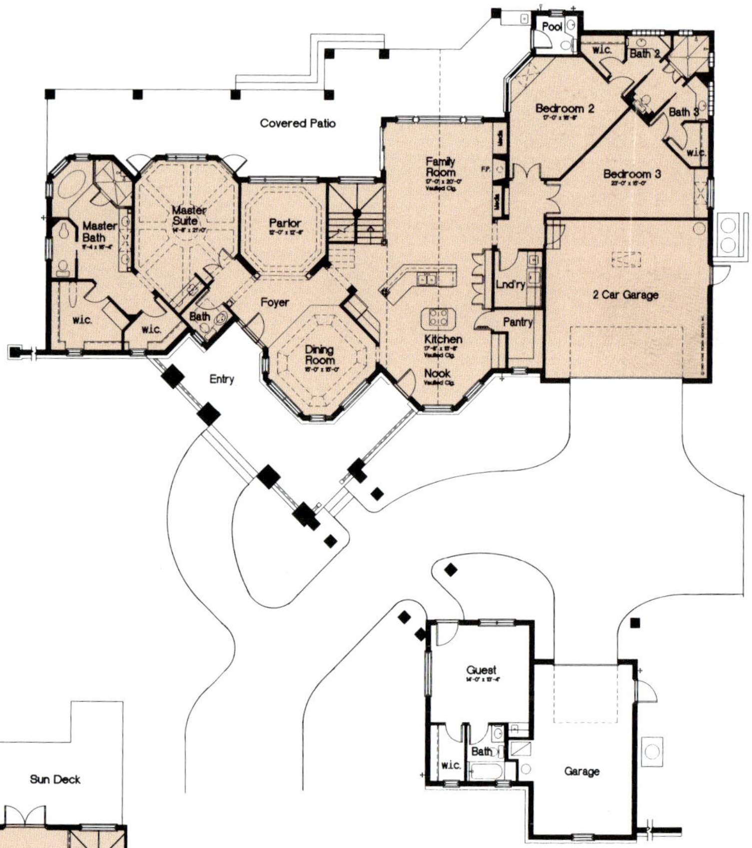

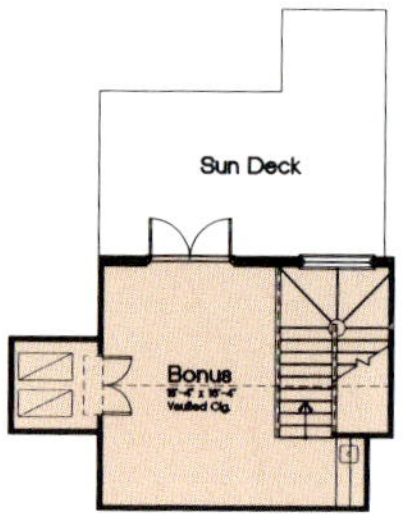

GREAT ROOMS

plan # HPK0300037

STYLE: GEORGIAN
SQUARE FOOTAGE: 3,190
BONUS SPACE: 305 SQ. FT.
BEDROOMS: 4
BATHROOMS: 3½
WIDTH: 74' - 0"
DEPTH: 84' - 6"
FOUNDATION: BASEMENT, CRAWLSPACE

SEARCH ONLINE @ EPLANS.COM

THIS SOUTHERN COLONIAL BEAUTY

will be the showpiece of any neighborhood, with prominent columns, multipane window dormers and flower-box accents. Inside, it is instantly clear that this luxurious home is designed with your ultimate comfort in mind. Columns define the dining room from the raised-ceiling foyer; both the dining room and nearby guest suite have French-door access to the front porch. The vaulted great room makes an elegant statement with a bookshelf-framed fireplace and rear French doors topped by a radius window. The island kitchen is definitely made for gourmet entertaining, complete with a butler's pantry and a serving bar to the bayed breakfast nook. The adjacent vaulted keeping room is perfect for cozy gatherings. The left wing is devoted to the master suite, which boasts a sitting bay and a vaulted bath with a step-up tub. Expansion options include a fifth bedroom and full bath.

GREAT ROOMS

plan# HPK0300038

STYLE: FARMHOUSE
FIRST FLOOR: 2,928 SQ. FT.
SECOND FLOOR: 1,296 SQ. FT.
TOTAL: 4,224 SQ. FT.
BEDROOMS: 4
BATHROOMS: 3½
WIDTH: 67' - 0"
DEPTH: 70' - 10"
FOUNDATION: CRAWLSPACE, BASEMENT

SEARCH ONLINE @ EPLANS.COM

WHAT APPEARS TO BE A TRADITIONAL BRICK COUNTRY

farmhouse on the exterior is actually a luxurious home, filled with all the comforts that new homeowners desire. French doors lead to the two-story foyer; a living room/study greets guests on the right. Columns to the left define a formal dining room. A butler's pantry makes service from the open island kitchen effortless. To the rear, a vaulted keeping room is hearth-warmed and filled with natural light. The two-story grand room surveys the rear property, courtesy of a prominent bowed window wall. The right wing is devoted to the master suite, rich with a trayed foyer, vaulted sitting room, and magnificent spa bath. Three generous upstairs bedrooms each enjoy unique amenities.

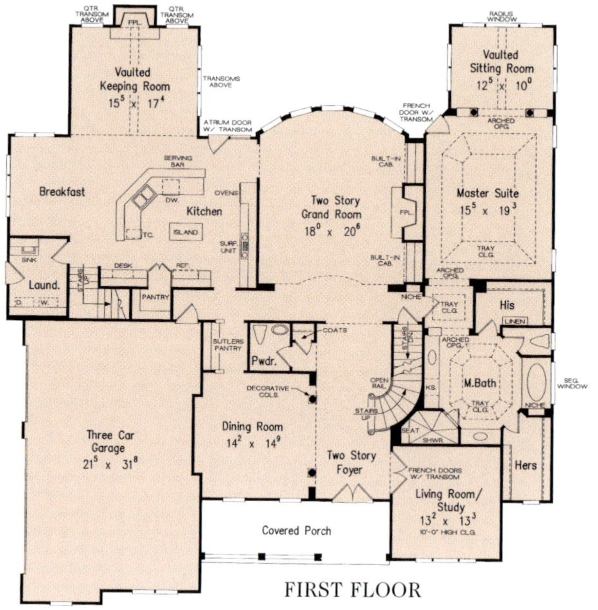

FIRST FLOOR

SECOND FLOOR

ORDER BLUEPRINTS 24 HOURS, 7 DAYS A WEEK, AT 1-800-521-6797

GREAT ROOMS

plan # HPK0300039

STYLE: FARMHOUSE
FIRST FLOOR: 1,706 SQ. FT.
SECOND FLOOR: 776 SQ. FT.
TOTAL: 2,482 SQ. FT.
BONUS SPACE: 414 SQ. FT.
BEDROOMS: 4
BATHROOMS: 2½
WIDTH: 54' - 8"
DEPTH: 43' - 0"

SEARCH ONLINE @ EPLANS.COM

THE SMALL APPEARANCE OF THIS COUNTRY farmhouse belies the spaciousness that lies within. A large great room is directly beyond the foyer and boasts a fireplace, shelves, a vaulted ceiling, and a door to the rear deck. A bayed breakfast room, located just off the kitchen, looks to a covered breezeway that leads from the house to the garage. The first-floor master bedroom is enhanced with a sitting area, walk-in closet, and full bath with a garden tub and dual sinks. The second floor overlooks the great room and includes three additional bedrooms, one with a cathedral ceiling.

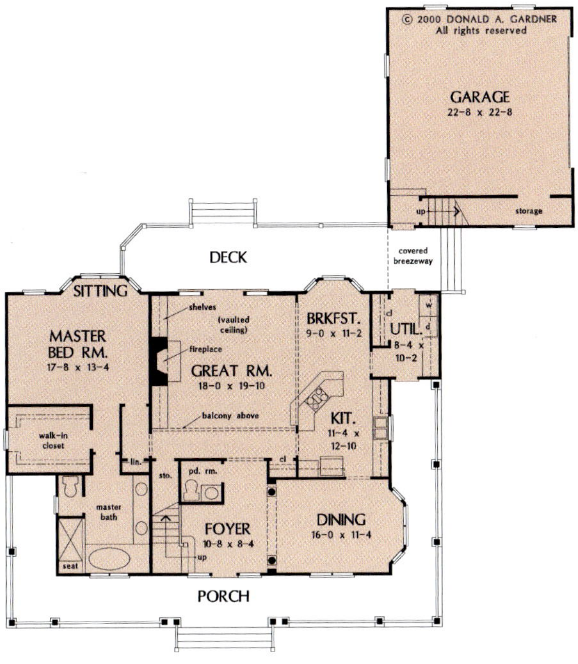

FIRST FLOOR

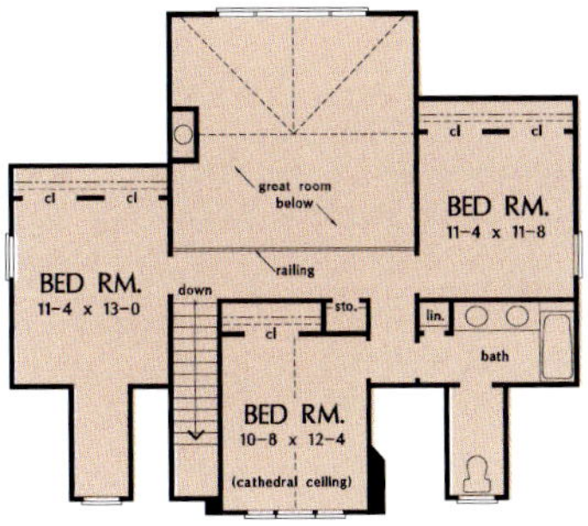

SECOND FLOOR

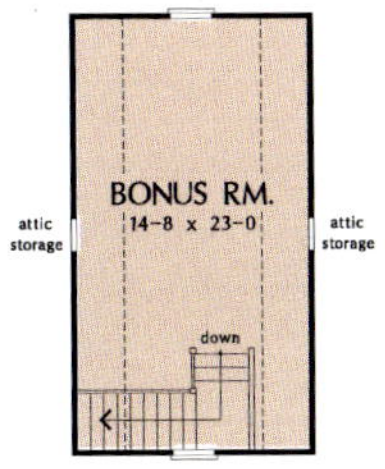

48   ROOMS FOR LIVING

ORDER BLUEPRINTS 24 HOURS, 7 DAYS A WEEK, AT 1-800-521-6797

GREAT ROOMS

plan # HPK03000040

STYLE: COUNTRY COTTAGE
FIRST FLOOR: 1,704 SQ. FT.
SECOND FLOOR: 734 SQ. FT.
TOTAL: 2,438 SQ. FT.
BONUS SPACE: 479 SQ. FT.
BEDROOMS: 3
BATHROOMS: 3½
WIDTH: 50' - 0"
DEPTH: 82' - 6"
FOUNDATION: CRAWLSPACE

SEARCH ONLINE @ EPLANS.COM

ELEGANT COUNTRY—that's one way to describe this attractive three-bedroom home. Inside, comfort is evidently the theme, with the formal dining room flowing into the U-shaped kitchen and casual dining taking place in the sunny breakfast area. The spacious, vaulted great room offers a fireplace and built-ins. The first-floor master suite is complete with a walk-in closet, a whirlpool tub, and a separate shower. Upstairs, the sleeping quarters include two family bedrooms with private baths and walk-in closets.

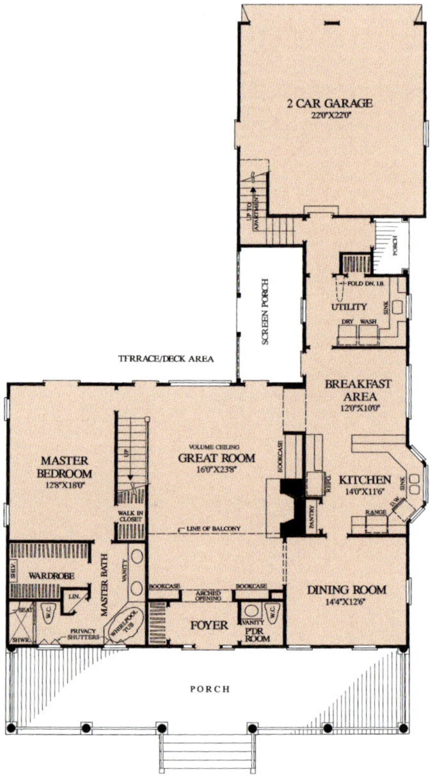

FIRST FLOOR

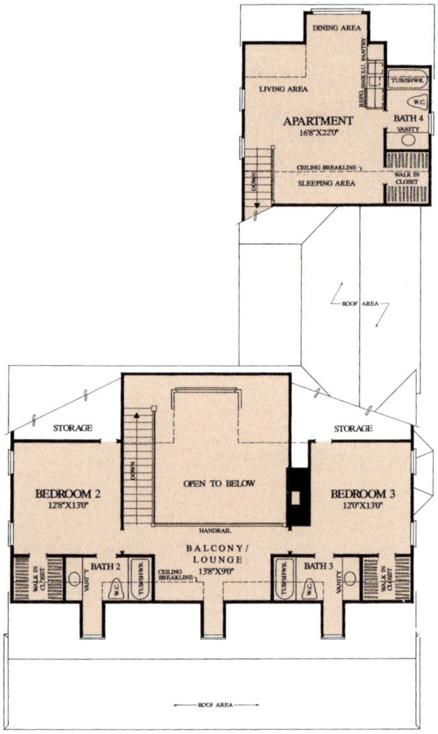

SECOND FLOOR

GREAT ROOMS

plan # HPK0300041

STYLE: SOUTHERN COLONIAL
SQUARE FOOTAGE: 1,927
BEDROOMS: 3
BATHROOMS: 2
WIDTH: 54' - 0"
DEPTH: 55' - 0"
FOUNDATION: CRAWLSPACE

SEARCH ONLINE @ EPLANS.COM

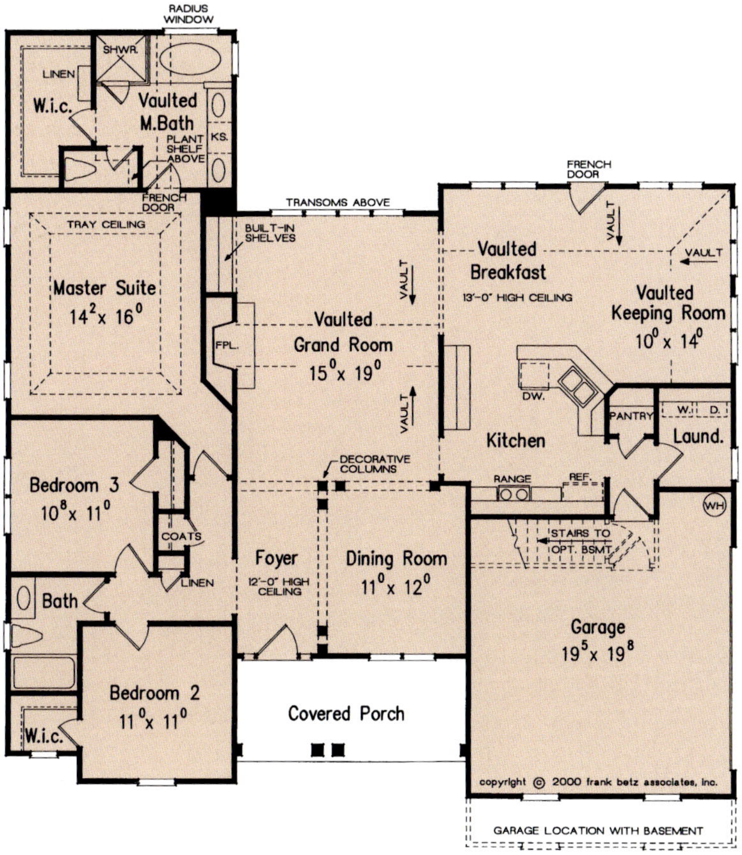

THIS SWEET BUNGALOW utilizes every square inch of space for a functional floor plan that will exceed your expectations. Inside, a 12-foot foyer ceiling makes a grand impression. Decorative columns set off the dining room; a vaulted ceiling in the great room is enhanced by tall transom windows. Vaulted ceilings continue in the breakfast nook and keeping room, for an appearance of expanded spaces. Sleeping quarters on the left side of the home include two family bedrooms and a lavish master suite with a vaulted spa bath.

GREAT ROOMS

THE FRONT PORCH OF THIS HOME OFFERS SANCTUARY

from the elements and welcoming charm. To the right, the formal dining room features a tray ceiling and pocket-door access to the kitchen. To the left, a study or guest bedroom also features a tray ceiling and accesses a full bath. The great room sits at the center with a fireplace, built-ins, a cathedral ceiling, and rear-deck access. With the breakfast area soaking up natural light from its many windows and the gourmet kitchen just steps away, the family will enjoy ease of service and a casual atmosphere. The master suite offers a cathedral ceiling, a spacious walk-in closet, and a bath with dual vanities.

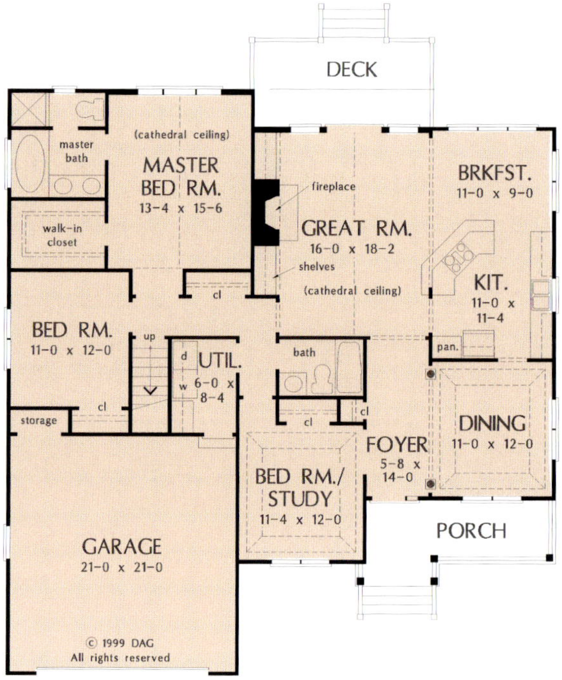

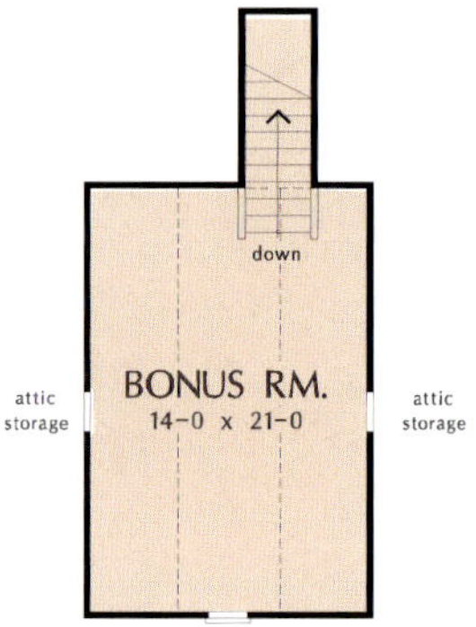

plan # HPK0300042

STYLE: COUNTRY
SQUARE FOOTAGE: 1,671
BONUS SPACE: 348 SQ. FT.
BEDROOMS: 3
BATHROOMS: 2
WIDTH: 50' - 8"
DEPTH: 52' - 4"

SEARCH ONLINE @ EPLANS.COM

© 1999 Donald A. Gardner, Inc.

GREAT ROOMS

plan # HPK0300043

STYLE: FARMHOUSE
MAIN LEVEL: 1,709 SQ. FT.
LOWER LEVEL: 1,051 SQ. FT.
TOTAL: 2,760 SQ. FT.
BEDROOMS: 3
BATHROOMS: 3½
WIDTH: 60' - 10"
DEPTH: 69' - 3"
FOUNDATION: SLAB,
BASEMENT

SEARCH ONLINE @ EPLANS.COM

A LOVELY TRADITIONAL FACADE COMPLEMENTS THIS

up-to-date ranch-style plan. Inside, an elegant arch connects the kitchen and breakfast room to the main living area beyond. The great room features a cozy fireplace and the dining room is easily served from the kitchen. The first-floor master suite features a roomy walk-in closet, double vanities, and a separate shower and whirlpool tub. Downstairs, Bedrooms 2 and 3 share a bath and are located on either side of a casual den.

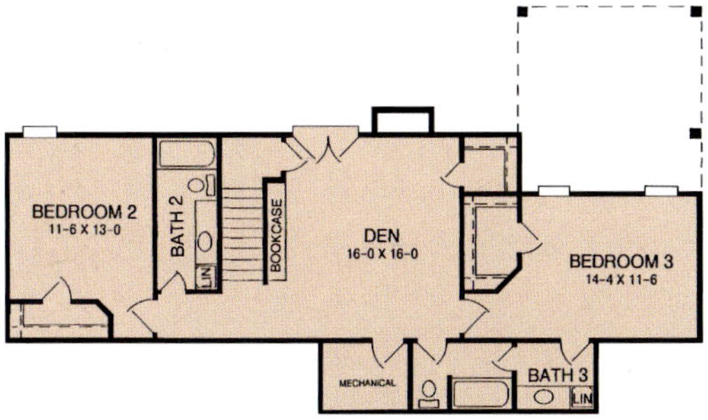

LOWER LEVEL

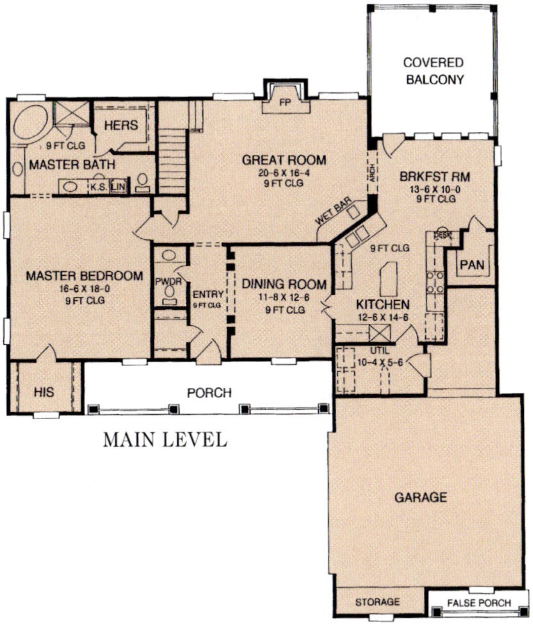

MAIN LEVEL

52   ROOMS FOR LIVING

ORDER BLUEPRINTS 24 HOURS, 7 DAYS A WEEK, AT 1-800-521-6797

GREAT ROOMS

plan# HPK0300044

STYLE: TRADITIONAL
SQUARE FOOTAGE: 3,270
BEDROOMS: 4
BATHROOMS: 3½
WIDTH: 101' - 0"
DEPTH: 48' - 1"
FOUNDATION:
CRAWLSPACE, SLAB

SEARCH ONLINE @ EPLANS.COM

A DISTINCTIVE EXTERIOR, COMPLETE WITH SIDING, stone, and brick, presents a welcoming facade on this four-bedroom home. The large family room includes a cathedral ceiling, a fireplace, and built-ins. The island kitchen has plenty of work space and direct access to a sunny, bay-windowed breakfast room. A study and formal dining room flank the tiled entryway, which leads straight into a formal living room. Three family bedrooms are arranged across the front of the house. The master suite offers plenty of seclusion as well as two walk-in closets, a lavish bath, and direct access to the rear patio. A stairway leads to the attic.

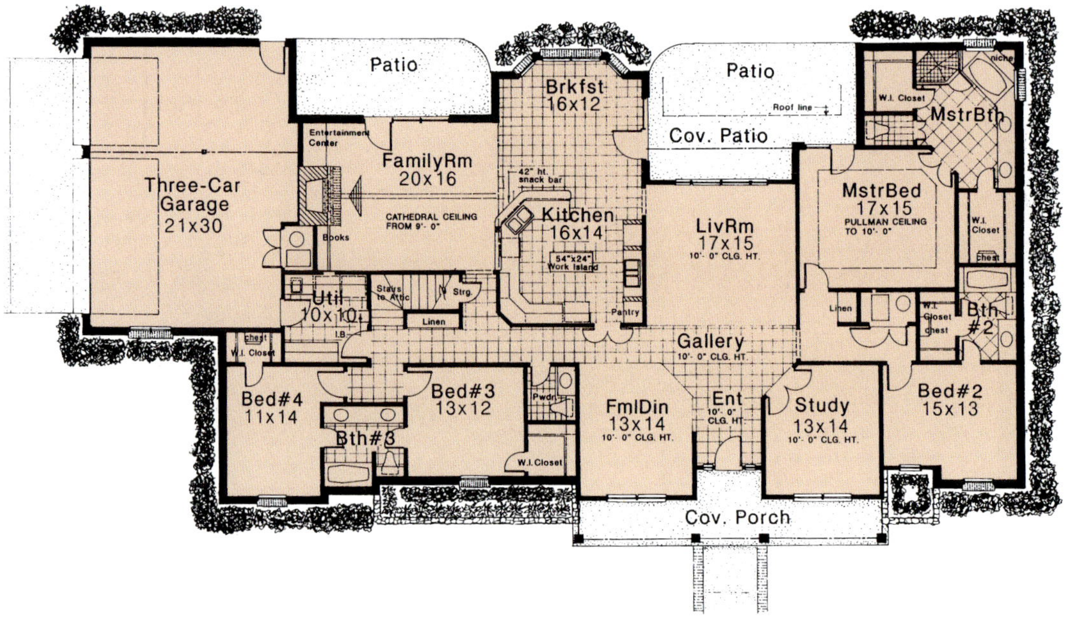

ORDER BLUEPRINTS 24 HOURS, 7 DAYS A WEEK, AT 1-800-521-6797

ROOMS FOR LIVING 53

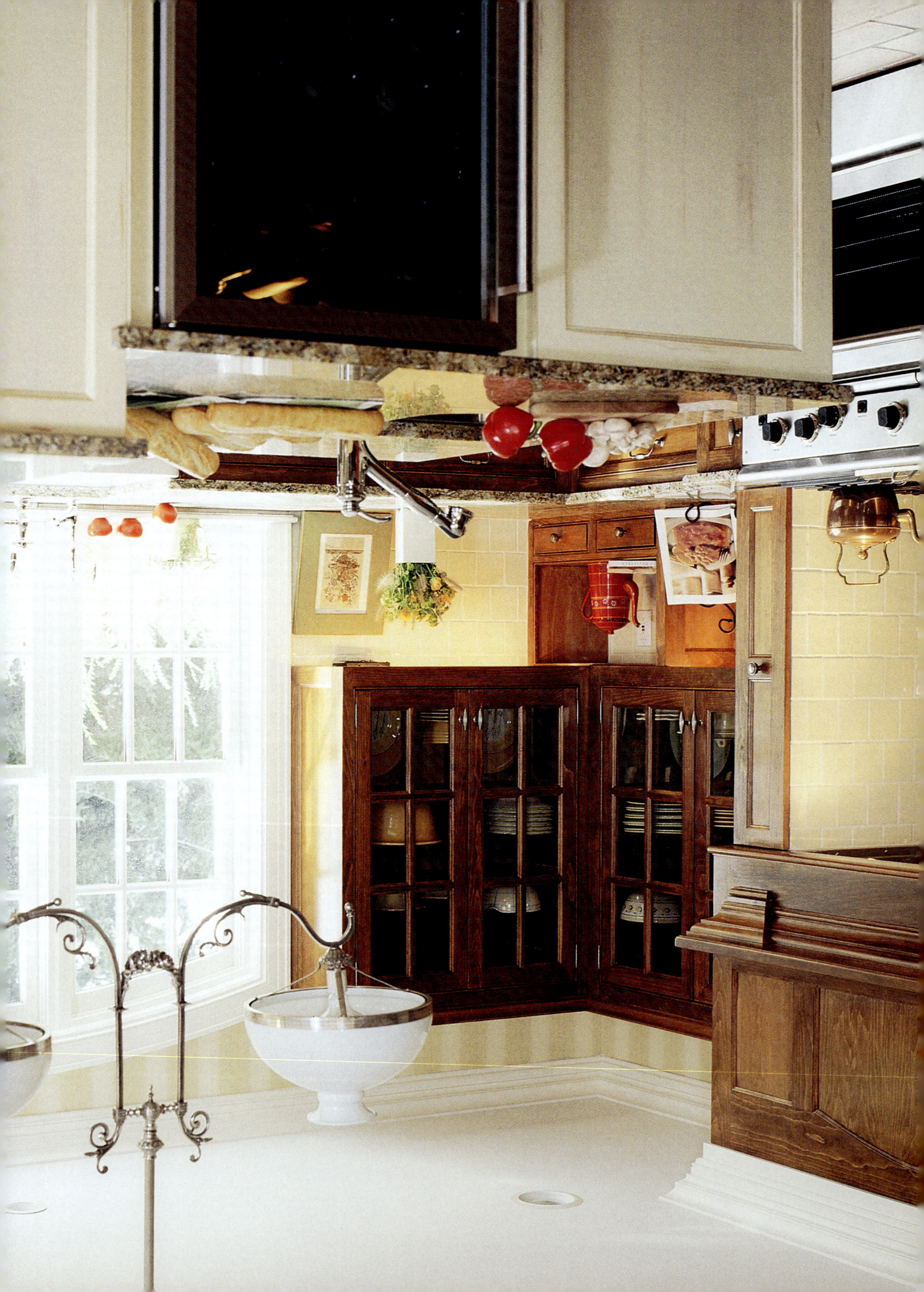

Rooms For Living
KITCHENS

A kitchen today—not unlike a skilled chef— needs to be able to handle a number of chores all at once. It serves as a gathering place for family and friends, so it's a place to both unwind and entertain. It needs to have plenty of space to prepare and serve meals, from snacks on the run to elaborate dinners. And storage is critical for everything from fine china and everyday dishes to cookbooks and wine bottles. The best kitchens not only pull all this off, but they do it in a style that fits the homeowner and the rest of the house.

Above: Mahogany cabinets and stainless-steel appliances combine to give this kitchen a truly elegant feel. The lighting—which can be subtle thanks to the wealth of windows—adds a distinctive touch as well.

Right Top: Thoughts of a perfect country kitchen probably include sun-filled windows over a deep farmhouse sink. Granite countertops and custom pine cabinetry contribute to this kitchen's appeal as well.

Right Bottom: This built-in hutch is not only convenient and beautiful itself, but also showcases the homeowner's collection of china. In addition, the tiles above play off the simple blue and white color scheme.

KITCHENS

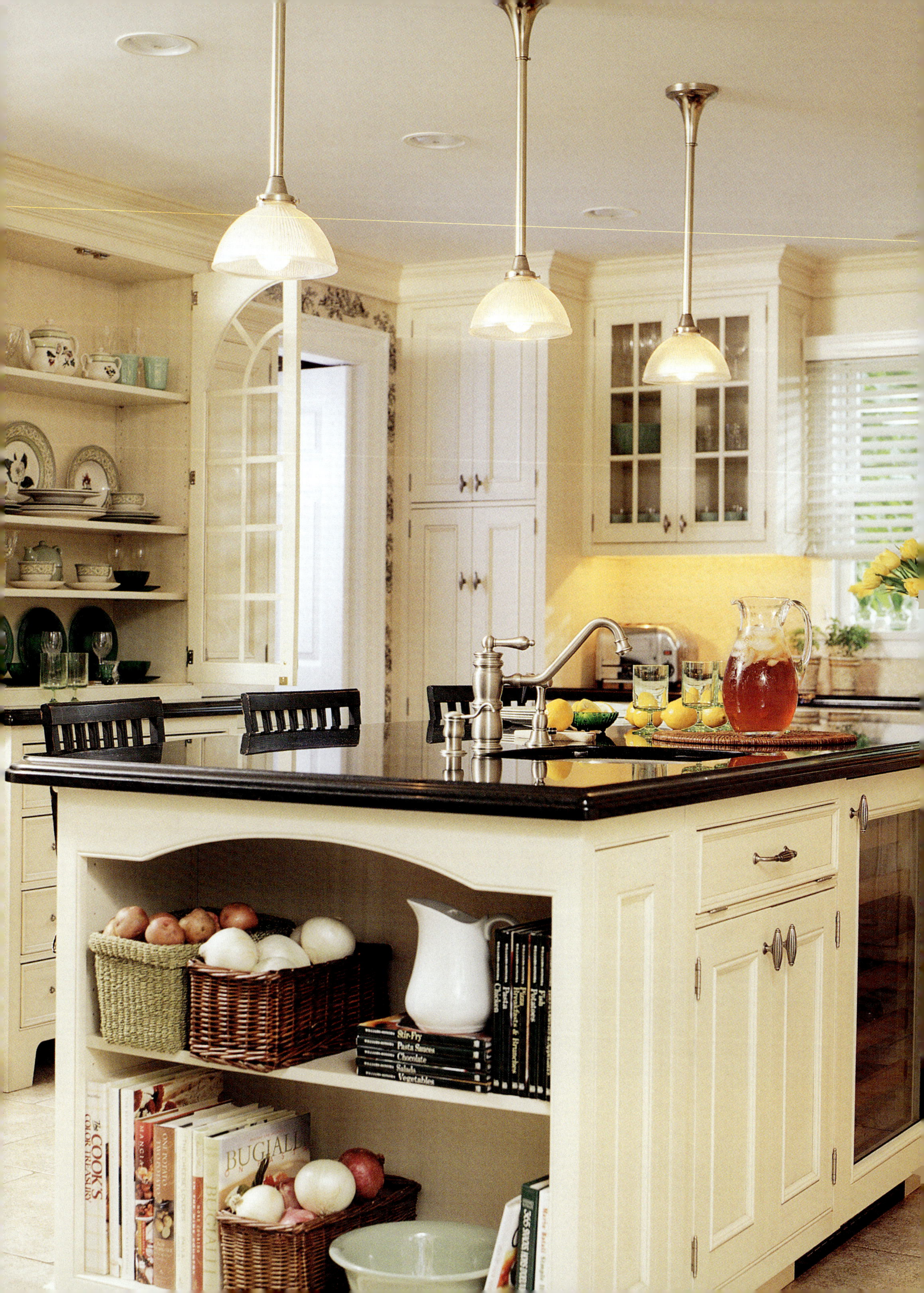

Above: The stainless-steel range in this kitchen is a focal point with Colonial charm, thanks to its surrounding cabinetry that resembles a fireplace. The narrow cabinet doors on either side of the range open to reveal slide-out spice racks.

Left: This island has it all: storage space for everything from bowls to wine bottles, work space and a second sink for helping hands, and a snack bar for serving casual meals.

Tile Style

Using decorative tiles behind a range or sink is a good way to add color or character to your kitchen. If you can't afford an entire wall of custom tile, be creative—pick out a few decorative pieces and arrange them with more affordable tiles. Here, in Design HPK3000054 (page 71), the two rows of unique tiles stand out thanks to their design and size.

Paint, like this light blue, is a popular alternative to tile when you want to add color to your kitchen without the long-term commitment. Use high-gloss or semi-gloss paint in kitchens for their ease of cleaning.

Grand Manor

Hipped rooflines, sunburst windows, and French-style shutters are the defining elements of this home's exterior. Inside, the foyer is flanked by the dining room and the study. Further on, the lavish great room can be entered through two stately columns and is complete with a fireplace, built-in shelves, a vaulted ceiling, and views to the rear patio. The island kitchen is a gourmet's dream. It has plenty of space, plus added details like a pantry and built-in desk. Its open design connects to the bayed breakfast area and the great room. The first-floor master bedroom enjoys a fireplace, two walk-in closets, and an amenity-filled private bath.

Clockwise from top left: Huge windows, including two with arched tops, adorn the front of this beautiful home. The elegant dining room is illuminated with natural light and sweeping outdoor views. The staircase rises from the dining room. A fireplace adds charm to the master bedroom.

the kitchen features
clever storage
such as the work-island shelves

KITCHENS

plan # HPK0300045

STYLE: TRADITIONAL
FIRST FLOOR: 2,270 SQ. FT.
SECOND FLOOR: 685 SQ. FT.
TOTAL: 2,955 SQ. FT.
BONUS SPACE: 563 SQ. FT.
BEDROOMS: 3
BATHROOMS: 2½
WIDTH: 75' - 1"
DEPTH: 53' - 6"

SEARCH ONLINE @ EPLANS.COM

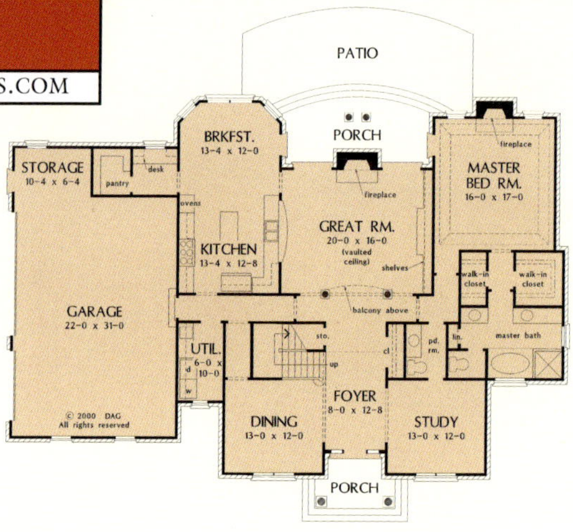

FIRST FLOOR

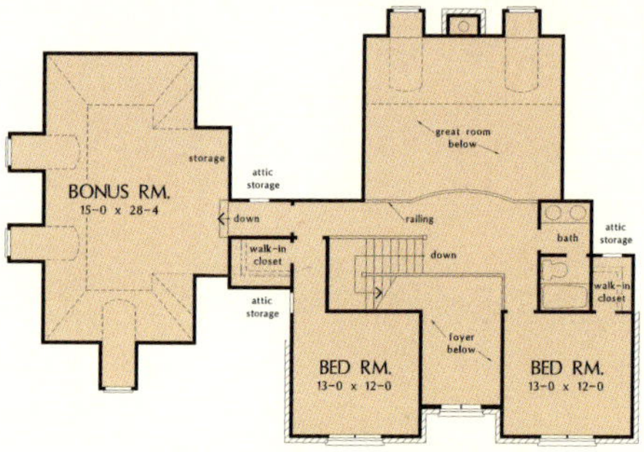

SECOND FLOOR

ORDER BLUEPRINTS 24 HOURS, 7 DAYS A WEEK, AT 1-800-521-6797

ROOMS FOR LIVING   61

Southern Charm

This magnificent Southern-style mansion offers all the features needed for graceful entertaining and refined living. From the stately columns that welcome visitors at the entry to the splendid spiral stairway winding up to the second level, this home is stunning. An octagonal library towards the front guarantees private quietude. An expansive deck with a covered porch at one end and a pampering hot tub at the other will bring hours of enjoyment. Fantastic meals can be prepared in the spacious country kitchen. A resplendent master suite on the main floor enjoys a roomy dressing area; upstairs three more bedrooms, one of them a posh guest suite, offer delightful sleeping accommodations. In addition to the formal dining area and impressive hearth room, the first floor also enjoys a music room and a convenient mudroom.

Clockwise from top left: The exterior of this home presents the image of stately Southern elegance, something that's maintained as you step inside to the foyer. The basement offers room to relax in a casual setting, while the living room has a more formal feel. The sun-drenched breakfast area is surrounded by windows.

KITCHENS

rich wood colors and decorative lighting give this kitchen classic appeal

plan# HPK03000046

STYLE: PLANTATION
FIRST FLOOR: 4,011 SQ. FT.
SECOND FLOOR: 2,198 SQ. FT.
TOTAL: 6,209 SQ. FT.
BEDROOMS: 4
BATHROOMS: 3½ + ½
WIDTH: 136' - 0"
DEPTH: 69' - 2"
FOUNDATION: BASEMENT

SEARCH ONLINE @ EPLANS.COM

FIRST FLOOR

SECOND FLOOR

BASEMENT

KITCHENS

COURTESY OF MASCO CORPORATION AND BETTER HOMES AND GARDENS SPECIAL INTEREST PUBLICATIONS

plan# HPK0300047

STYLE: TRADITIONAL
FIRST FLOOR: 3,297 SQ. FT.
SECOND FLOOR: 1,453 SQ. FT.
TOTAL: 4,750 SQ. FT.
BEDROOMS: 5
BATHROOMS: 4½
WIDTH: 80' - 10"
DEPTH: 85' - 6"
FOUNDATION: SLAB

SEARCH ONLINE @ EPLANS.COM

THIS ELEGANT HOME COMBINES A TRADITIONAL exterior with a contemporary interior and provides a delightful setting for both entertaining and individual solitude. A living room and bay-windowed dining room provide an open area for formal entertaining, which can spill outside to the entertainment terrace or to the nearby gathering room with its dramatic fireplace. On the opposite side of the house, French doors make it possible for the study/guest room to be closed off from the rest of the first floor. The master suite is also a private retreat, offering a fireplace as well as an abundance of natural light, and a bath designed to pamper. The entire family will enjoy the second-floor media loft from which a balcony overlooks the two-story gathering room below.

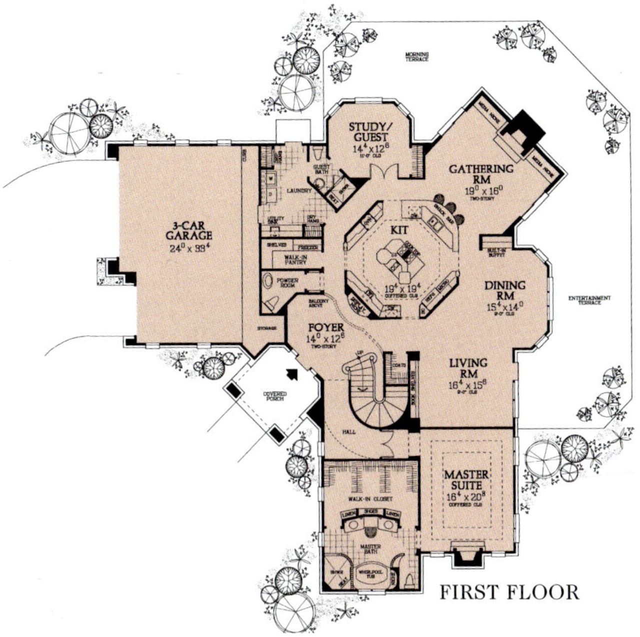

FIRST FLOOR

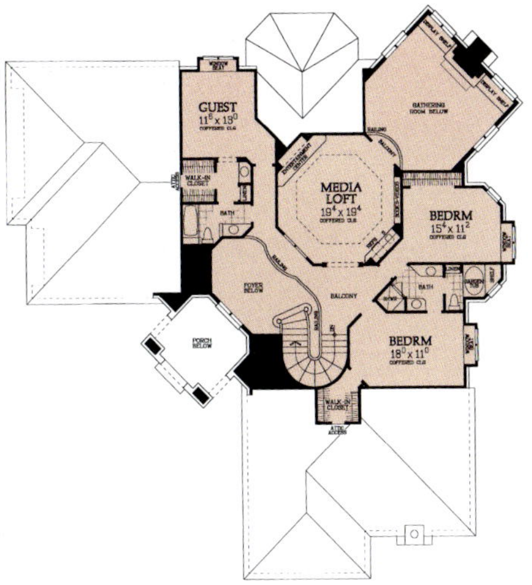

SECOND FLOOR

64   ROOMS FOR LIVING   ORDER BLUEPRINTS 24 HOURS, 7 DAYS A WEEK, AT 1-800-521-6797

KITCHENS

FOR MORE DETAILED INFORMATION, PLEASE CHECK THE FLOOR PLANS CAREFULLY.

plan # HPK0300048

STYLE: TRADITIONAL
SQUARE FOOTAGE: 2,625
BONUS SPACE: 447 SQ. FT.
BEDROOMS: 4
BATHROOMS: 2½
WIDTH: 63' - 1"
DEPTH: 90' - 2"

SEARCH ONLINE @ EPLANS.COM

THIS STATELY BRICK FACADE

features a columned, covered porch that ushers visitors into the large foyer. An expansive great room with a fireplace and access to a covered rear porch awaits. The centrally located kitchen is within easy reach of the great room, formal dining room, and skylit breakfast area. Split-bedroom planning places the master bedroom and elegant master bath to the right of the home. Two bedrooms with abundant closet space are placed to the left; an optional bedroom or study with a Palladian window faces the front. A large bonus room is located above the garage.

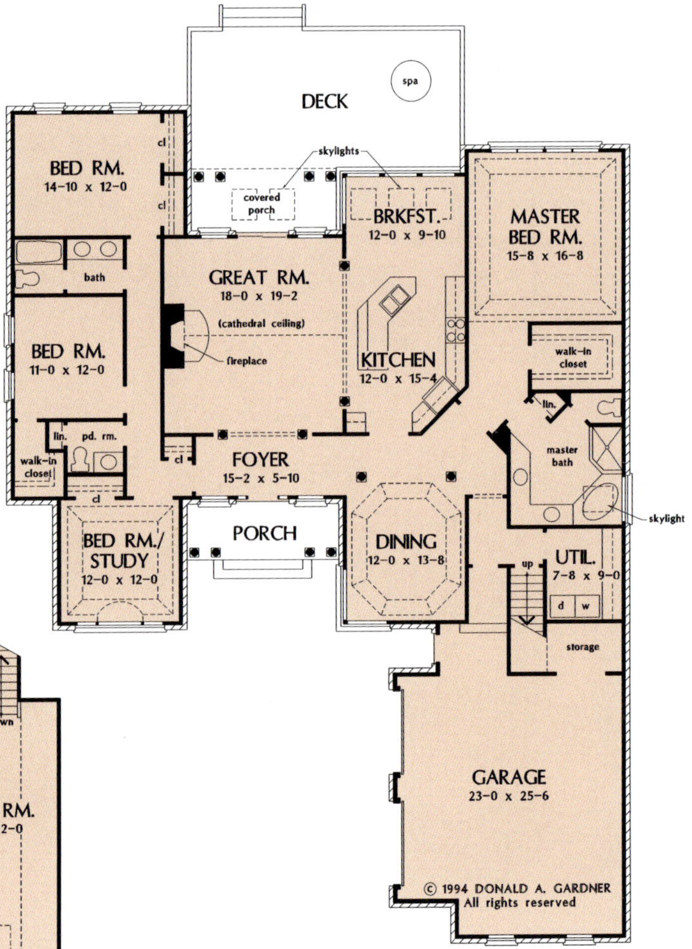

DECK
spa

BED RM.
14-10 x 12-0
cl
cl
bath

skylights

covered porch

BRKFST.
12-0 x 9-10

MASTER BED RM.
15-8 x 16-8

GREAT RM.
18-0 x 19-2
(cathedral ceiling)

BED RM.
11-0 x 12-0

fireplace

KITCHEN
12-0 x 15-4

walk-in closet

lin.
pd. rm.
walk-in closet

lin.

master bath

FOYER
15-2 x 5-10

cl

skylight

BED RM./
STUDY
12-0 x 12-0

PORCH

DINING
12-0 x 13-8

UTIL.
7-8 x 9-0

up
d w

storage

BONUS RM.
15-0 x 22-0

down

GARAGE
23-0 x 25-6

© 1994 DONALD A. GARDNER
All rights reserved

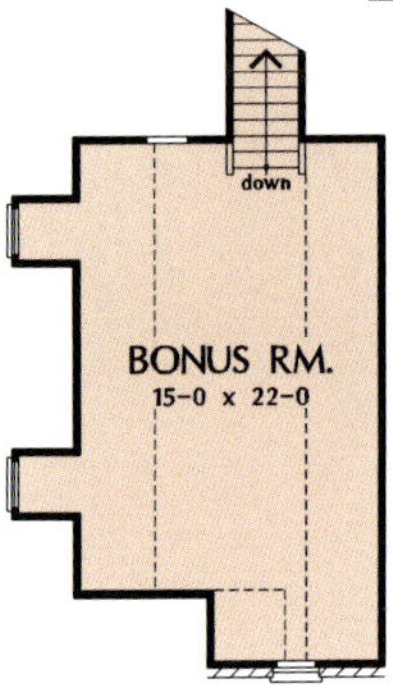

ORDER BLUEPRINTS 24 HOURS, 7 DAYS A WEEK, AT 1-800-521-6797

ROOMS FOR LIVING   65

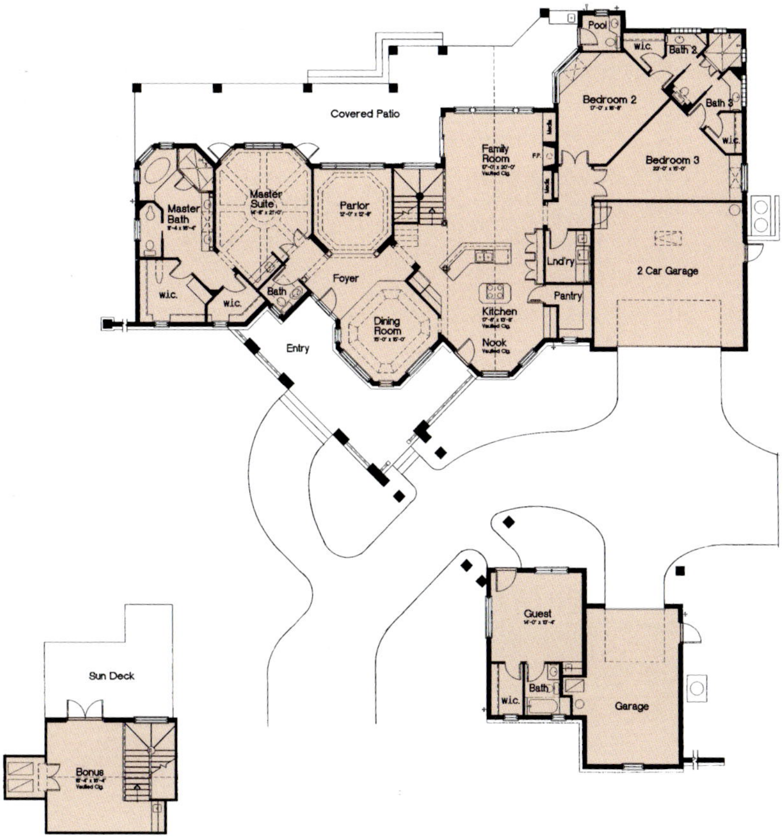

THOUGH DESIGNED AS a grand estate, this home retains the warmth of a country manor with intimate details, on the inside and out. A one-of-a-kind drive court leads to private parking and ends in a two-car garage; a separate guest house is replete with angled walls and sculptured ceilings. A continuous vault follows from the family room through the kitchen and nook. The vault soars even higher in the bonus room with a sundeck upstairs. Two exquisitely appointed family bedrooms with window seats and walk-in closets share a full bath. The master suite has pampering details such as a juice bar and media wall, walk-in closets, and covered patio access.

---

plan # HPK0300049

STYLE: COUNTRY COTTAGE
FIRST FLOOR: 3,146 SQ. FT.
BONUS SPACE: 330 SQ. FT.
TOTAL: 3,436 SQ. FT.
BEDROOMS: 4
BATHROOMS: 3½ + ½
WIDTH: 94' - 0"
DEPTH: 113' - 5"
FOUNDATION: SLAB

SEARCH ONLINE @ EPLANS.COM

KITCHENS

plan# HPK0300050

STYLE: TRADITIONAL
FIRST FLOOR: 3,414 SQ. FT.
SECOND FLOOR: 1,238 SQ. FT.
TOTAL: 4,652 SQ. FT.
BEDROOMS: 4
BATHROOMS: 3½
WIDTH: 90' - 6"
DEPTH: 78' - 9"
FOUNDATION: BASEMENT

SEARCH ONLINE @ EPLANS.COM

COUNTRY MEETS TRADITIONAL IN THIS SPLENDID design.

A covered front porch offers a place to enjoy the sunrise or place a porch swing. With the formal areas flanking the foyer, an open flow is established between the column-accented dining room and the library with its distinguished beam ceiling. The two-story great room features a wall of windows looking out to the rear grounds. On the left, the gourmet kitchen serves up casual and formal meals to the breakfast and hearth rooms with the dining room just steps away. The master bedroom enjoys a sitting area with an array of view-catching windows, a spacious dressing area, and an accommodating walk-in closet. Three family bedrooms—one with a private bath—complete the second level.

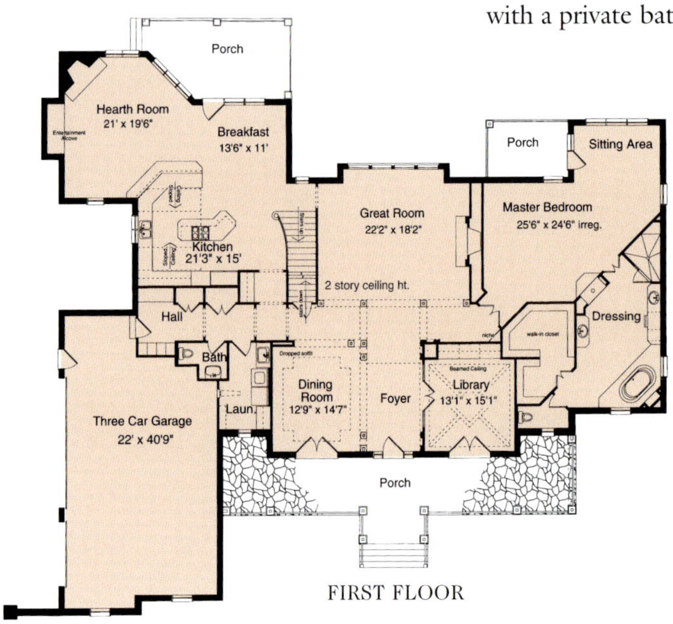

FIRST FLOOR

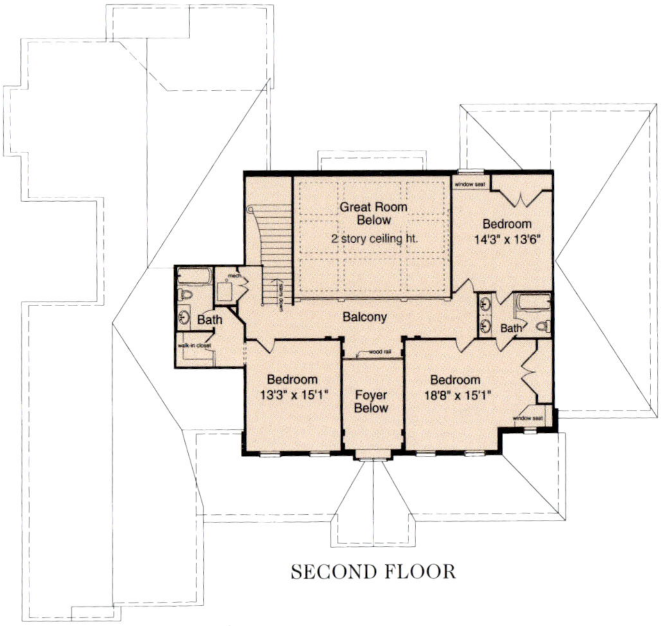

SECOND FLOOR

KITCHENS

A GENTLY SLOPING, HIGH-PITCHED ROOF complements keystones, arch-top windows, and a delicate balcony balustrade, calling up a sense of cozy elegance. The foyer opens to a grand room with a focal-point fireplace and access to a screened room that leads to the veranda. The gourmet kitchen offers a walk-in pantry, acres of counter space, and a morning room with outdoor flow. An island wardrobe highlights the master suite, which boasts a secluded lounge with a door to a private area of the veranda. Upstairs, two secondary bedrooms enjoy a balcony overlook to the foyer, and each room has its own access to an outdoor deck.

plan # **HPK0300051**

STYLE: EUROPEAN COTTAGE
FIRST FLOOR: 1,862 SQ. FT.
SECOND FLOOR: 1,044 SQ. FT.
TOTAL: 2,906 SQ. FT.
BONUS SPACE: 259 SQ. FT.
BEDROOMS: 3
BATHROOMS: 3½
WIDTH: 60' - 0"
DEPTH: 60' - 0"
FOUNDATION: CRAWLSPACE

SEARCH ONLINE @ EPLANS.COM

PHOTO COURTESY OF LIVING CONCEPTS HOME PLANNING

plan # HPK03000052

STYLE: TRADITIONAL
FIRST FLOOR: 2,345 SQ. FT.
SECOND FLOOR: 1,336 SQ. FT.
TOTAL: 3,681 SQ. FT.
BEDROOMS: 4
BATHROOMS: 3½
WIDTH: 65' - 0"
DEPTH: 66' - 0"
FOUNDATION: CRAWLSPACE

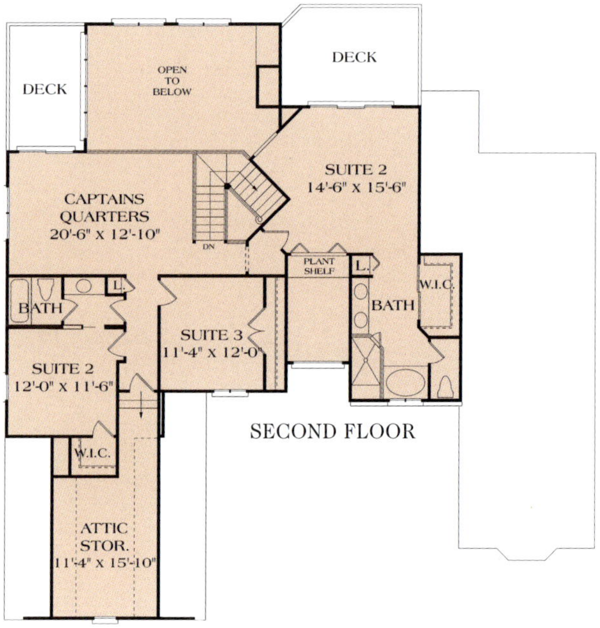

SEARCH ONLINE @ EPLANS.COM

AN EYE-CATCHING ROOFLINE AND A GENTLY ARCHED

entry draw attention to this home's exterior; the interior contains a wide variety of amenity-packed rooms. On the first floor, the central grand room overlooks both the rear screened porch and a side deck; a wet bar sits just outside the nearby dining room. The gourmet kitchen offers a walk-in pantry and adjoins a cozy "good morning" room, suitable for quiet family meals and open to a small dining deck. A library and gathering room round out the first-floor living space, and a luxurious master suite with a private lounge provides the sleeping space. Three more family bedrooms—one with a private bath and deck—are found upstairs.

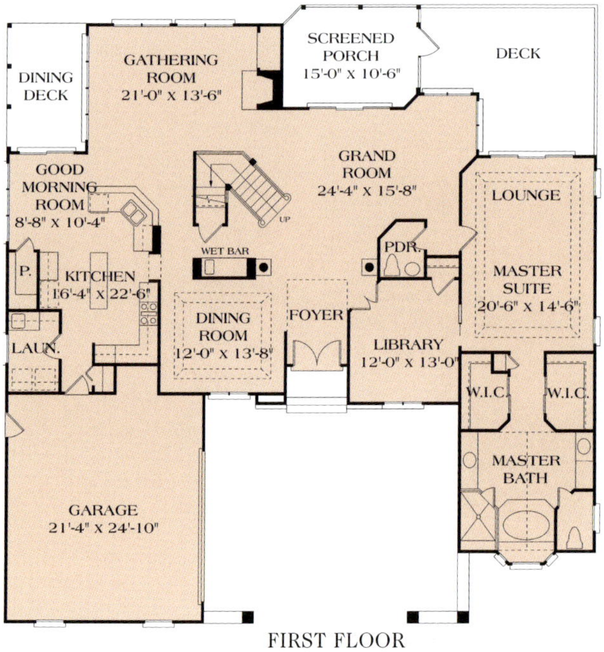

KITCHENS

GABLES, VARIED ROOFLINES, INTERESTING DORMERS,

arched windows, a recessed entry—the detailing on this stone manor is exquisite! The foyer opens through arches to the formal dining room, an elegant stair hall, and the grand room, with its fireplace, built-ins, and French doors to the lanai. The informal zone includes a kitchen with an oversized work island and pantry, a breakfast nook, and a family room with a fireplace and its own screened porch. An anteroom outside the master suite gives the homeowners added privacy and allows the option of a private entrance to the study. The master bath is loaded with extras, including a stairway to the upstairs exercise room. The second floor also offers a home theater and a home office, as well as four bedroom suites and a mother-in-law or maid's apartment. Note that there are four sets of stairs to aid in the traffic flow and a laundry room on each level.

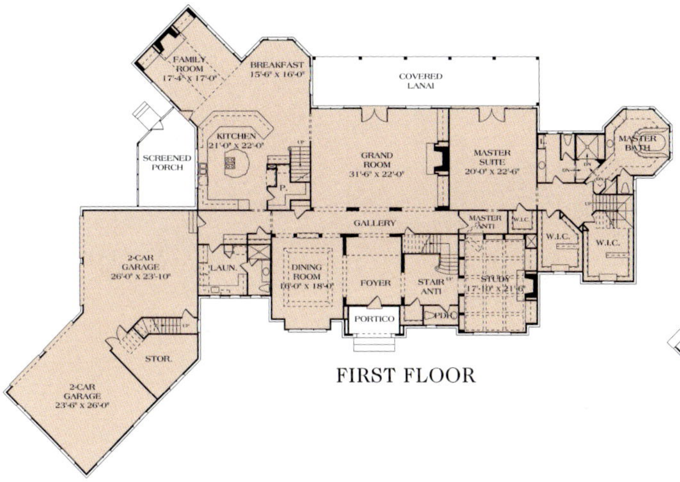

plan# HPK0300053

STYLE: COUNTRY COTTAGE
FIRST FLOOR: 5,200 SQ. FT.
SECOND FLOOR: 4,177 SQ. FT.
TOTAL: 9,377 SQ. FT.
BEDROOMS: 6
BATHROOMS: 7½
WIDTH: 155' - 9"
DEPTH: 107' - 11"
FOUNDATION: CRAWLSPACE

SEARCH ONLINE @ EPLANS.COM

FIRST FLOOR

SECOND FLOOR

70   ROOMS FOR LIVING

ORDER BLUEPRINTS 24 HOURS, 7 DAYS A WEEK, AT 1-800-521-6797

KITCHENS

plan # HPK0300054

STYLE: FRENCH COUNTRY
FIRST FLOOR: 2,390 SQ. FT.
SECOND FLOOR: 765 SQ. FT.
TOTAL: 3,155 SQ. FT.
BONUS SPACE: 433 SQ. FT.
BEDROOMS: 4
BATHROOMS: 3½
WIDTH: 87' - 11"
DEPTH: 75' - 2"
FOUNDATION: CRAWLSPACE

SEARCH ONLINE @ EPLANS.COM

THE GRAND EXTERIOR OF THIS NORMANDY COUNTRY

design features a steeply pitched gable roofline. Arched dormers repeat the window accents. Inside, the promise of space is fulfilled with a large gathering room that fills the center of the house and opens to a long trellised veranda. The den or guest suite with a fireplace, the adjacent powder room, and the master suite with a vaulted ceiling and access to the veranda reside in the right wing. Two additional bedrooms with two baths and a loft overlooking the gathering room are upstairs. A large bonus room is found over the garage and can be developed later as office or hobby space.

FIRST FLOOR

- GARAGE 23'4" x 23'4"
- UTIL
- PORTICO
- LOGGIA
- Den/GUEST SUITE 15'2" x 12'8"
- DINING ROOM 12'8" x 13'6"
- FOYER
- PDR
- W.I.C.
- MASTER BATH
- KITCHEN 14'0" x 19'6"
- GATHERING ROOM 20'4" x 20'4"
- MORNING 9'8" x 11'0"
- MASTER SUITE 15'2" x 19'4"
- Veranda

SECOND FLOOR

- BONUS ROOM 23'2" x 16'0"
- PDR
- SUITE 3 12'8" x 13'6"
- BATH
- SUITE 2 15'8" x 13'2"
- OPEN TO BELOW
- Loft

KITCHENS

THE HEART OF THIS MAGNIFICENT DESIGN IS THE TWO-

story living room with its fireplace and built-in bookshelves. To the right rear of the plan lie the more casual rooms—the vaulted family room, island kitchen with pantry, and the breakfast nook. A formal dining room awaits elegant meals at the front of the plan. The private master wing features a secluded study, bayed sitting area, and deluxe vaulted bath. Upstairs, three bedrooms, each with ample closet space, share two full baths and a loft and a gallery that overlook the first floor.

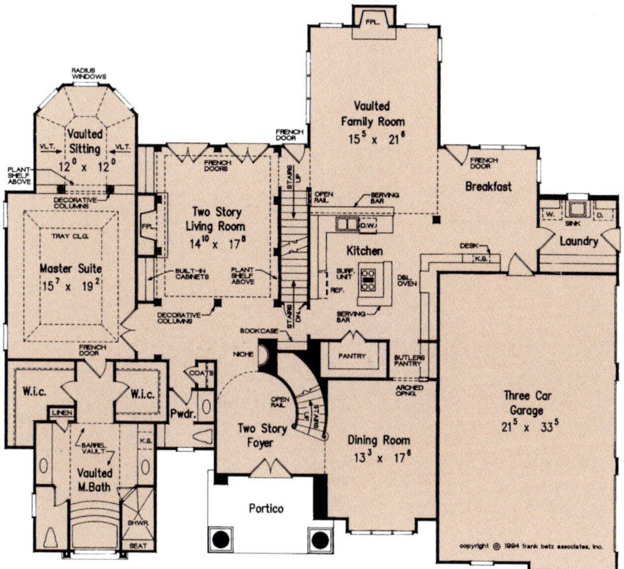

plan# HPK0300055

STYLE: FRENCH
FIRST FLOOR: 2,764 SQ. FT.
SECOND FLOOR: 1,598 SQ. FT.
TOTAL: 4,362 SQ. FT.
BEDROOMS: 4
BATHROOMS: 3½
WIDTH: 74' - 6"
DEPTH: 65' - 10"
FOUNDATION: BASEMENT, CRAWLSPACE

SEARCH ONLINE @ EPLANS.COM

FIRST FLOOR

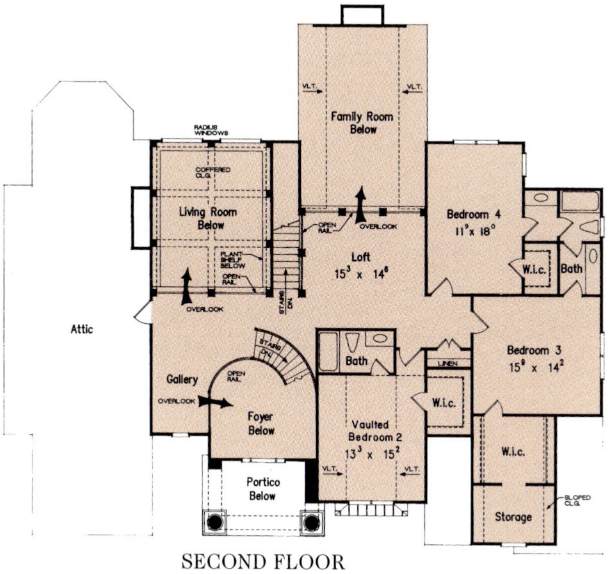

SECOND FLOOR

72   ROOMS FOR LIVING

ORDER BLUEPRINTS 24 HOURS, 7 DAYS A WEEK, AT 1-800-521-6797

KITCHENS

plan# HPK0300056

STYLE: FRENCH
FIRST FLOOR: 1,900 SQ. FT.
SECOND FLOOR: 890 SQ. FT.
TOTAL: 2,790 SQ. FT.
BEDROOMS: 4
BATHROOMS: 2½
WIDTH: 63' - 0"
DEPTH: 51' - 0"
FOUNDATION: WALKOUT
BASEMENT

SEARCH ONLINE @ EPLANS.COM

A PERFECT BLEND OF STUCCO AND STACKED STONE sets off keystones, transoms, and arches in this French Country facade to inspire an elegant spirit. The foyer is flanked by the spacious dining room and study, accented by a vaulted ceiling and a fireplace. A great room with a full wall of glass connects the interior with the outdoors. A first-floor master suite offers both style and intimacy with a coffered ceiling and a secluded bath.

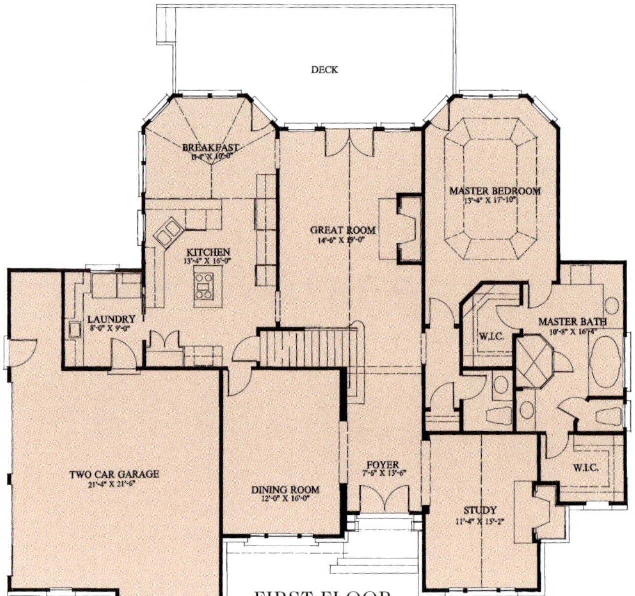

FIRST FLOOR

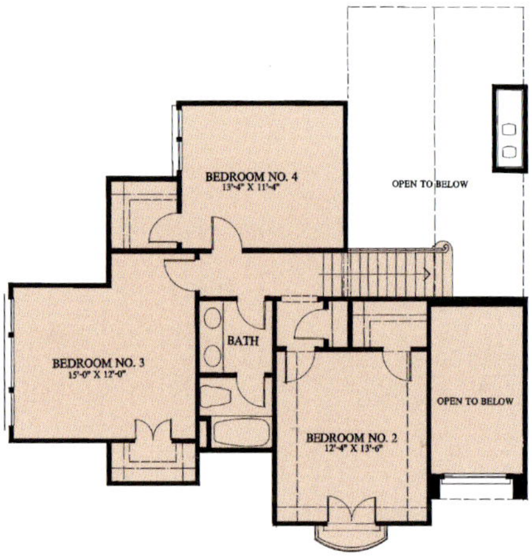

SECOND FLOOR

ORDER BLUEPRINTS 24 HOURS, 7 DAYS A WEEK, AT 1-800-521-6797

KITCHENS

plan # HPK0300057

STYLE: TRADITIONAL
FIRST FLOOR: 2,095 SQ. FT.
SECOND FLOOR: 1,954 SQ. FT.
TOTAL: 4,049 SQ. FT.
BEDROOMS: 5
BATHROOMS: 4½
WIDTH: 56' - 0"
DEPTH: 63' - 0"
FOUNDATION: BASEMENT,
CRAWLSPACE

SEARCH ONLINE @ EPLANS.COM

THE FRENCH COUNTRY FACADE OF THIS LOVELY design hints at the enchanting amenities found within. A two-story foyer welcomes you inside. To the right, a bayed living room is separated from the formal dining room by graceful columns. A butler's pantry leads to the gourmet island kitchen. The breakfast room accesses a rear covered porch and shares a casual area with the two-story family room. Here, a fireplace flanked by built-ins adds to the relaxing atmosphere. Bedroom 5 with a private bath converts to an optional study. Upstairs, the master suite offers palatial elegance. Here, the sitting room is warmed by a fireplace flanked by built-ins, and the suite accesses a private second-floor porch. A dressing room leads to the vaulted master bath and enormous His and Hers walk-in closets. Three additional bedrooms are available on the second floor.

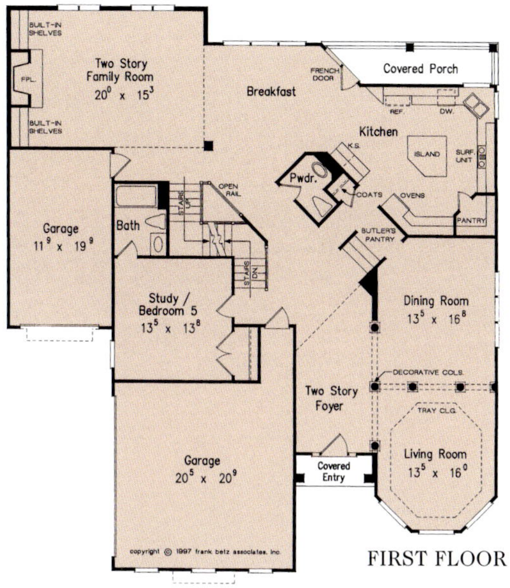

FIRST FLOOR

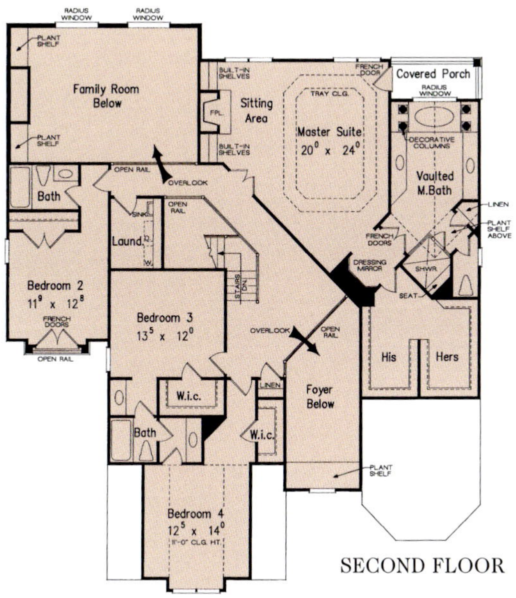

SECOND FLOOR

74   ROOMS FOR LIVING

ORDER BLUEPRINTS 24 HOURS, 7 DAYS A WEEK, AT 1-800-521-6797

EUROPEAN DETAILS BRING CHARM AND A TOUCH OF joie

de vivre to this traditional home. Casual living space includes a two-story family room with a centered fireplace. A sizable kitchen, with an island serving bar and a French door to the rear property, leads to the formal dining room through a convenient butler's pantry. The second floor includes a generous master suite with a sitting room defined by decorative columns and five lovely windows. Bedroom 2 has a private bath, and two additional bedrooms share a hall bath with compartmented vanities.

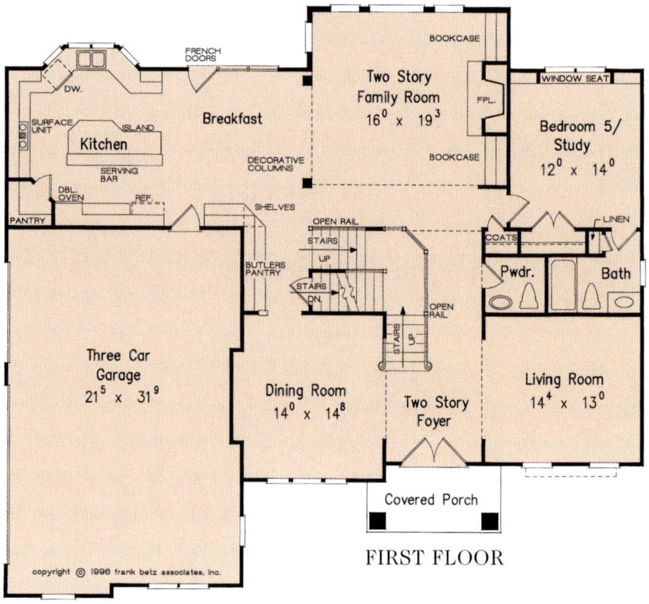

plan # HPK0300058

STYLE: EUROPEAN COTTAGE
FIRST FLOOR: 1,786 SQ. FT.
SECOND FLOOR: 1,739 SQ. FT.
TOTAL: 3,525 SQ. FT.
BEDROOMS: 5
BATHROOMS: 4½
WIDTH: 59' - 0"
DEPTH: 53' - 0"
FOUNDATION: BASEMENT, CRAWLSPACE, SLAB

SEARCH ONLINE @ EPLANS.COM

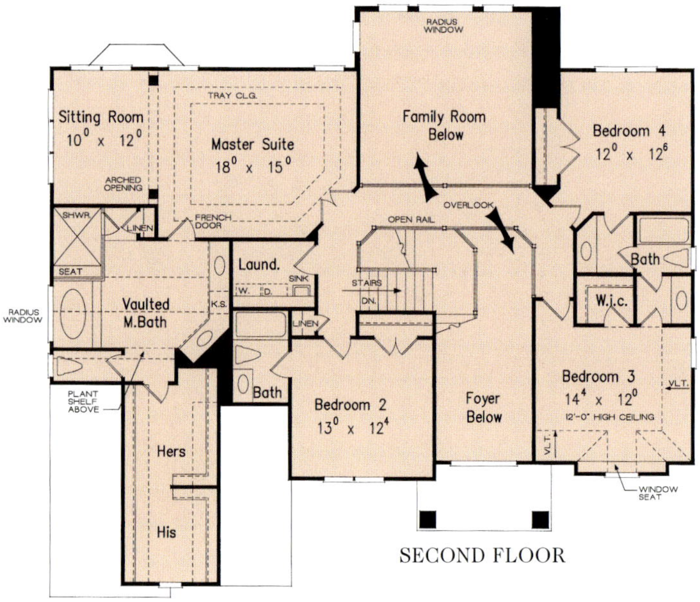

76 ROOMS FOR LIVING ORDER BLUEPRINTS 24 HOURS, 7 DAYS A WEEK, AT 1-800-521-6797

KITCHENS

GRACEFUL DETAILS COMBINE WITH A COVERED entryway to welcome friends and family to come on in. The canted bay sitting area in the master suite provides sunny respite and quiet solitude. To be the center of attention, invite everyone to party in the vaulted great room, which spills over into the big airy kitchen. Guests can make use of the optional study/bedroom. Upstairs, secondary bedrooms share a full bath and a balcony overlook. A spacious central hall leads to a bonus room that provides wardrobe space.

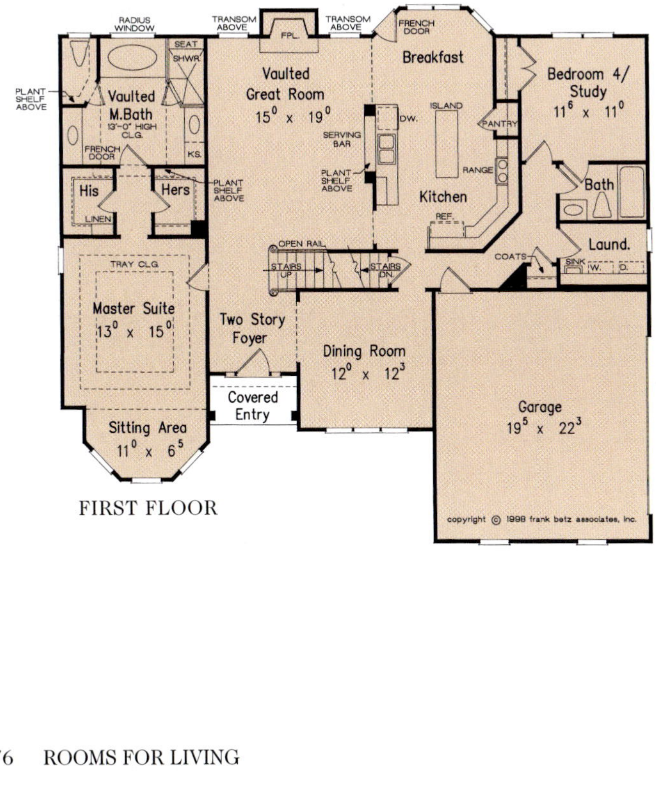

plan # HPK03000059

STYLE: COUNTRY COTTAGE
FIRST FLOOR: 1,688 SQ. FT.
SECOND FLOOR: 558 SQ. FT.
TOTAL: 2,246 SQ. FT.
BONUS SPACE: 269 SQ. FT.
BEDROOMS: 4
BATHROOMS: 3
WIDTH: 54' - 0"
DEPTH: 48' - 0"
FOUNDATION: BASEMENT, CRAWLSPACE, SLAB

SEARCH ONLINE @ EPLANS.COM

FIRST FLOOR

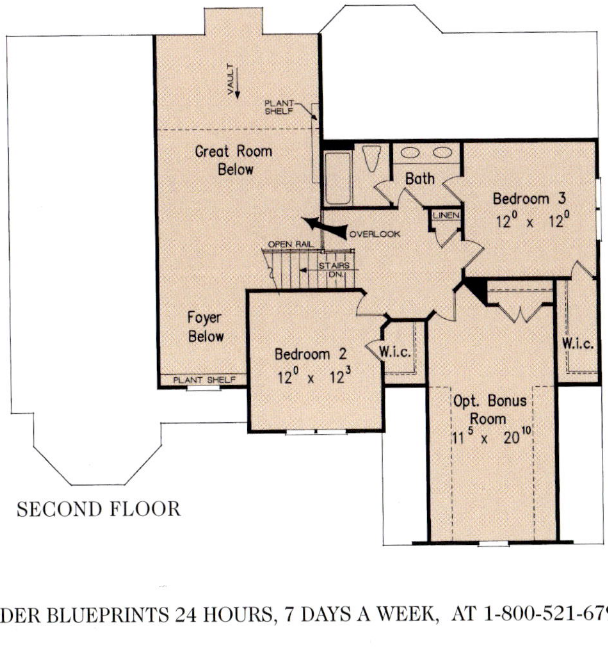

SECOND FLOOR

plan # HPK0300060

STYLE: COUNTRY COTTAGE
FIRST FLOOR: 3,261 SQ. FT.
SECOND FLOOR: 1,920 SQ. FT.
TOTAL: 5,181 SQ. FT.
BEDROOMS: 4
BATHROOMS: 3½
WIDTH: 86' - 2"
DEPTH: 66' - 10"
FOUNDATION: CRAWLSPACE, BASEMENT

SEARCH ONLINE @ EPLANS.COM

THIS HOME IS ELEGANTLY STYLED IN THE FRENCH

Country tradition. A large dining room and a study open off the two-story grand foyer. The large formal living room accesses the covered patio. A more informal family room is conveniently located off the kitchen and breakfast room. The roomy master suite includes a sitting area, a luxurious private bath, and its own entrance to the study. The second floor can be reached from the formal front stair or a well-placed rear staircase. Three large bedrooms and a game room are located on this floor. A walkout basement can be expanded to provide more living space.

KITCHENS

WITH EUROPEAN AND SOUTHERN COLONIAL

influences, this striking five-bedroom stucco home allows plenty of room for family and friends, and every amenity on your wish list. A stylish, open foyer presents access to all living areas. The library/study will delight with a beamed ceiling, built-in shelves, and French doors to a private porch. The formal dining room and two-story living room are elegant and bathed in natural light. The guest suite offers a private bath and double doors to the loggia. A country kitchen, bayed breakfast nook and leisure room (with a fireplace) are open to each other, a popular feature. Upstairs, three generous family suites access private baths and balconies. The sprawling master suite is lovely and bright, with a private sunporch and a spa bath with a corner whirlpool tub. Not to be missed: a convenient utility room on the upper level.

plan # HPK0300061

STYLE: EUROPEAN COTTAGE
FIRST FLOOR: 2,164 SQ. FT.
SECOND FLOOR: 2,311 SQ. FT.
TOTAL: 4,475 SQ. FT.
BEDROOMS: 5
BATHROOMS: 5½
WIDTH: 58' - 0"
DEPTH: 65' - 0"
FOUNDATION: SLAB

SEARCH ONLINE @ EPLANS.COM

FIRST FLOOR

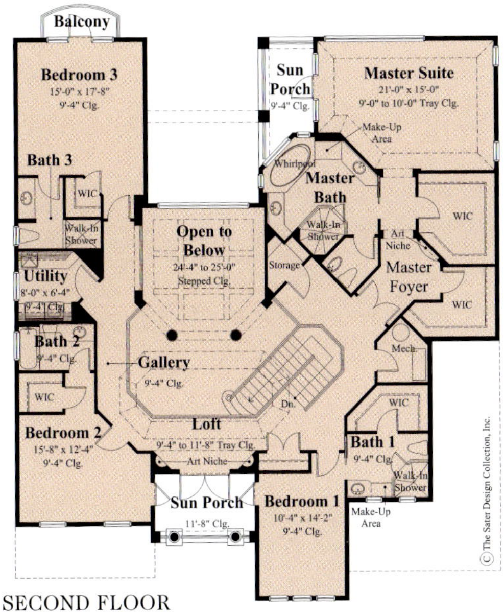

SECOND FLOOR

plan # HPK0300004

STYLE: FRENCH
FIRST FLOOR: 2,232 SQ. FT.
SECOND FLOOR: 1,269 SQ. FT.
TOTAL: 3,501 SQ. FT.
BEDROOMS: 4
BATHROOMS: 4½
WIDTH: 63' - 9"
DEPTH: 80' - 0"
FOUNDATION: SLAB

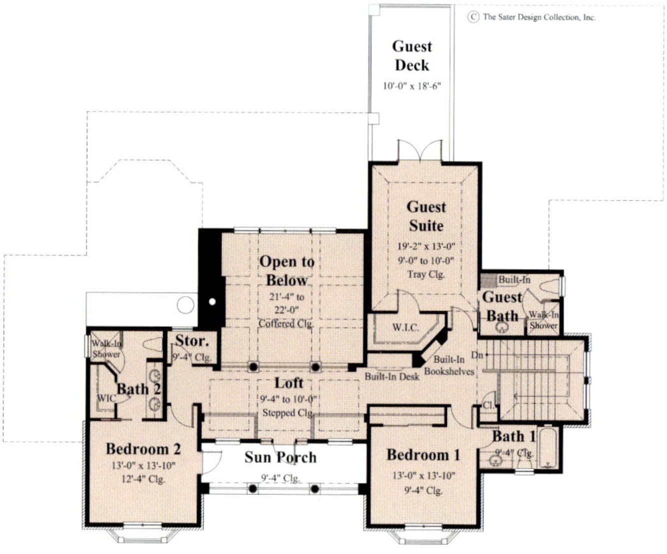

SEARCH ONLINE @ EPLANS.COM

AN IMPRESSIVE ITALIAN RENAISSANCE MANOR, THIS

stone-and-stucco home is stunning from the curb and pure rapture inside. Twin bays at the front of the plan hold a study with a star-stepped ceiling and a dining room with coffer accents and decorative columns. The great room offers a warming fireplace and a soaring coffered ceiling. Not to be missed: an outdoor kitchen in addition to the modern country kitchen and bayed breakfast nook inside. The master suite is a dream come true; a large bay window, oversize walk-in closets and a pampering bath with a corner tub will delight. Upstairs, three bedrooms all have private baths and large walk-in closets. Two bedrooms enjoy deck access.

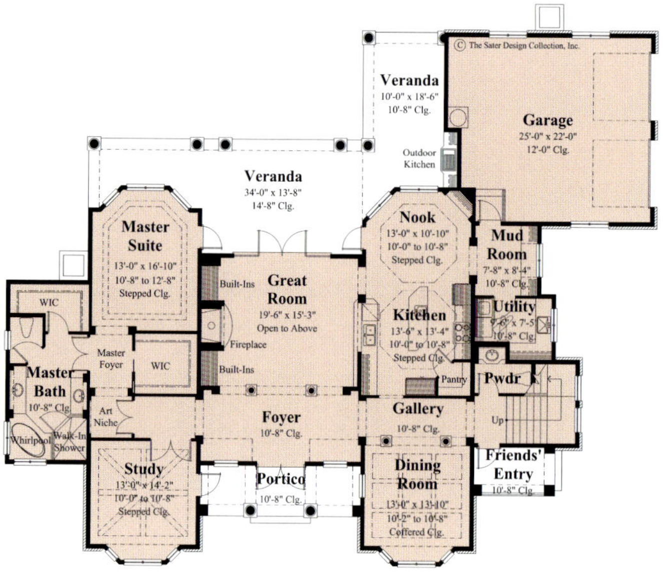

KITCHENS

MEDITERRANEAN ACCENTS ENHANCE THE FACADE OF

this contemporary estate home. Two fanciful turret bays add a sense of grandeur to the exterior. Double doors open inside to a grand two-story foyer. A two-sided fireplace warms the study and living room, with a two-story coffered ceiling. To the right, the master suite includes a private bath, two walk-in closets, and double-door access to the sweeping rear veranda. Casual areas of the home include the gourmet island kitchen, breakfast nook and leisure room warmed by a fireplace. A spiral staircase leads upstairs, where a second-floor balcony separates two family bedrooms from the luxurious guest suite.

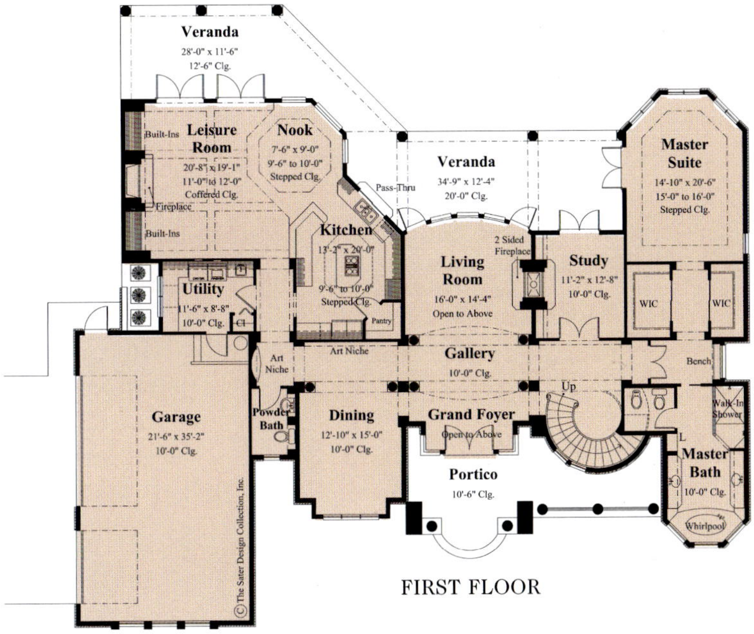

plan# HPK0300062

STYLE: EUROPEAN COTTAGE
FIRST FLOOR: 2,834 SQ. FT.
SECOND FLOOR: 1,143 SQ. FT.
TOTAL: 3,977 SQ. FT.
BEDROOMS: 4
BATHROOMS: 3½
WIDTH: 85' - 0"
DEPTH: 76' - 8"
FOUNDATION: SLAB

SEARCH ONLINE @ EPLANS.COM

FIRST FLOOR

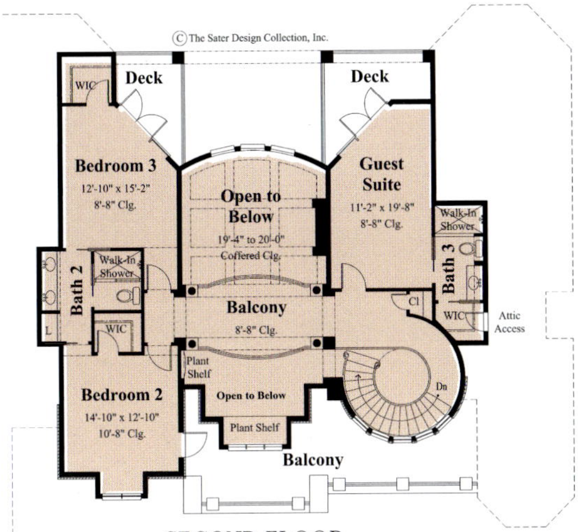

SECOND FLOOR

80   ROOMS FOR LIVING

ORDER BLUEPRINTS 24 HOURS, 7 DAYS A WEEK, AT 1-800-521-6797

KITCHENS

plan# HPK0300063

STYLE: EUROPEAN COTTAGE
FIRST FLOOR: 2,219 SQ. FT.
SECOND FLOOR: 1,085 SQ. FT.
TOTAL: 3,304 SQ. FT.
BONUS SPACE: 404 SQ. FT.
BEDROOMS: 4
BATHROOMS: 3½
WIDTH: 91' - 0"
DEPTH: 52' - 8"
FOUNDATION: SLAB

SEARCH ONLINE @ EPLANS.COM

THIS HOME FEATURES TWO
levels of pampering luxury filled with the most up-to-date amenities. Touches of Mediterranean detail add to the striking facade. A wrapping front porch welcomes you inside to a formal dining room and two-story great room warmed by a fireplace. Double doors from the master suite, great room, and breakfast nook access the rear veranda. The first-floor master suite enjoys a luxury bath, roomy walk-in closet, and close access to the front-facing office/study. Three additional bedrooms reside upstairs. The bonus room above the garage is great for an apartment or storage space.

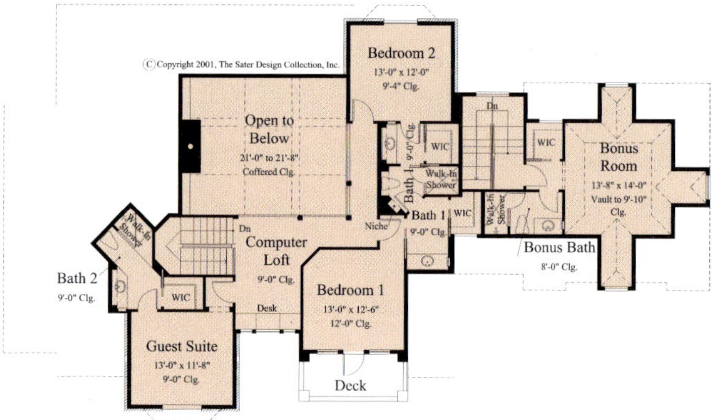

SECOND FLOOR

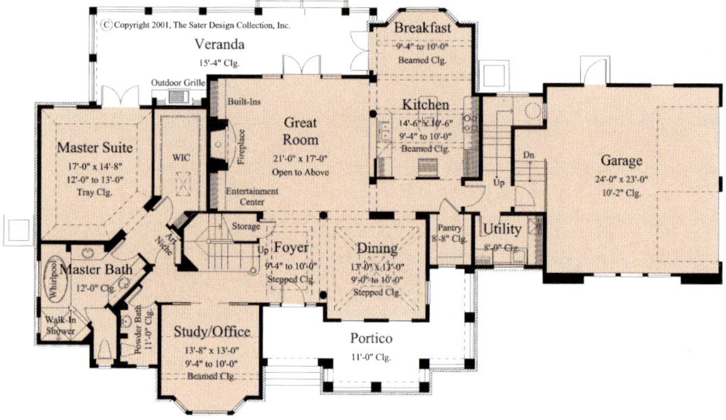

FIRST FLOOR

ORDER BLUEPRINTS 24 HOURS, 7 DAYS A WEEK, AT 1-800-521-6797

ROOMS FOR LIVING   81

KITCHENS

plan # HPK0300064

STYLE: FLORIDIAN
FIRST FLOOR: 2,254 SQ. FT.
SECOND FLOOR: 608 SQ. FT.
TOTAL: 2,862 SQ. FT.
BEDROOMS: 4
BATHROOMS: 3
WIDTH: 66' - 0"
DEPTH: 78' - 10"
FOUNDATION: SLAB

SEARCH ONLINE @ EPLANS.COM

INDOOR AND OUTDOOR LIVING ARE ENHANCED BY the beautiful courtyard that decorates the center of this home. A gallery leads to a kitchen featuring a center work island and adjacent breakfast room. To the left, the gallery leads to the formal living room and master suite. The secluded master bedroom features a tray ceiling and double doors that lead to a covered patio. The second floor contains a full bath shared by two family bedrooms and a loft that provides flexible space.

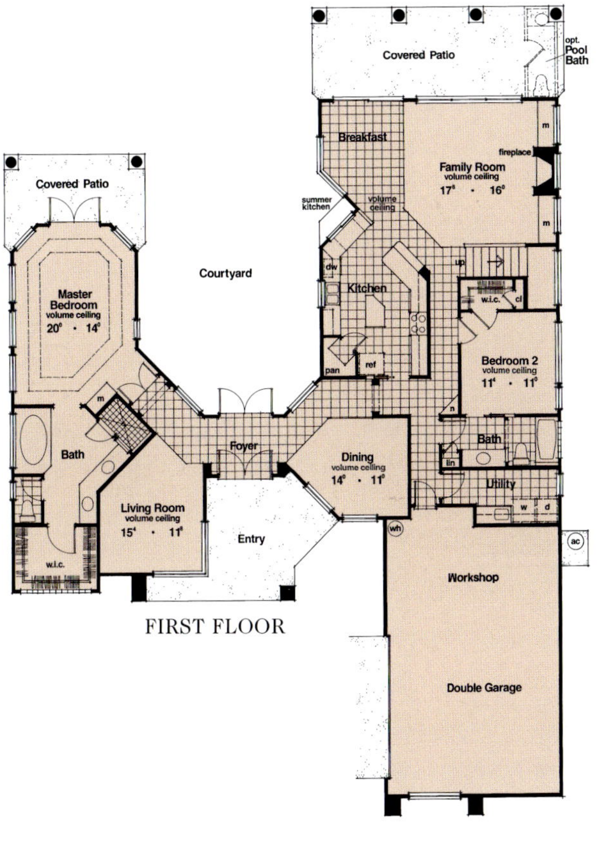

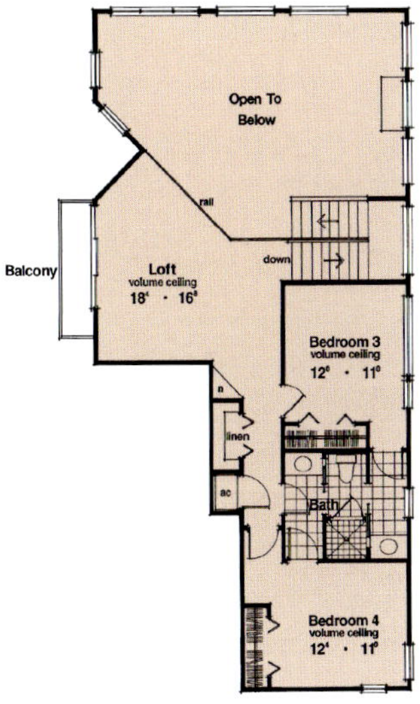

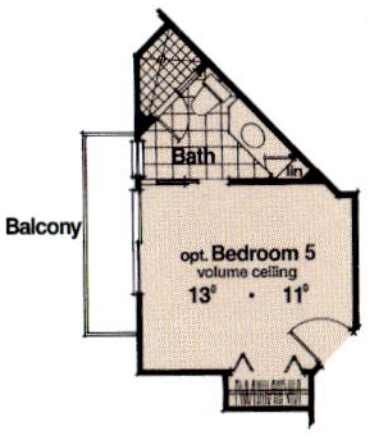

plan# HPK0300065

STYLE: TRADITIONAL
SQUARE FOOTAGE: 2,597
BEDROOMS: 4
BATHROOMS: 3
WIDTH: 96' - 6"
DEPTH: 50' - 0"
FOUNDATION: SLAB

SEARCH ONLINE @ EPLANS.COM

THE ANGLES IN THIS HOME CREATE UNLIMITED VIEWS

and space. Majestic columns of brick add warmth to a striking facade. Inside, the foyer commands a special perspective on living areas including the living room, dining room, and den. The island kitchen serves the breakfast nook and the family room. A large pantry provides ample space for food storage. Nearby, in the master suite, mitered glass and a private bath set the tone for simple luxury. Two secondary bedrooms share privacy and quiet at the front of the house. The den may also convert to a fourth bedroom, if desired.

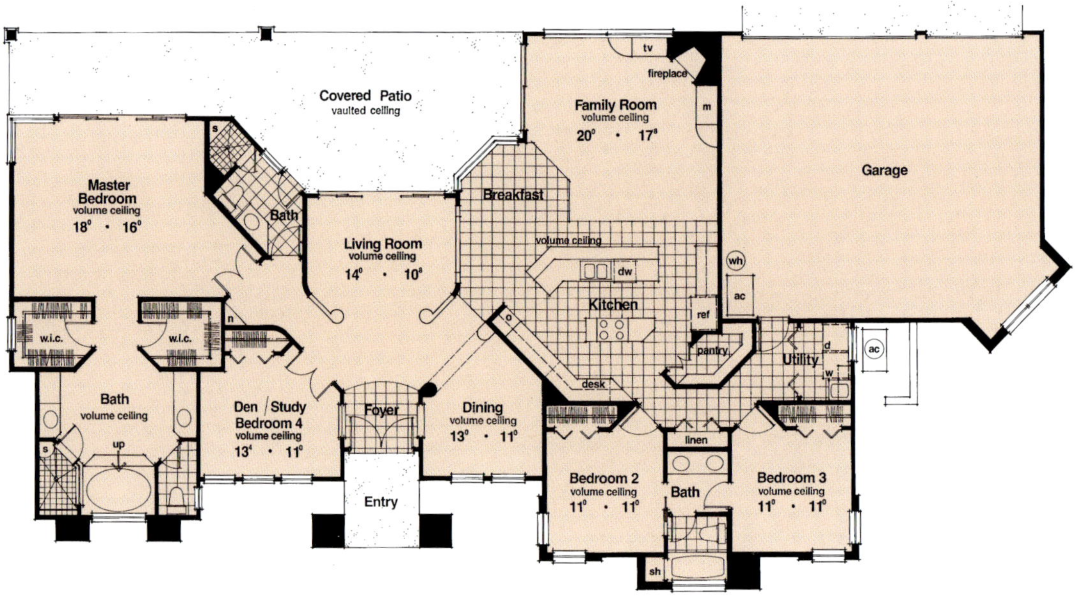

KITCHENS

KITCHENS

THIS MAJESTIC EARLY AMERICAN MANSION PRESENTS A

sturdy, formal outside appearance; inside, it is especially well suited for a large family that likes big informal get-togethers. The huge family room, with a corner fireplace that merges with a dining nook and adjoins the country-style kitchen, will surely be the center of activity. Five bedrooms are placed throughout the home's two levels, including a glorious master suite with all the comforts you've ever dreamed about. A game room joins three bedrooms upstairs. For formal socializing, the dining area and living room are easily entered from the foyer, which guests reach through the impressive pillars of the covered entry. A den, or make it a study, is also located near the front. To the rear is a covered patio, perfect for meals alfresco.

plan# HPK03000066

STYLE: FEDERAL
FIRST FLOOR: 3,505 SQ. FT.
SECOND FLOOR: 1,302 SQ. FT.
TOTAL: 4,807 SQ. FT.
BEDROOMS: 5
BATHROOMS: 4½
WIDTH: 89' - 4"
DEPTH: 87' - 0"
FOUNDATION: SLAB

SEARCH ONLINE @ EPLANS.COM

FIRST FLOOR

SECOND FLOOR

plan# HPK0300067

STYLE: COLONIAL
FIRST FLOOR: 2,814 SQ. FT.
SECOND FLOOR: 979 SQ. FT.
TOTAL: 3,793 SQ. FT.
BEDROOMS: 4
BATHROOMS: 3½
WIDTH: 98' - 0"
DEPTH: 45' - 10"
FOUNDATION: BASEMENT, SLAB

SEARCH ONLINE @ EPLANS.COM

A COVERED, COLUMNED PORCH AND SYMMETRICALLY

placed windows welcome you to this elegant brick home. The formal living room offers built-in bookshelves and one of two fireplaces, the other being found in the spacious family room. A gallery running between these rooms leads to the sumptuous master suite, which includes a sitting area, a private covered patio, and a bath with two walk-in closets, dual vanities, a large shower, and a garden tub. The step-saving kitchen features a work island and a snack bar. The breakfast and family rooms offer doors to the large covered veranda. Upstairs, you'll find three bedrooms and attic storage space. The three-car garage even has room for a golf cart.

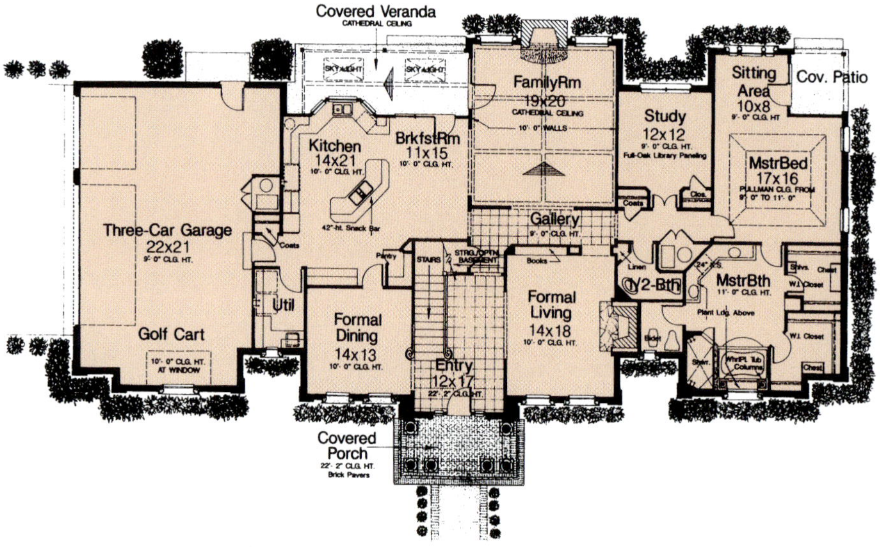

FIRST FLOOR

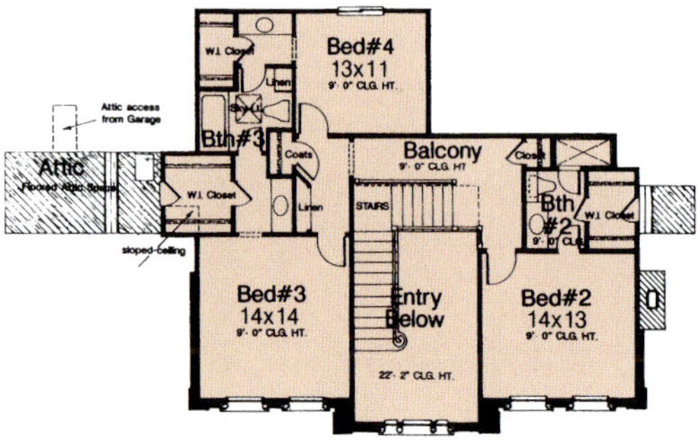

SECOND FLOOR

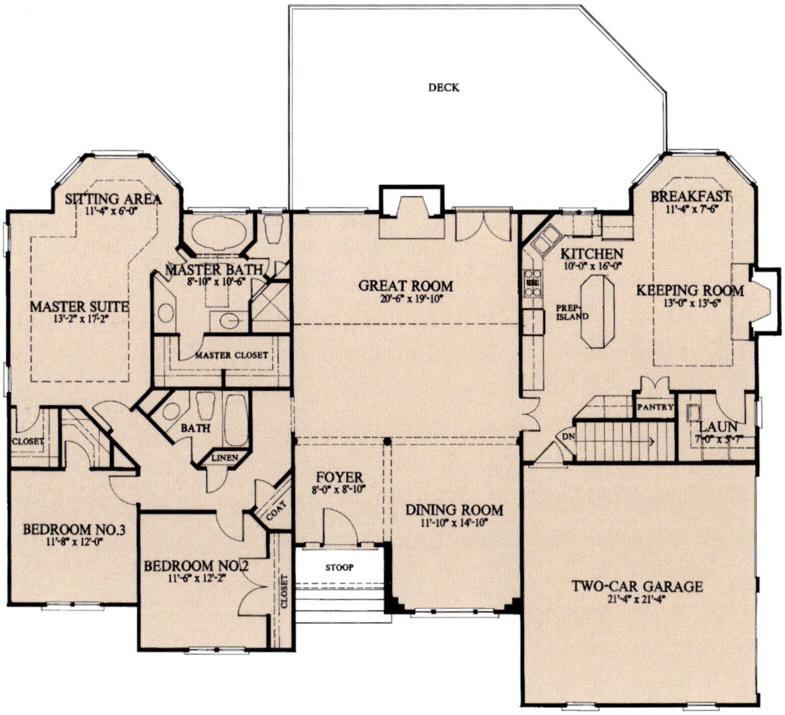

THE ABUNDANCE OF DETAILS

in this plan makes it the finest in one-story living. The great room and formal dining room are loosely defined by a simple column at the entry foyer, allowing for an open, dramatic sense of space. The kitchen with a prep island shares the right side of the plan with a bayed breakfast area and a keeping room with a fireplace. Sleeping accommodations to the left of the plan include a master suite with a sitting area, two closets, and a separate tub and shower. Two family bedrooms share a full bath. Additional living and sleeping space can be developed in the walkout basement.

plan# HPK0300068

STYLE: FRENCH
SQUARE FOOTAGE: 2,295
BEDROOMS: 3
BATHROOMS: 2
WIDTH: 69' – 0"
DEPTH: 49' – 6"
FOUNDATION: WALKOUT BASEMENT

SEARCH ONLINE @ EPLANS.COM

KITCHENS

plan # HPK0300069

STYLE: FRENCH
SQUARE FOOTAGE: 2,150
BEDROOMS: 3
BATHROOMS: 2½
WIDTH: 64' - 0"
DEPTH: 60' - 4"
FOUNDATION: WALKOUT BASEMENT

SEARCH ONLINE @ EPLANS.COM

THIS HOME DRAWS its inspiration from both French and English Country homes. The great room and dining room combine to form an impressive gathering space, with the dining area subtly defined by columns and a large triple window. The kitchen, with its work island, adjoins the breakfast area and keeping room with a fireplace. The home is completed by a master suite with a bay window and a garden tub. Space on the lower level can be developed later.

Cost to build? See page 157 to order complete cost estimate to build this house in your area!

QUOTE ONE®

KITCHENS

THIS GRAND COUNTRY FARMHOUSE WITH A wraparound porch offers comfortable living at its finest. The open floor plan is accented by the great room's cathedral ceiling and the entrance foyer with clerestory windows. The large kitchen has lots of counter space, a sunny breakfast nook, and a cooktop island with a bumped-out snack bar. The master suite has beautiful bay windows, a well-designed private bath, and a spacious walk-in closet. The second level has two large bedrooms, a full bath, and plenty of attic storage.

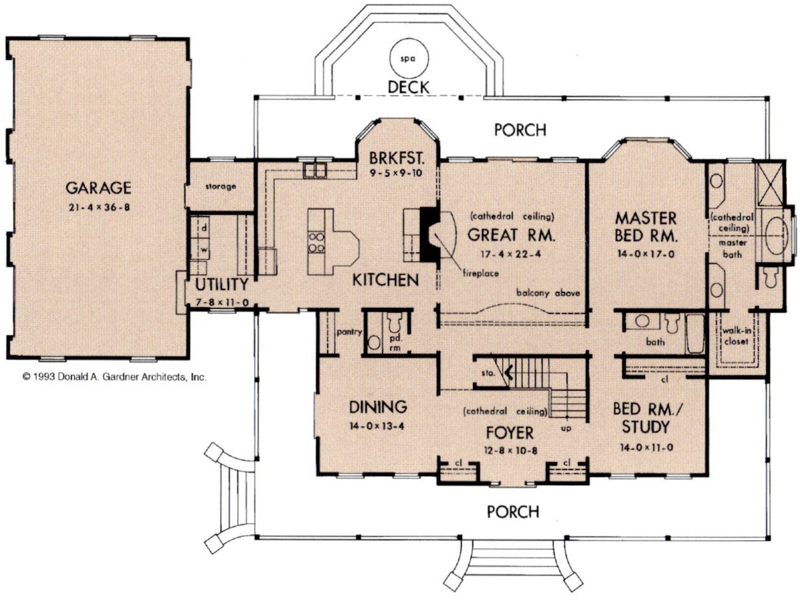

plan # HPK0300070

STYLE: FARMHOUSE
FIRST FLOOR: 2,238 SQ. FT.
SECOND FLOOR: 768 SQ. FT.
TOTAL: 3,006 SQ. FT.
BEDROOMS: 4
BATHROOMS: 3½
WIDTH: 94' - 1"
DEPTH: 59' - 10"

SEARCH ONLINE @ EPLANS.COM

FIRST FLOOR

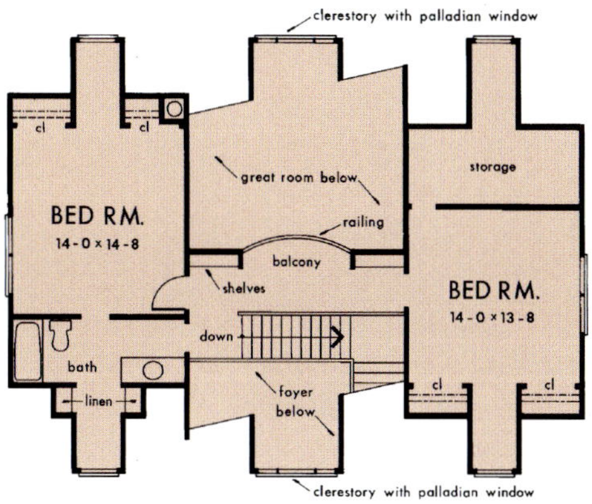

SECOND FLOOR

88   ROOMS FOR LIVING

ORDER BLUEPRINTS 24 HOURS, 7 DAYS A WEEK, AT 1-800-521-6797

K I T C H E N S

plan# HPK0300071

STYLE: FARMHOUSE
FIRST FLOOR: 2,064 SQ. FT.
SECOND FLOOR: 594 SQ. FT.
TOTAL: 2,658 SQ. FT.
BONUS SPACE: 483 SQ. FT.
BEDROOMS: 4
BATHROOMS: 3½
WIDTH: 92' - 0"
DEPTH: 57' - 8"

SEARCH ONLINE @ EPLANS.COM

MEANDERING THROUGH THIS FOUR-BEDROOM farmhouse with its wraparound porch, you'll find country living at its best. A front Palladian dormer window and rear clerestory windows in the great room add exciting visual elements to the exterior and provide natural light to the interior. The large great room boasts a fireplace, bookshelves, and a raised cathedral ceiling, allowing a curved balcony overlook above. The great room, master bedroom, and breakfast room are accessible to the rear porch for greater circulation and flexibility. Special features such as the large cooktop island in the kitchen, the wet bar, the bedroom/study, the generous bonus room over the garage, and ample storage space set this plan apart.

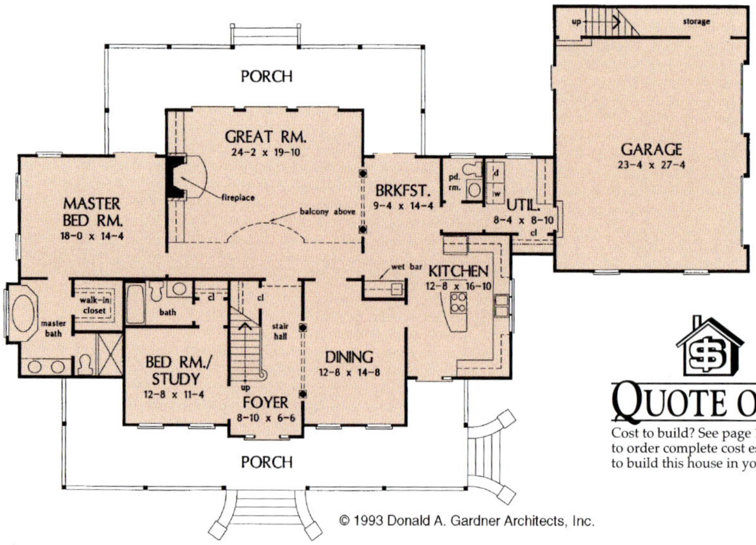

FIRST FLOOR

SECOND FLOOR

BONUS RM.
27-4 x 14-0

Quote One®
Cost to build? See page 157
to order complete cost estimate
to build this house in your area!

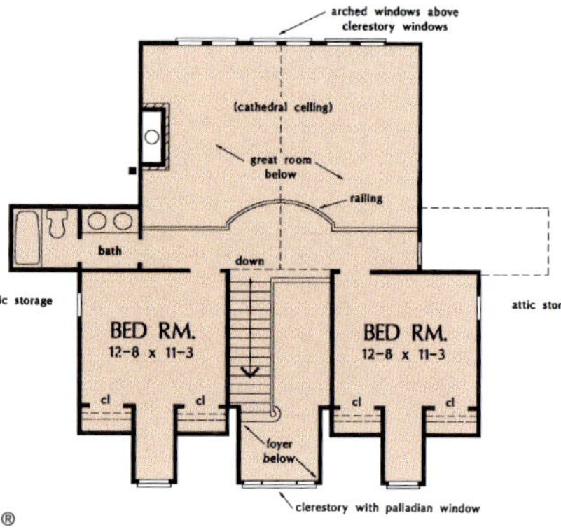

© 1993 Donald A. Gardner Architects, Inc.

ORDER BLUEPRINTS 24 HOURS, 7 DAYS A WEEK, AT 1-800-521-6797

ROOMS FOR LIVING   89

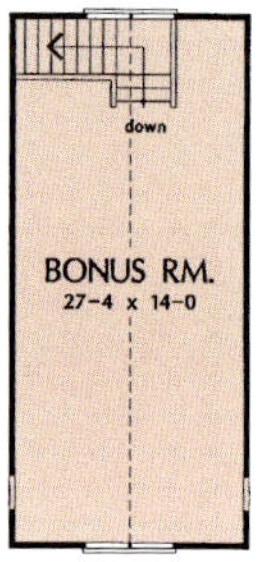

KITCHENS

plan # HPK0300072

STYLE: FARMHOUSE
SQUARE FOOTAGE: 2,078
BEDROOMS: 4
BATHROOMS: 2
WIDTH: 75' - 0"
DEPTH: 47' - 10"
FOUNDATION: SLAB

SEARCH ONLINE @ EPLANS.COM

COLONIAL STYLE MEETS FARMHOUSE CHARM IN THIS

plan, furnishing old-fashioned charisma with a flourish. From the entry, double doors open to the country dining room and a large island kitchen. Nearby, the spacious great room takes center stage and is warmed by a fireplace flanked by large windows. Tucked behind the three-car garage, the secluded master suite features a vaulted ceiling in the bedroom. The master bath contains a relaxing tub, double-bowl vanity, separate shower, and compartmented toilet. Beyond the bath is a huge walk-in closet with two built-in chests. Three family bedrooms—one doubles as a study or home office—a full bath, and a utility room complete the plan.

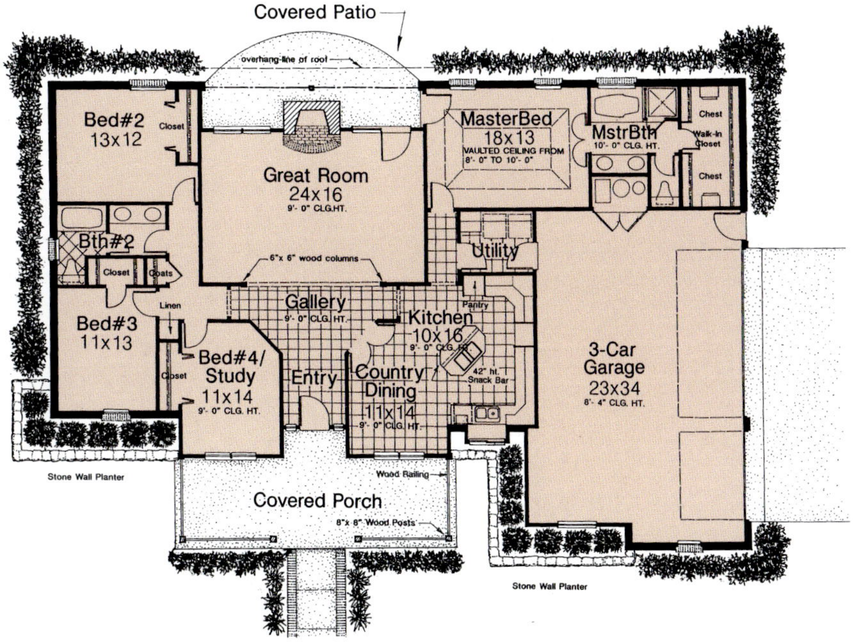

90   ROOMS FOR LIVING   ORDER BLUEPRINTS 24 HOURS, 7 DAYS A WEEK, AT 1-800-521-6797

KITCHENS

DORMER WINDOWS AND FLOWER BOXES LEND charming country style to this home. Inside, the foyer leads directly to the living room, where a fireplace is flanked by built-in shelves. The nearby kitchen, conveniently close to the dining room, opens to a sun room. A rear bedroom, tucked to the left side of the plan behind the garage, can serve as a home office. To the right, the master suite boasts a lavish bath and a walk-in closet. Upstairs, two additional bedrooms share a full bath.

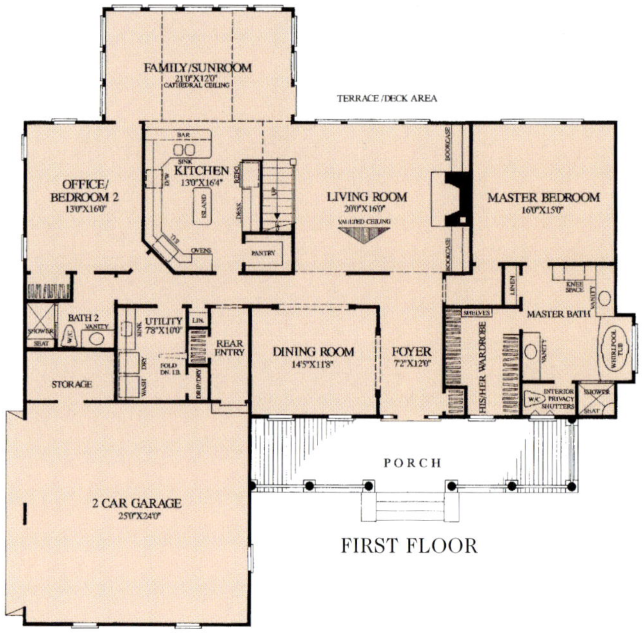

---

plan # **HPK0300073**

STYLE: COUNTRY COTTAGE
FIRST FLOOR: 2,357 SQ. FT.
SECOND FLOOR: 772 SQ. FT.
TOTAL: 3,129 SQ. FT.
BONUS SPACE: 450 SQ. FT.
BEDROOMS: 4
BATHROOMS: 3
WIDTH: 69' - 4"
DEPTH: 67' - 4"
FOUNDATION: CRAWLSPACE

SEARCH ONLINE @ EPLANS.COM

FIRST FLOOR

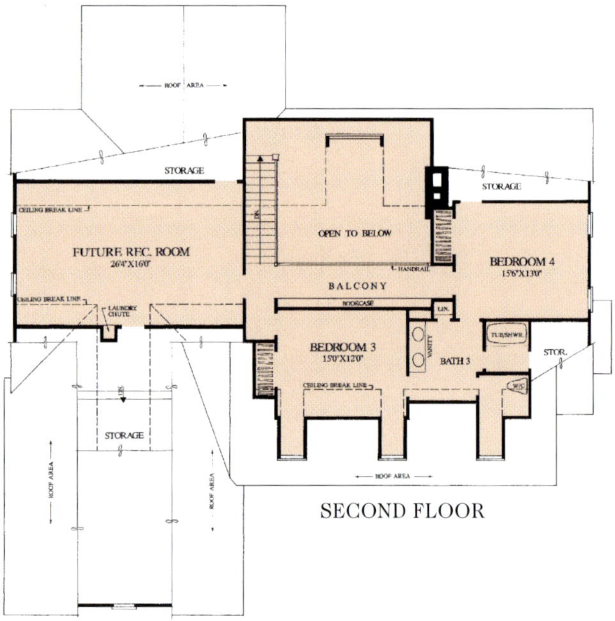

SECOND FLOOR

FIRST FLOOR

SECOND FLOOR

FINELY CRAFTED PORCHES—FRONT, SIDE, AND REAR—make this home a classic in traditional Southern living. Past the large French doors, the impressive foyer is flanked by the formal living and dining rooms. Beyond the stair is a vaulted great room with an expanse of windows, a fireplace, and built-in bookcases. From here, the breakfast room and kitchen are easily accessible and open to a private side porch. The master suite provides a large bath, two spacious closets, and a fireplace. The second floor contains three bedrooms with private bath access and a playroom.

plan # HPK03000074

STYLE: PLANTATION
FIRST FLOOR: 2,380 SQ. FT.
SECOND FLOOR: 1,295 SQ. FT.
TOTAL: 3,675 SQ. FT.
BEDROOMS: 4
BATHROOMS: 3½
WIDTH: 77' – 4"
DEPTH: 58' – 4"
FOUNDATION: WALKOUT BASEMENT

SEARCH ONLINE @ EPLANS.COM

KITCHENS

THIS ELEGANTLY APPOINTED HOME IS A BEAUTY INSIDE

and out. A centerpiece stair rises gracefully from the two-story grand foyer. The kitchen, breakfast room, and family room provide open space for the gathering of family and friends. The beam-ceilinged study and the dining room flank the grand foyer, and each includes a fireplace. The master bedroom features a cozy sitting area and a luxury master bath with His and Hers vanities and walk-in closets. Three large bedrooms and a game room complete the second floor. A large expandable area is available at the top of the rear stair.

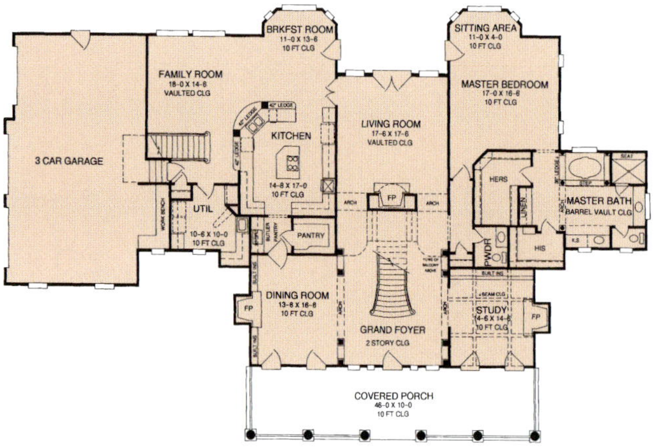

---

plan # HPK03000075

STYLE: SOUTHERN COLONIAL
FIRST FLOOR: 3,170 SQ. FT.
SECOND FLOOR: 1,914 SQ. FT.
TOTAL: 5,084 SQ. FT.
BONUS SPACE: 445 SQ. FT.
BEDROOMS: 4
BATHROOMS: 3½
WIDTH: 100' - 10"
DEPTH: 65' - 5"
FOUNDATION: CRAWLSPACE

SEARCH ONLINE @ EPLANS.COM

FIRST FLOOR

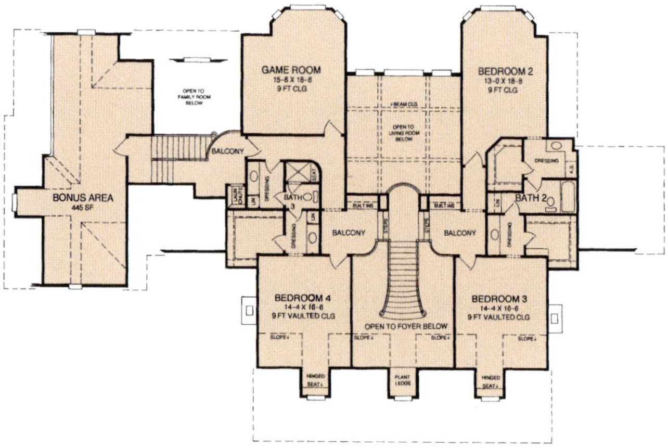

SECOND FLOOR

SIDING AND SHINGLES GIVE THIS HOME A CRAFTSMAN look

while columns and gables suggest a more traditional style. The foyer opens to a short flight of stairs that leads to the great room, which features a lovely coffered ceiling, a fireplace, built-ins and French doors to the rear veranda. To the left, the open, island kitchen enjoys a pass-through to the great room and easy service to the dining bay. The secluded master suite has two walk-in closets, a luxurious bath and veranda access. Upstairs, two family bedrooms enjoy their own full baths and share a loft area.

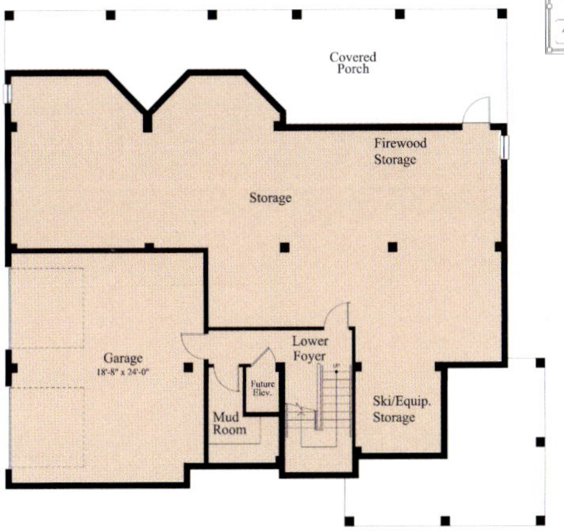

plan # HPK03000076

STYLE: BUNGALOW
FIRST FLOOR: 2,096 SQ. FT.
SECOND FLOOR: 892 SQ. FT.
TOTAL: 2,988 SQ. FT.
BEDROOMS: 3
BATHROOMS: 3½
WIDTH: 56' - 0"
DEPTH: 54' - 0"
FOUNDATION: BASEMENT

SEARCH ONLINE @ EPLANS.COM

plan# HPK03000077

STYLE: PLANTATION
FIRST FLOOR: 2,113 SQ. FT.
SECOND FLOOR: 2,098 SQ. FT.
TOTAL: 4,211 SQ. FT.
BEDROOMS: 5
BATHROOMS: 4½
WIDTH: 68' - 6"
DEPTH: 53' - 0"
FOUNDATION: BASEMENT, SLAB, CRAWLSPACE

SEARCH ONLINE @ EPLANS.COM

THIS TWO-STORY FARMHOUSE HAS MUCH TO OFFER, with the most exciting feature being the opulent master suite, which takes up almost the entire width of the upper level. French doors access the large master bedroom with its coffered ceiling. Steps lead to a separate sitting room with a fireplace and sun-filled bay window. His and Hers walk-in closets lead the way to a vaulted private bath with separate vanities and a lavish whirlpool tub. On the first floor, an island kitchen and a bayed breakfast room flow into a two-story family room with a raised-hearth fireplace, built-in shelves, and French-door access to the rear yard.

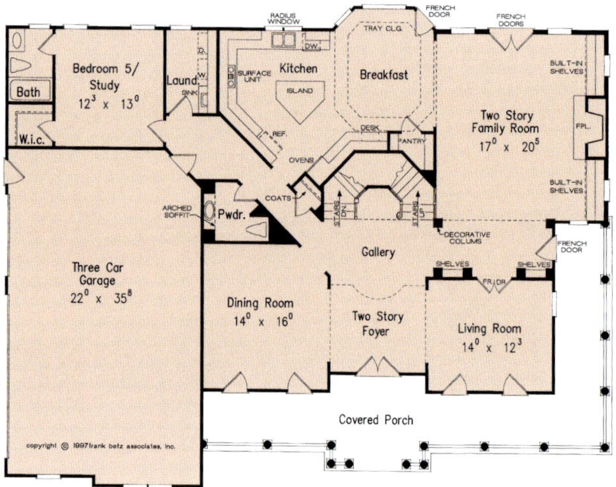

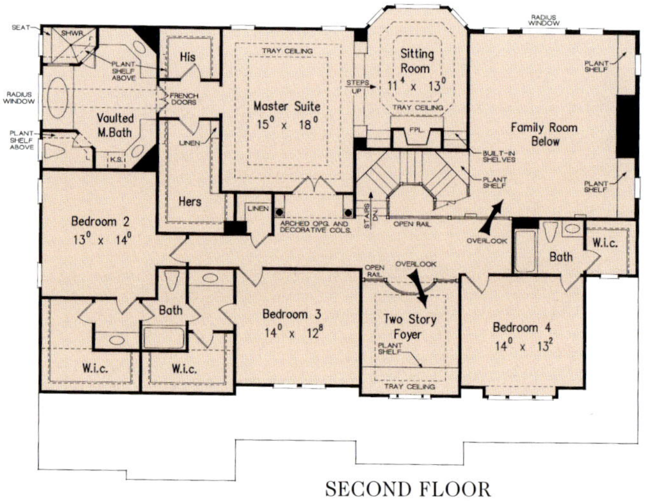

KITCHENS

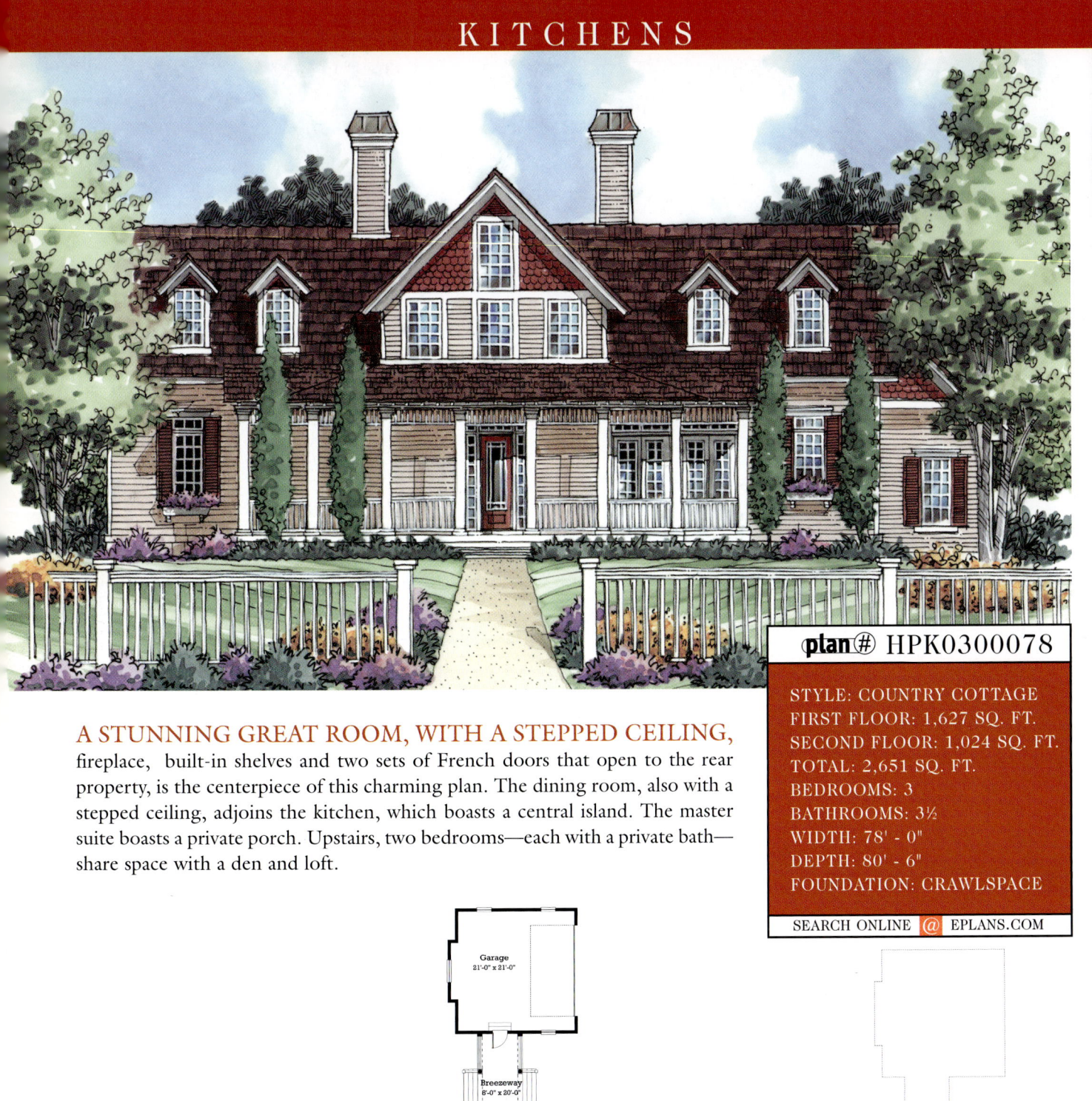

A STUNNING GREAT ROOM, WITH A STEPPED CEILING,

fireplace, built-in shelves and two sets of French doors that open to the rear property, is the centerpiece of this charming plan. The dining room, also with a stepped ceiling, adjoins the kitchen, which boasts a central island. The master suite boasts a private porch. Upstairs, two bedrooms—each with a private bath—share space with a den and loft.

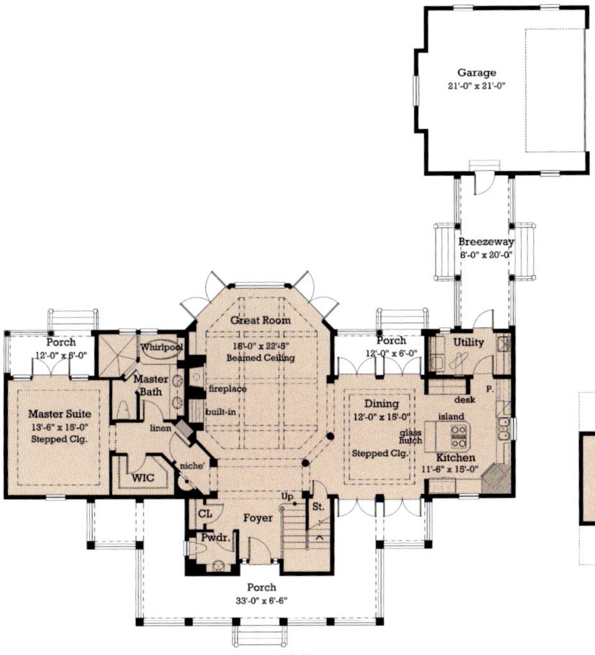

plan# HPK0300078

STYLE: COUNTRY COTTAGE
FIRST FLOOR: 1,627 SQ. FT.
SECOND FLOOR: 1,024 SQ. FT.
TOTAL: 2,651 SQ. FT.
BEDROOMS: 3
BATHROOMS: 3½
WIDTH: 78' - 0"
DEPTH: 80' - 6"
FOUNDATION: CRAWLSPACE

SEARCH ONLINE @ EPLANS.COM

FIRST FLOOR

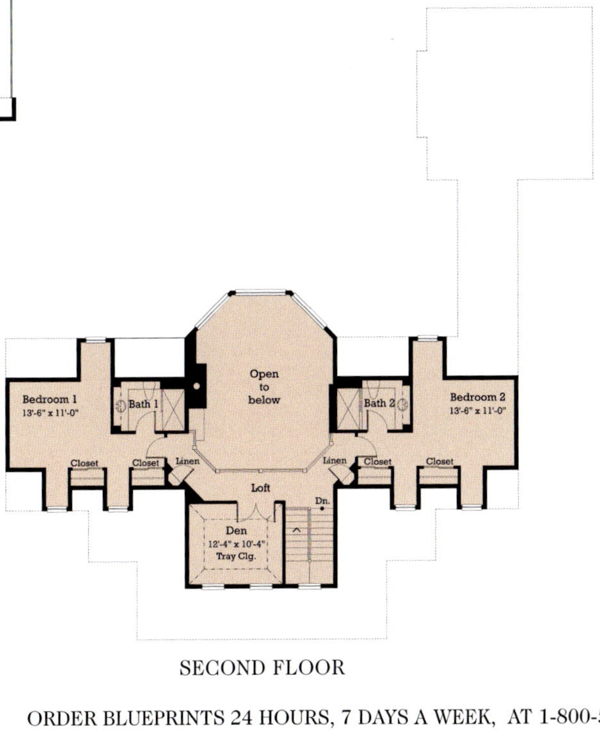

SECOND FLOOR

96   ROOMS FOR LIVING

ORDER BLUEPRINTS 24 HOURS, 7 DAYS A WEEK, AT 1-800-521-6797

KITCHENS

plan # HPK0300079

STYLE: TIDEWATER
FIRST FLOOR: 1,855 SQ. FT.
SECOND FLOOR: 901 SQ. FT.
TOTAL: 2,756 SQ. FT.
BEDROOMS: 3
BATHROOMS: 3½
WIDTH: 66' - 0"
DEPTH: 50' - 0"
FOUNDATION: BASEMENT

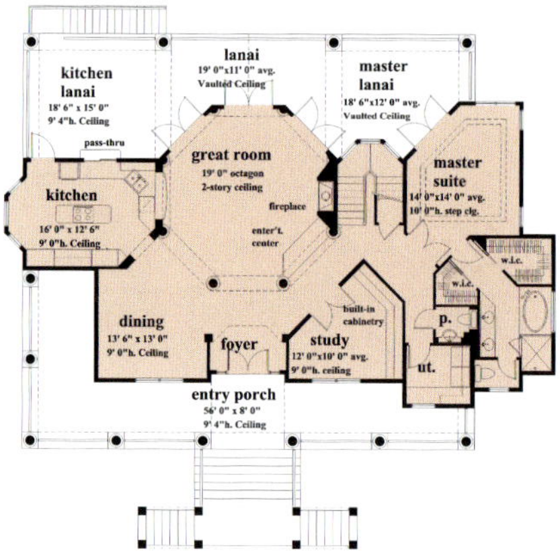

SEARCH ONLINE @ EPLANS.COM

THIS SOUTHERN TIDEWATER COTTAGE IS THE PERFECT

vacation hideaway. An octagonal great room with a multifaceted vaulted ceiling illuminates the interior. The island kitchen is brightened by a bumped-out window and a pass-through to the lanai. Two walk-in closets and a whirlpool bath await to indulge the homeowner in the master suite. A set of double doors opens to the vaulted master lanai for quiet comfort. The U-shaped staircase leads to a loft, which overlooks the great room and the foyer. Two additional family bedrooms offer private baths. A computer center and a morning kitchen complete the upper level.

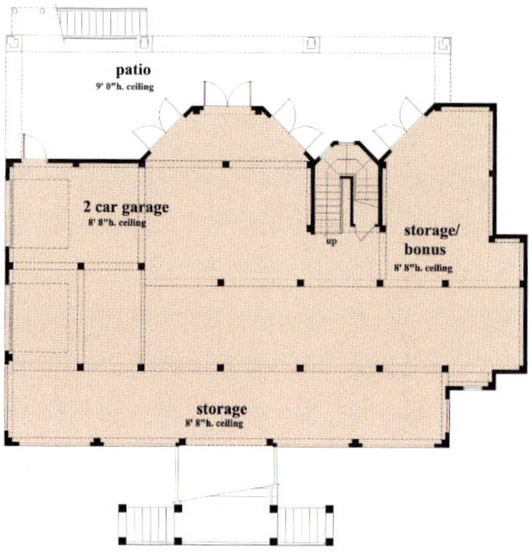

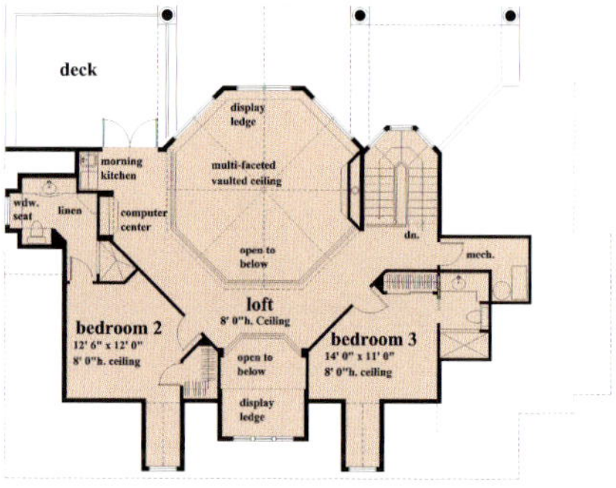

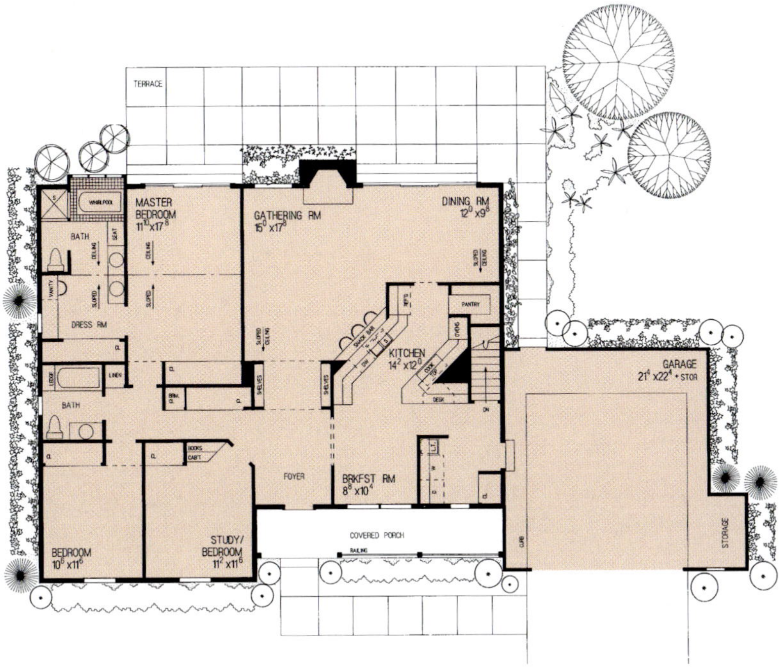

THIS CHARMING ONE-STORY

traditional home greets visitors with a covered porch. A uniquely shaped galley-style kitchen shares a snack bar with the spacious gathering room where a fireplace is the focal point. The dining room furnishes sliding glass doors to the rear terrace as does the master bedroom. This bedroom area also includes a luxury bath with a whirlpool tub and separate dressing room. Two additional bedrooms, one that could double as a study, are located at the front of the home. The two-car garage features a large storage area and can be reached through the service entrance or from the rear terrace.

plan# HPK0300080

STYLE: FARMHOUSE
SQUARE FOOTAGE: 1,830
BEDROOMS: 3
BATHROOMS: 2
WIDTH: 75' - 0"
DEPTH: 43' - 5"
FOUNDATION: BASEMENT

SEARCH ONLINE @ EPLANS.COM

KITCHENS

plan# HPK0300081

STYLE: COUNTRY COTTAGE
SQUARE FOOTAGE: 2,170
BEDROOMS: 4
BATHROOMS: 3
WIDTH: 62' - 0"
DEPTH: 61' - 6"
FOUNDATION: WALKOUT
BASEMENT

SEARCH ONLINE @ EPLANS.COM

THIS CLASSIC COTTAGE

boasts a stone-and-wood exterior with a welcoming arch-top entry that leads to a columned foyer. An extended-hearth fireplace is the focal point of the family room, and a nearby sunroom with covered porch access opens up the living area to the outdoors. The gourmet island kitchen opens through double doors from the living area; the breakfast area looks out to a porch. Sleeping quarters include a master wing with a spacious, angled bath and a sitting room or den that has its own full bath—perfect for a guest suite. On the opposite side of the plan, two family bedrooms share a full bath.

Quote One®
Cost to build? See page 157
to order complete cost estimate
to build this house in your area!

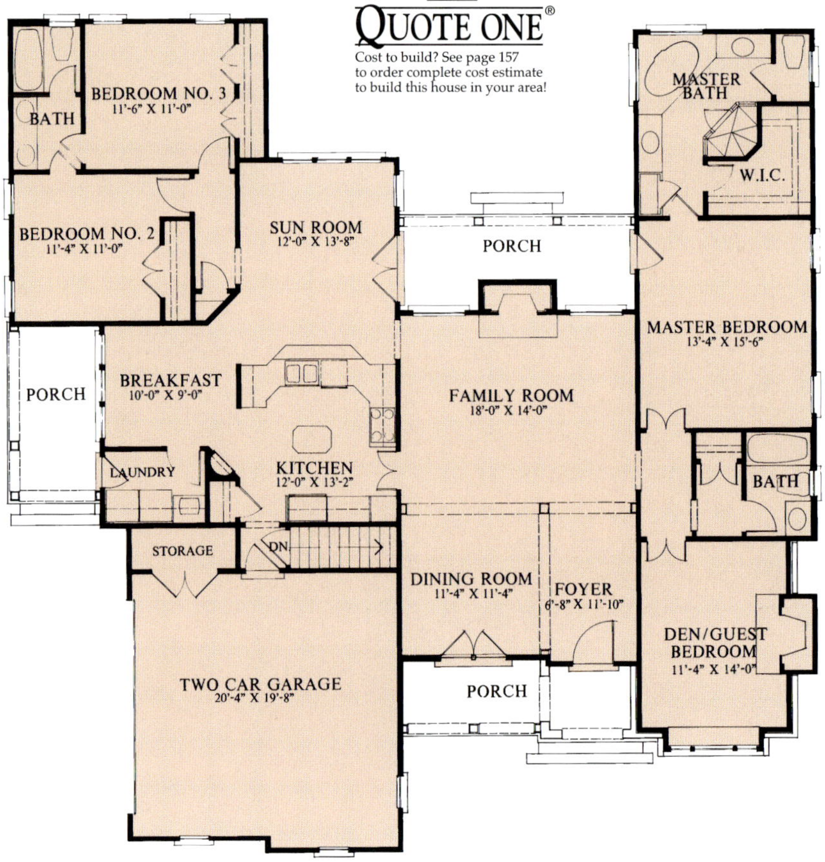

ORDER BLUEPRINTS 24 HOURS, 7 DAYS A WEEK, AT 1-800-521-6797

ROOMS FOR LIVING   99

KITCHENS

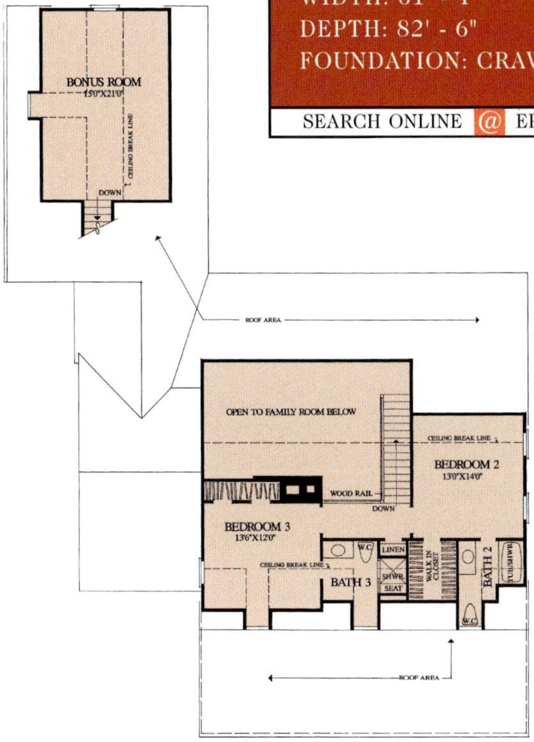

SPECIAL FEATURES IN THIS COZY COTTAGE INCLUDE an expansive family room with a fireplace, a lavish master suite with a whirlpool bath, and a spacious kitchen with an island, pantry, and built-in desk. Both the family room and master bedroom open to the covered rear porch. Two second-floor bedrooms boast private baths.

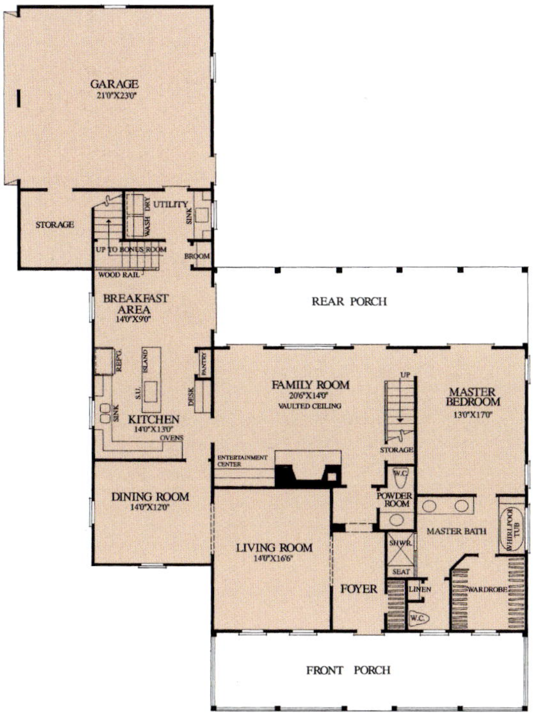

plan# HPK0300082

STYLE: COUNTRY COTTAGE
FIRST FLOOR: 1,892 SQ. FT.
SECOND FLOOR: 608 SQ. FT.
TOTAL: 2,500 SQ. FT.
BONUS SPACE: 370 SQ. FT.
BEDROOMS: 3
BATHROOMS: 3½
WIDTH: 61' - 4"
DEPTH: 82' - 6"
FOUNDATION: CRAWLSPACE

SEARCH ONLINE @ EPLANS.COM

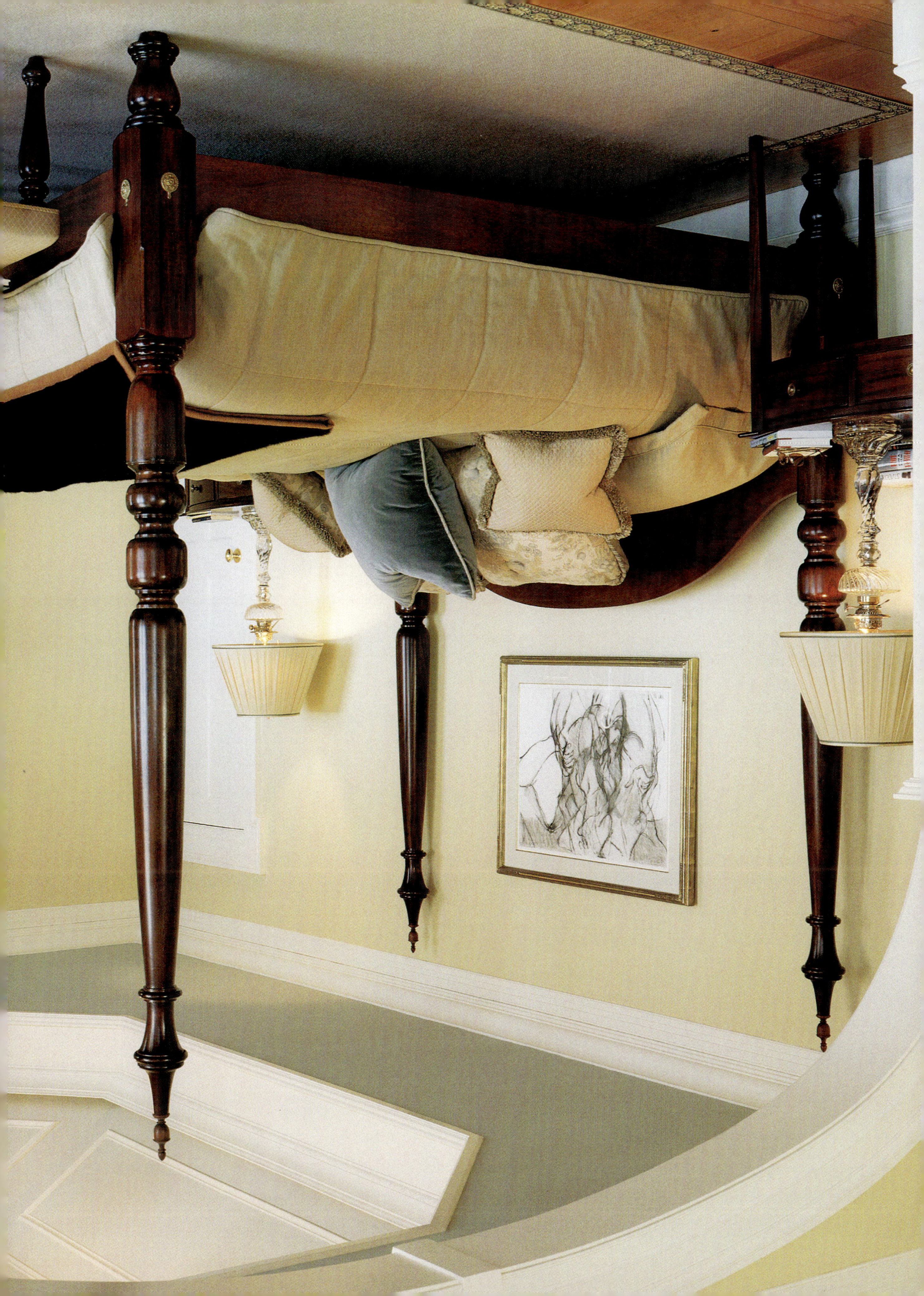

Rooms For Living
MASTER SUITES

Every homeowner spends time planning and decorating the public spaces in their homes, like the great rooms and kitchens showcased in the first two chapters of this book. But it's equally important to focus on the space where you spend the most time: your master suite. A secluded haven to call your own, the best master suites become almost a vacation home within a home. Whether soaking in a luxurious whirlpool tub or relaxing in a comfortable bed, a well-designed master suite offers everything you need to unwind after a long day, and it does so in a style that reflects your personal taste and the rest of your home's design.

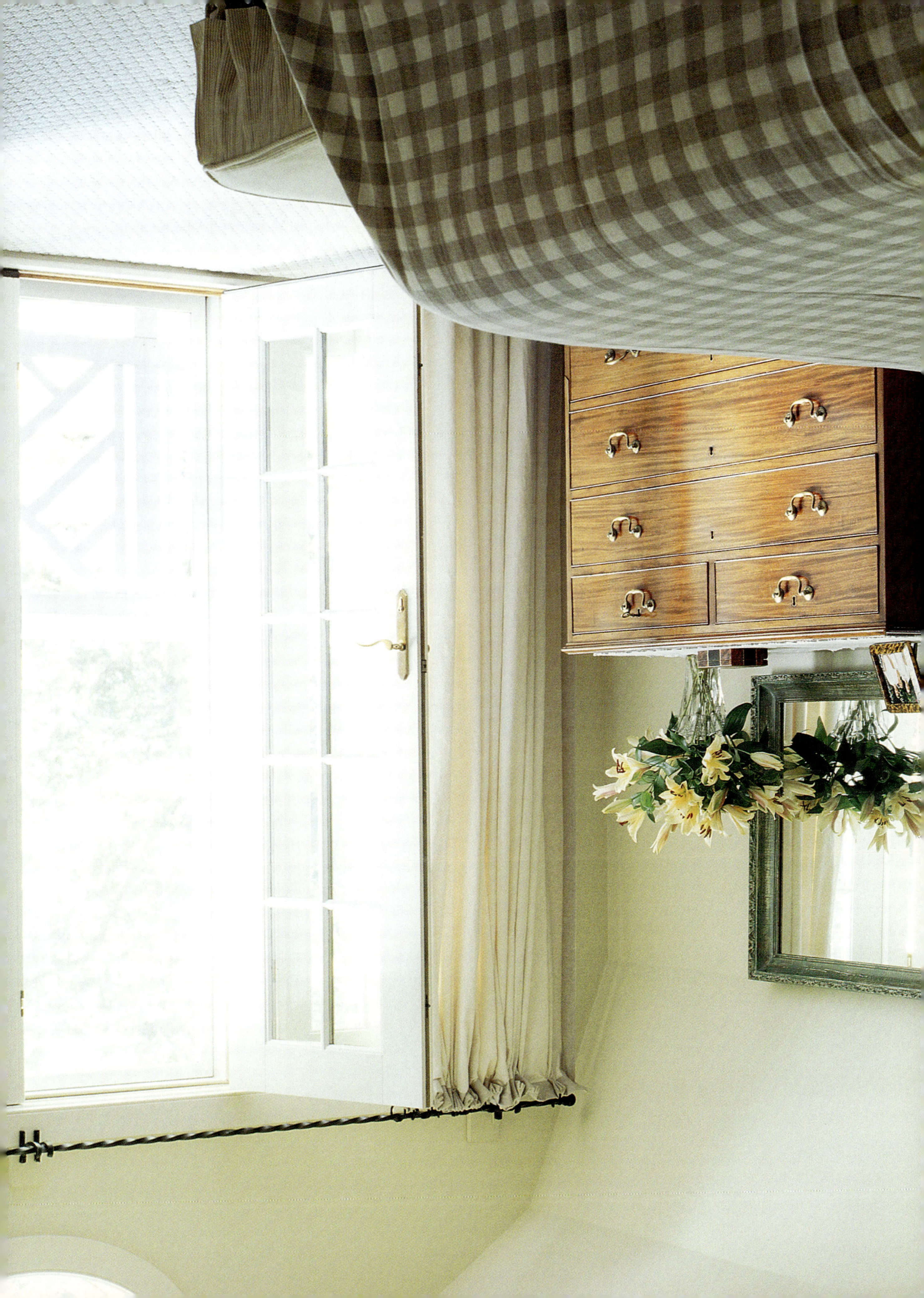

KITCHENS

plan # HPK0300083

STYLE: FARMHOUSE
SQUARE FOOTAGE: 2,555
BEDROOMS: 3
BATHROOMS: 2½
WIDTH: 70' - 6"
DEPTH: 76' - 6"
FOUNDATION: CRAWLSPACE

SEARCH ONLINE @ EPLANS.COM

SHINGLES, STONE, AND STURDY

porch pillars make this farmhouse an eye-catching retreat. Inside, the foyer is flanked by formal rooms—a dining room with a stepped ceiling and a study with a beamed ceiling and built-in bookshelves. Family living space is to the center of the plan—the kitchen includes a built-in planning desk and an adjoining breakfast nook. The great room features a coffered ceiling, a fireplace, built-in shelves, and three sets of French doors that open to the rear porch. The split-bedroom plan—family bedrooms to the right, and the master suite to the left—allows everyone plenty of privacy.

ORDER BLUEPRINTS 24 HOURS, 7 DAYS A WEEK, AT 1-800-521-6797

ROOMS FOR LIVING   101

MASTER SUITES

Above: A whirlpool bath beneath a wall of windows is a true sign of luxury in the master suite. Decorative mosaic tiles surround the tub to give it a unique look.

Left: This antique bed fits perfectly in this elegant master bedroom. The fireplace and decorative tray ceiling add to the room's formal appeal as well.

ROOMS FOR LIVING 105

MASTER SUITES

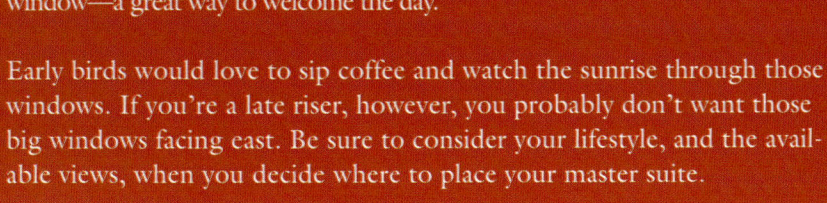

Setting Your Sites

Above: Where you situate a new master suite is a critical decision. This bedroom, from Design HPK0300086 (page 112), enjoys gorgeous views from its bay window—a great way to welcome the day.

Early birds would love to sip coffee and watch the sunrise through those windows. If you're a late riser, however, you probably don't want those big windows facing east. Be sure to consider your lifestyle, and the available views, when you decide where to place your master suite.

An antique table works well as the centerpiece of this spacious bath, and matches the country-style faucets and hardware. A Palladian window and vaulted ceiling add to the sense of space.

Suite Escape

Looking a bit like a mountain resort, this fine Rustic-style home is sure to be the envy of your neighborhood. Entering through the elegant front door, one finds an open staircase to the right and a spacious great room directly ahead. Here, a fireplace and a wall of windows give a cozy welcome. A lavish master suite begins with a sitting room complete with a fireplace and continues to a private porch, large walk-in closet, and sumptuous bedroom area. The gourmet kitchen adjoins a sunny dining room that offers access to a screened porch.

Clockwise from top right: This stunning resort-style home successfully incorporates many Craftsman design elements. Dramatic views—of the waterfront and the lower-level media room—are available from the great room's convenient sitting area. The spacious great room's rustic look is solidified with the grand fireplace and cathedral ceiling.

MASTER SUITES

the luxurious master suite is
illuminated with light
and panoramic views

plan # HPK0300084

STYLE: CRAFTSMAN
MAIN LEVEL: 3,040 SQ. FT.
LOWER LEVEL: 1,736 SQ. FT.
TOTAL: 4,776 SQ. FT.
BEDROOMS: 5
BATHROOMS: 4½ + ½
WIDTH: 106' - 5"
DEPTH: 104' - 2"

SEARCH ONLINE @ EPLANS.COM

MAIN LEVEL

LOWER LEVEL

ROOMS FOR LIVING   109

ORDER BLUEPRINTS 24 HOURS, 7 DAYS A WEEK, AT 1-800-521-6797

Outer Space

This Italianate plan is designed to take full advantage of its fabulous surroundings. A lanai that stretches the length of the back of the home and plentiful windows embrace the outdoors at every turn. Scrolled columns, mosaic tiles, and arched windows lend Mediterranean details throughout. Open design connects the family room, kitchen, and dinette, all of which feature spectacular views. A centrally located living room will awe guests as they step through the arched front doorway. To the right of the plan is the gorgeous master suite, which includes impressive extras like a pair of walk-in closets, a garden patio, and a spacious exercise room. It also includes access to the lanai, just steps away from the gazebo and outdoor kitchen.

Below: Pillars and arches define the impressive entrance to this Mediterranean home. Right, top to bottom: The dinette offers a charming spot with plenty of room for casual family meals. With a large fireplace and views of the lanai, the family room is the perfect spot to relax. Even the bathrooms feature the earth tones and archways that characterize this home.

MASTER SUITES

the master suite provides a seamless transition between indoors and out

plan # HPK0300085

STYLE: MEDITERRANEAN
FIRST FLOOR: 3,633 SQ. FT.
SECOND FLOOR: 695 SQ. FT.
TOTAL: 4,328 SQ. FT.
BEDROOMS: 5
BATHROOMS: 5½
WIDTH: 115' - 7"
DEPTH: 109' - 8"
FOUNDATION: SLAB

SEARCH ONLINE @ EPLANS.COM

FIRST FLOOR

SECOND FLOOR

MASTER SUITES

©LAURENCE TAYLOR PHOTOGRAPHY

plan# HPK0300086

STYLE: FLORIDIAN
FIRST FLOOR: 2,853 SQ. FT.
SECOND FLOOR: 627 SQ. FT.
TOTAL: 3,480 SQ. FT.
BEDROOMS: 3
BATHROOMS: 2½
WIDTH: 80' - 0"
DEPTH: 96' - 0"
FOUNDATION: SLAB

SEARCH ONLINE @ EPLANS.COM

A UNIQUE COURTYARD PROVIDES A HAPPY MEDIUM for indoor/outdoor living in this design. Inside, the foyer opens to a grand salon with a wall of glass, providing unobstructed views of the backyard. Informal areas include a leisure room with an entertainment center and glass doors that open to a covered pool-side lanai. An outdoor fireplace enhances casual gatherings. The master suite is filled with amenities that include a bayed sitting area, access to the rear lanai, His and Hers closets, and a soaking tub. Upstairs, two family bedrooms—both with private decks—share a full bath. A detached guest house has a cabana bath and an outdoor grill area.

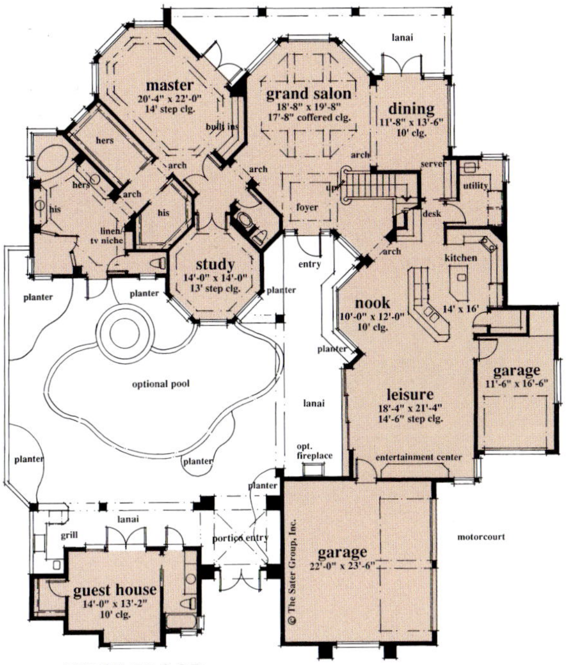

FIRST FLOOR

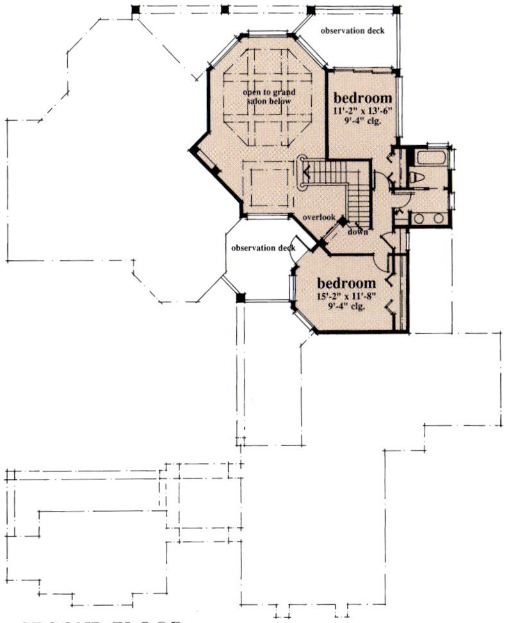

SECOND FLOOR

112   ROOMS FOR LIVING

ORDER BLUEPRINTS 24 HOURS, 7 DAYS A WEEK, AT 1-800-521-6797

MASTER SUITES

FOR MORE DETAILED INFORMATION, PLEASE CHECK THE FLOOR PLANS CAREFULLY.

plan# HPK0300087

STYLE: FLORIDIAN
SQUARE FOOTAGE: 2,794
BEDROOMS: 3
BATHROOMS: 3
WIDTH: 70' - 0"
DEPTH: 98' - 0"
FOUNDATION: SLAB

SEARCH ONLINE @ EPLANS.COM

CLASSIC COLUMNS, circle-head windows, and a bay-windowed study give this stucco home a wonderful street presence. The foyer leads to the formal living and dining areas. An arched buffet server separates these rooms and contributes an open feeling. The kitchen, nook, and leisure room are grouped for informal living. A desk/message center in the island kitchen, art niches in the nook, and a fireplace with an entertainment center and shelves add custom touches. Two secondary suites have guest baths and offer full privacy from the master wing. The master suite hosts a private garden area; the bath features a walk-in shower that overlooks the garden and a water closet room with space for books or a television. Large His and Hers walk-in closets complete these private quarters.

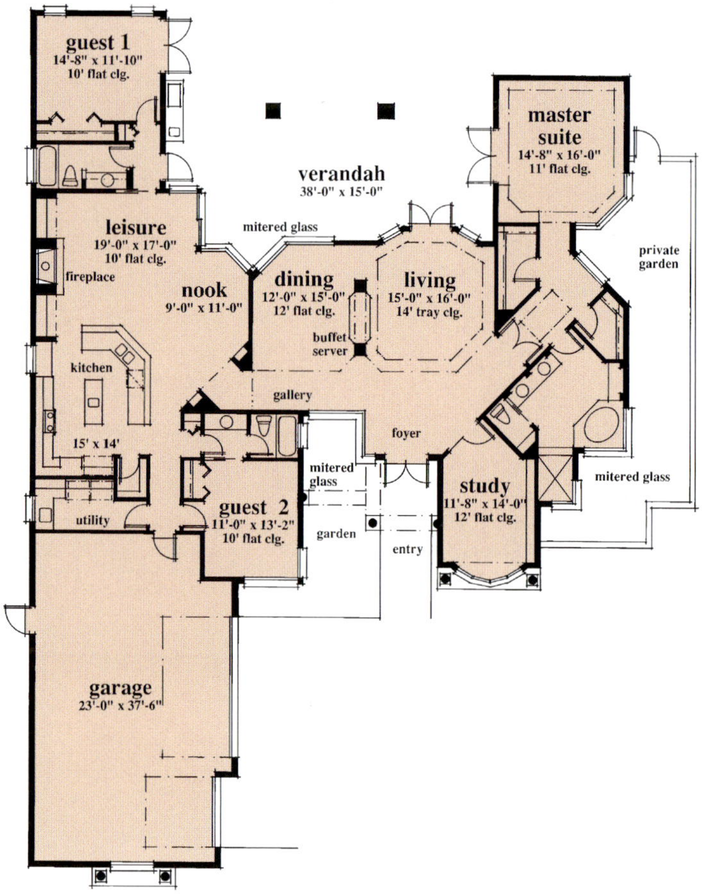

guest 1
14'-8" x 11'-10"
10' flat clg.

master suite
14'-8" x 16'-0"
11' flat clg.

verandah
38'-0" x 15'-0"

leisure
19'-0" x 17'-0"
10' flat clg.

mitered glass

private garden

fireplace

nook
9'-0" x 11'-0"

dining
12'-0" x 15'-0"
12' flat clg.

living
15'-0" x 16'-0"
14' tray clg.

kitchen

buffet server

15' x 14'

gallery

foyer

mitered glass

mitered glass

utility

guest 2
11'-0" x 13'-2"
10' flat clg.

garden

study
11'-8" x 14'-0"
12' flat clg.

entry

garage
23'-0" x 37'-6"

ORDER BLUEPRINTS 24 HOURS, 7 DAYS A WEEK, AT 1-800-521-6797

ROOMS FOR LIVING   113

MASTER SUITES

plan # HPK0300088

STYLE: TRADITIONAL
SQUARE FOOTAGE: 3,790
BEDROOMS: 4
BATHROOMS: 3½
WIDTH: 80' - 0"
DEPTH: 107' - 8"
FOUNDATION: SLAB

SEARCH ONLINE @ EPLANS.COM

A MAJESTIC DESERT OASIS, this well-planned home puts family comfort and privacy first. Enter under a keystone portico to the foyer; a dramatic dining room opens to the right. Just ahead, the living room is an inviting place to relax by the fireplace under the coffered ceiling. A unique kitchen supports gourmet meals or a quick snack enjoyed in the sunny nook. An entertainment center separates the leisure room and game room—or finish the space to include a fourth bedroom. The rear guest suite offers a private bath and access to the veranda, featuring an outdoor grill. For the ultimate in luxury, the master suite is peerless; a light-filled sitting area, angled bedroom, and indulgent bath make an inviting retreat for any homeowner.

Veranda
20'-0" x 19'-7"
Flat Clg.

Walk-In Shower

Outdoor Grille

Guest Suite
11'-8" x 16'-0"
Flat Clg.

Guest Bath

Tiled

WIC

Storage

Sitting Area
10'-0" x 7'-11"
Flat Clg.

Veranda
33'-11" x 14'-0"
Flat Clg.

Leisure Room
18'-8" x 15'-9"
Stepped Clg.

Game Room
12'-8" x 13'-11"
Stepped Clg.

Nook
7'-0" x 9'-8"
Flat Clg.

Entertainment Center

Master Suite
16'-10" x 16'-9"
Stepped Clg.

Living Room
18'-9" x 13'-10"
Coffered Clg.

Pwdr.

Fireplace

Built-Ins

Kitchen
14'-0" x 13'-0"
Stepped Clg.

Pantry

Bedroom 2
12'-2" x 13'-0"
Flat Clg.

Art Niche

Gallery

WIC

Bath 1/2

Walk-In Shower

Bedroom 1
12'-2" x 12'-0"
Flat Clg.

Master Bath
Flat Clg.

Make-up Area

Whirlpool

Walk-In Shower

WIC

Study
11'-0" x 15'-10"
Beamed Clg.

Foyer

Dining Room
12'-0" x 15'-2"
Stepped Clg.

Built-Ins

Portico
9'-0" x 11'-5"

Window Seat

Utility
8'-6" x 10'-?"

Garage
21'-0" x 37'-2"
Flat Clg.

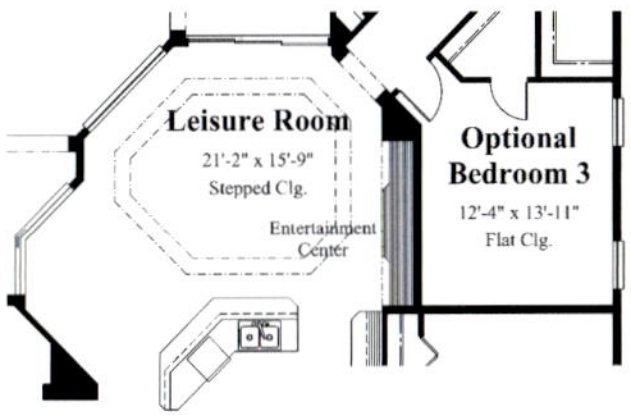

Leisure Room
21'-2" x 15'-9"
Stepped Clg.

Entertainment Center

Optional Bedroom 3
12'-4" x 13'-11"
Flat Clg.

ALTERNATE LAYOUT

114   ROOMS FOR LIVING

ORDER BLUEPRINTS 24 HOURS, 7 DAYS A WEEK, AT 1-800-521-6797

MASTER SUITES

plan# HPK0300089

STYLE: ITALIANATE
FIRST FLOOR: 1,266 SQ. FT.
SECOND FLOOR: 1,324 SQ. FT.
TOTAL: 2,590 SQ. FT.
BEDROOMS: 3
BATHROOMS: 2½
WIDTH: 34' - 0"
DEPTH: 63' - 2"
FOUNDATION: SLAB

SEARCH ONLINE @ EPLANS.COM

THIS MODERN TAKE ON THE
Italian villa boasts plenty of indoor/outdoor flow. Four sets of double doors wrap around the great room and dining area and open to the stunning veranda. The great room is enhanced by a coffered ceiling and built-in cabinetry, and the entire first floor is bathed in sunlight from a wall of glass doors overlooking the veranda. The dining room connects to a gourmet island kitchen. Upstairs, a beautiful deck wraps gracefully around the family bedrooms. The master suite is a skylit haven enhanced by a sitting bay, which features a vaulted octagonal ceiling and a cozy two-sided fireplace. Private double doors access the sundeck from the master suite, the secondary bedrooms, and the study.

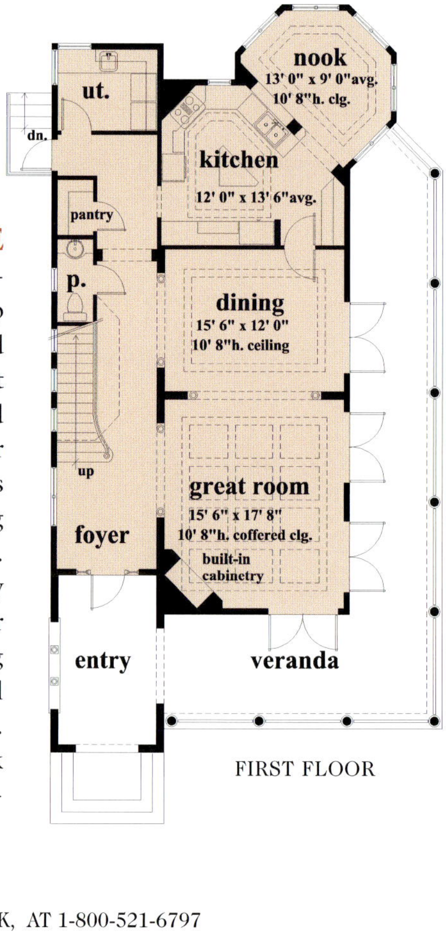

FIRST FLOOR

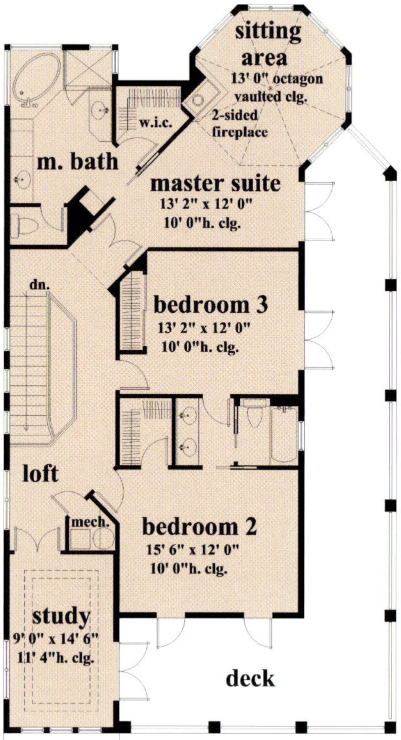

ut.
dn.
pantry
p.
nook
13' 0" x 9' 0"avg.
10' 8"h. clg.
kitchen
12' 0" x 13' 6"avg.
dining
15' 6" x 12' 0"
10' 8"h. ceiling
great room
15' 6" x 17' 8"
10' 8"h. coffered clg.
built-in cabinetry
up
foyer
entry
veranda

SECOND FLOOR

sitting area
13' 0" octagon
vaulted clg.
2-sided fireplace
w.i.c.
m. bath
master suite
13' 2" x 12' 0"
10' 0"h. clg.
dn.
bedroom 3
13' 2" x 12' 0"
10' 0"h. clg.
loft
mech.
bedroom 2
15' 6" x 12' 0"
10' 0"h. clg.
study
9' 0" x 14' 6"
11' 4"h. clg.
deck

ORDER BLUEPRINTS 24 HOURS, 7 DAYS A WEEK, AT 1-800-521-6797   ROOMS FOR LIVING   115

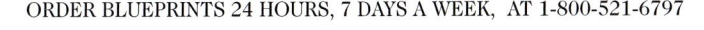

MASTER SUITES

plan# HPK0300090

STYLE: FLORIDIAN
SQUARE FOOTAGE: 2,385
BONUS SPACE: 1,271 SQ. FT.
BEDROOMS: 3
BATHROOMS: 2½
WIDTH: 60' - 4"
DEPTH: 59' - 4"
FOUNDATION: PIER, BLOCK

SEARCH ONLINE @ EPLANS.COM

A CLASSIC PEDIMENT AND LOW-PITCHED ROOF ARE topped by a cupola on this gorgeous coastal design, influenced by 19th-Century Caribbean plantation houses. Savory style blended with a contemporary seaside spirit invites entertaining as well as year-round living—plus room to grow. The beauty and warmth of natural light splash the spacious living area with a sense of the outdoors and a touch of joie de vivre. The great room features a wall of built-ins designed for even the most technology-savvy entertainment buff. Dazzling views through walls of glass are enlivened by the presence of a breezy porch. The master suite features a luxurious bath, a dressing area, and two walk-in closets. Glass doors open to the porch and provide generous views of the seascape; a nearby study offers an indoor retreat.

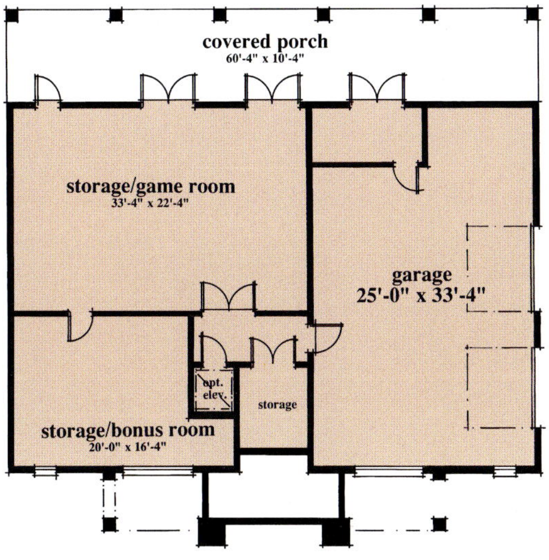

BASEMENT

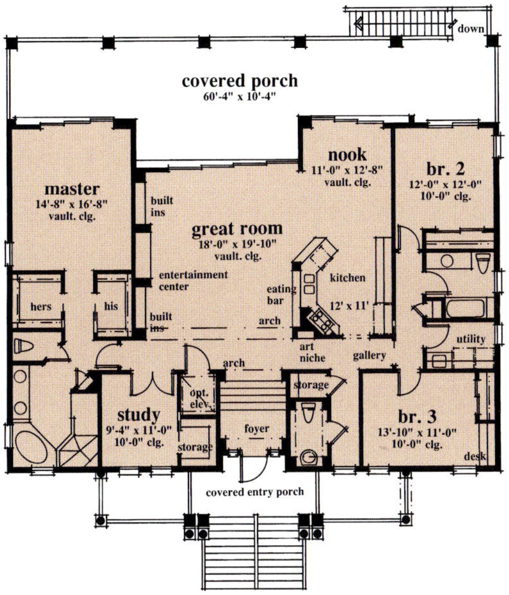

covered porch
60'-4" x 10'-4"

storage/game room
33'-4" x 22'-4"

garage
25'-0" x 33'-4"

storage/bonus room
20'-0" x 16'-4"

opt. elev.

storage

FIRST FLOOR

covered porch
60'-4" x 10'-4"

down

master
14'-8" x 16'-8"
vault. clg.

hers

his

built ins

built

great room
18'-0" x 19'-10"
vault. clg.

entertainment center

nook
11'-0" x 12'-8"
vault. clg.

br. 2
12'-0" x 12'-0"
10'-0" clg.

kitchen
12' x 11'

eating bar

arch

art niche

gallery

utility

study
9'-4" x 11'-0"
10'-0" clg.

opt. elev.

storage

arch

storage

foyer

br. 3
13'-10" x 11'-0"
10'-0" clg.

desk

covered entry porch

116   ROOMS FOR LIVING

ORDER BLUEPRINTS 24 HOURS, 7 DAYS A WEEK, AT 1-800-521-6797

MASTER SUITES

plan# HPK0300091

STYLE: ITALIANATE
FIRST FLOOR: 2,491 SQ. FT.
SECOND FLOOR: 1,290 SQ. FT.
TOTAL: 3,781 SQ. FT.
BEDROOMS: 5
BATHROOMS: 4½
WIDTH: 62' - 0"
DEPTH: 67' - 0"
FOUNDATION: BASEMENT

SEARCH ONLINE @ EPLANS.COM

CHIC AND GLAMOROUS, THIS MEDITERRANEAN FACADE

pairs ancient shapes, such as square columns, with a refined disposition set off by radius windows. A magnificent entry leads to an interior gallery and the great room. This extraordinary space is warmed by a two-sided fireplace and defined by extended views of the rear property. Sliding glass doors to a wraparound veranda create great indoor/outdoor flow. The gourmet kitchen easily serves any occasion and provides a pass-through to the outdoor kitchen. A powder room accommodates visitors, and an elevator leads to the sleeping quarters upstairs. Double doors open to the master suite, which features a walk-in closet, two-sided fireplace, and angled whirlpool bath. The master bedroom boasts a tray ceiling and doors to a spacious deck. The upper-level catwalk leads to a bedroom suite that can easily accommodate a guest or live-in relative. The basement level features future space and a two-car garage.

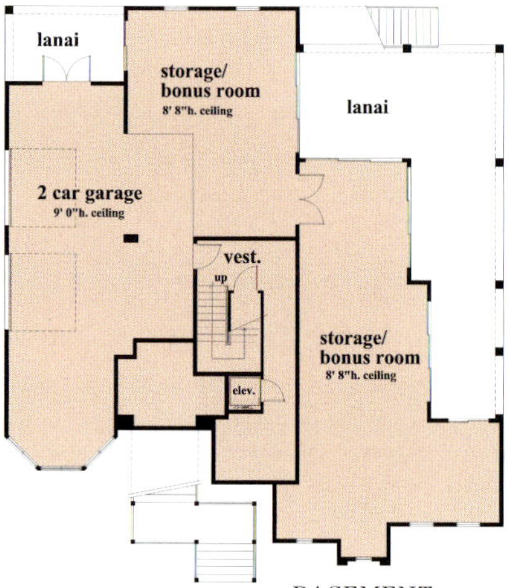

BASEMENT

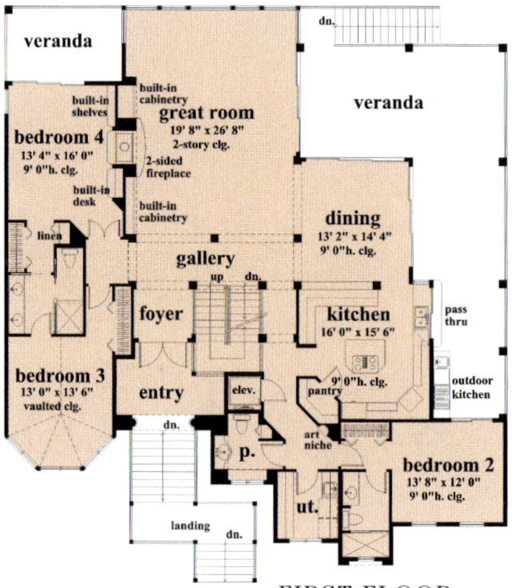

FIRST FLOOR

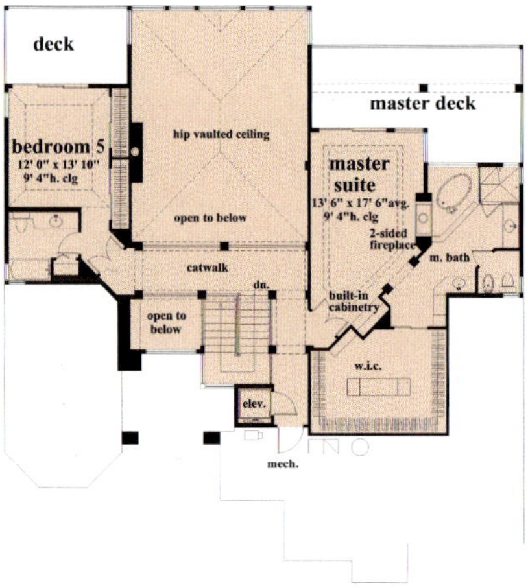

SECOND FLOOR

ORDER BLUEPRINTS 24 HOURS, 7 DAYS A WEEK, AT 1-800-521-6797

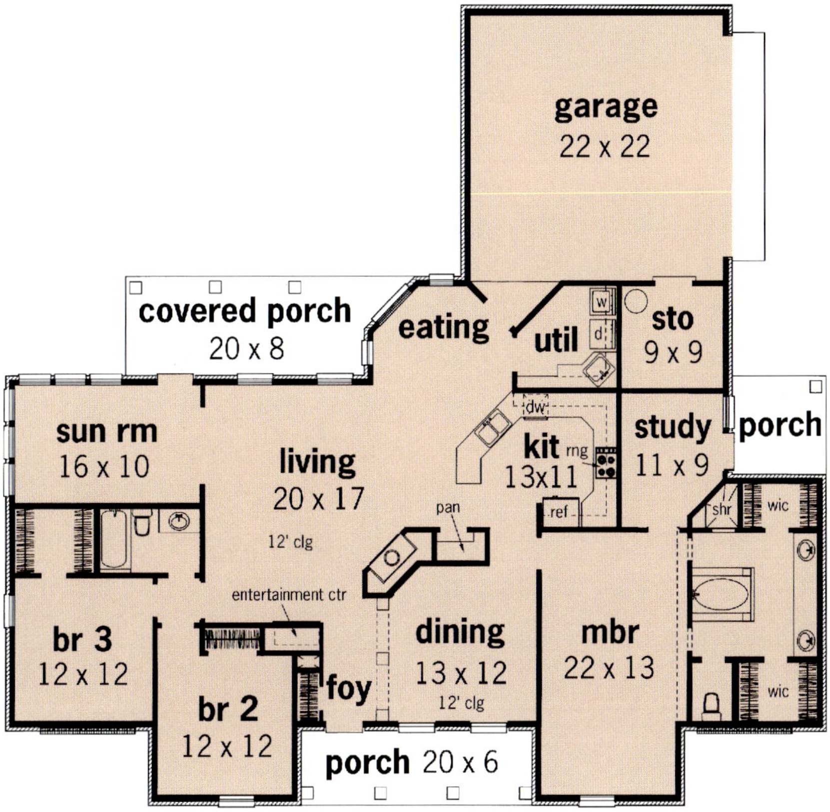

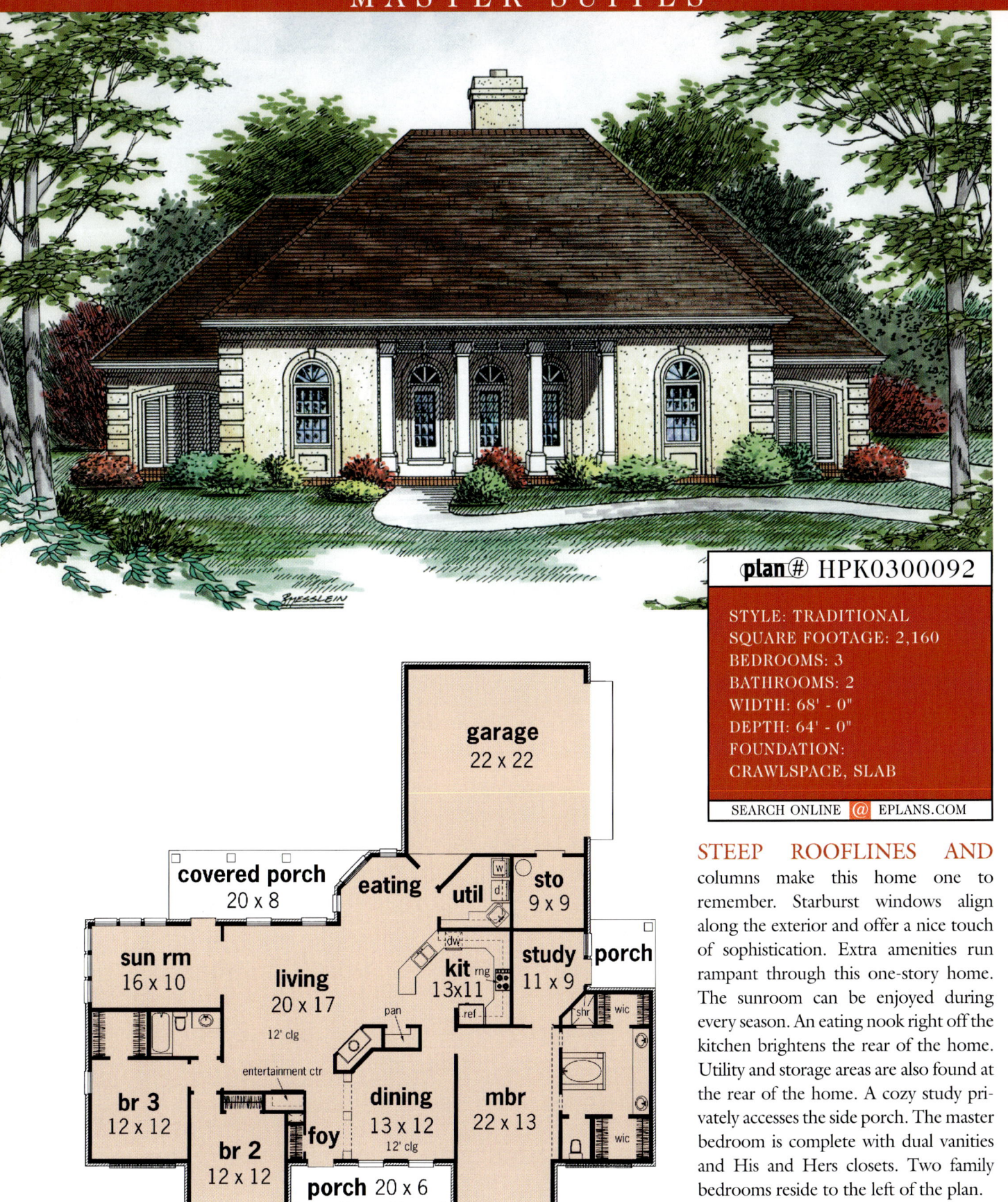

MASTER SUITES

plan # HPK0300092

STYLE: TRADITIONAL
SQUARE FOOTAGE: 2,160
BEDROOMS: 3
BATHROOMS: 2
WIDTH: 68' - 0"
DEPTH: 64' - 0"
FOUNDATION:
CRAWLSPACE, SLAB

SEARCH ONLINE @ EPLANS.COM

STEEP ROOFLINES AND columns make this home one to remember. Starburst windows align along the exterior and offer a nice touch of sophistication. Extra amenities run rampant through this one-story home. The sunroom can be enjoyed during every season. An eating nook right off the kitchen brightens the rear of the home. Utility and storage areas are also found at the rear of the home. A cozy study privately accesses the side porch. The master bedroom is complete with dual vanities and His and Hers closets. Two family bedrooms reside to the left of the plan.

garage
22 x 22

covered porch
20 x 8

eating

util

sto
9 x 9

sun rm
16 x 10

living
20 x 17
12' clg

kit
13x11

study
11 x 9

porch

pan

entertainment ctr

br 3
12 x 12

dining
13 x 12
12' clg

mbr
22 x 13

br 2
12 x 12

foy

porch 20 x 6

118   ROOMS FOR LIVING   ORDER BLUEPRINTS 24 HOURS, 7 DAYS A WEEK, AT 1-800-521-6797

MASTER SUITES

© The Sater Design Collection, Inc.

plan # HPK0300005

STYLE: EUROPEAN COTTAGE
SQUARE FOOTAGE: 3,640
BEDROOMS: 3
BATHROOMS: 3½
WIDTH: 106' - 4"
DEPTH: 102' - 4"
FOUNDATION: SLAB

SEARCH ONLINE @ EPLANS.COM

COME HOME TO luxurious living—all on one level—with this striking Mediterranean plan. Unique ceiling treatments highlight the living areas—the living and dining rooms, as well as the study, feature stepped ceilings, and the leisure room soars with a vaulted ceiling. The gourmet kitchen includes a spacious center island; another kitchen, this one outdoors, can be accessed from the leisure room. The master suite boasts plenty of amenities: a large, skylit walk-in closet, a bath with a whirlpool tub and walk-in shower, and private access to a charming garden area. Two suites, both with private baths, sit to the right of the plan.

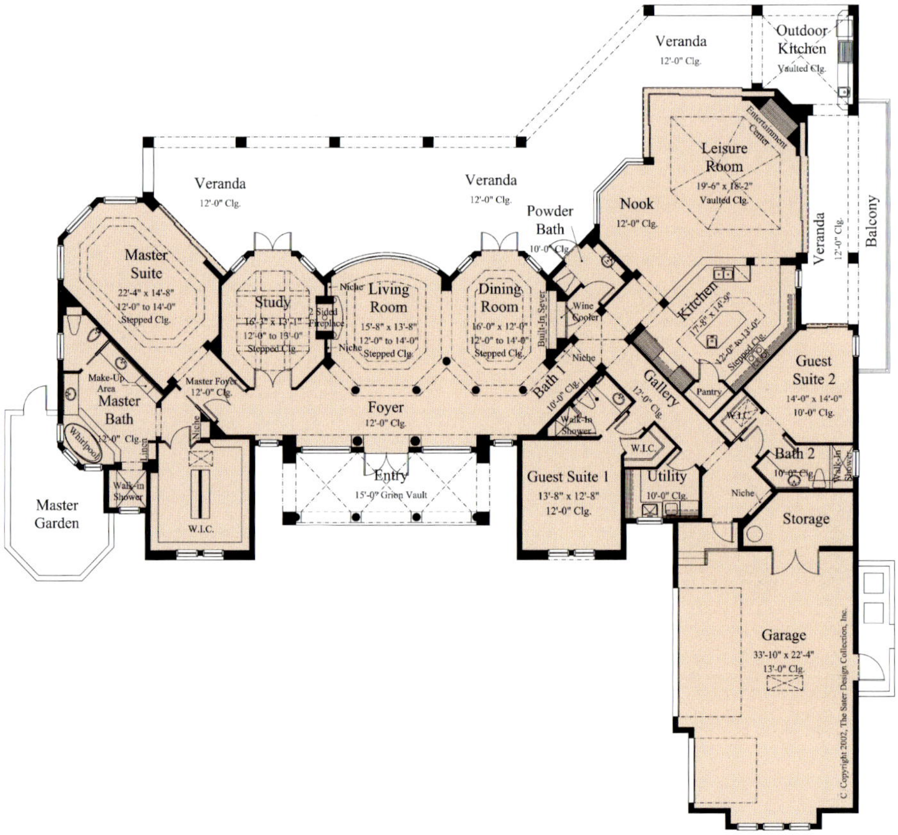

ORDER BLUEPRINTS 24 HOURS, 7 DAYS A WEEK, AT 1-800-521-6797

ROOMS FOR LIVING   119

MASTER SUITES

THIS CHARMING COUNTRY DESIGN SHOWCASES HINTS

of Victorian style. Inside, the family room boasts a fireplace flanked by built-in bookshelves. The living and dining rooms provide space for formal entertaining, with a handy powder room nearby. The kitchen, with an island cooktop, walk-in pantry, and built-in desk, adjoins a cozy breakfast nook. In the master suite, luxury reigns with two walk-in closets—both contain built-in shelves—and a beautiful bath with two vanities, a corner shower, and a whirlpool tub. Upstairs, a second master suite—also with a whirlpool tub—shares space with two additional bedrooms.

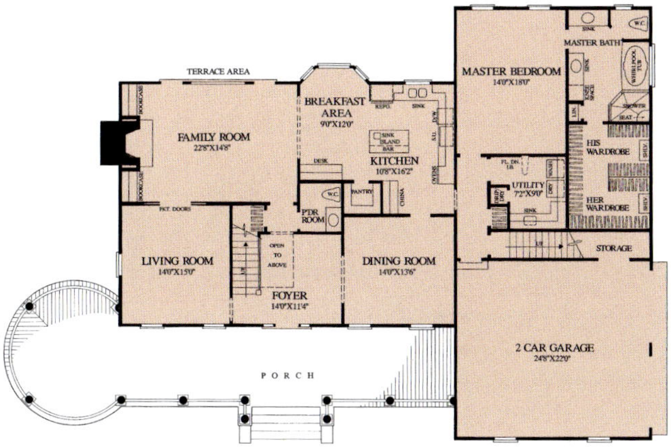

plan# HPK0300093

STYLE: VICTORIAN
FIRST FLOOR: 2,099 SQ. FT.
SECOND FLOOR: 1,260 SQ. FT.
TOTAL: 3,359 SQ. FT.
BONUS SPACE: 494 SQ. FT.
BEDROOMS: 4
BATHROOMS: 3½
WIDTH: 68' - 4"
DEPTH: 54' - 0"
FOUNDATION: CRAWLSPACE

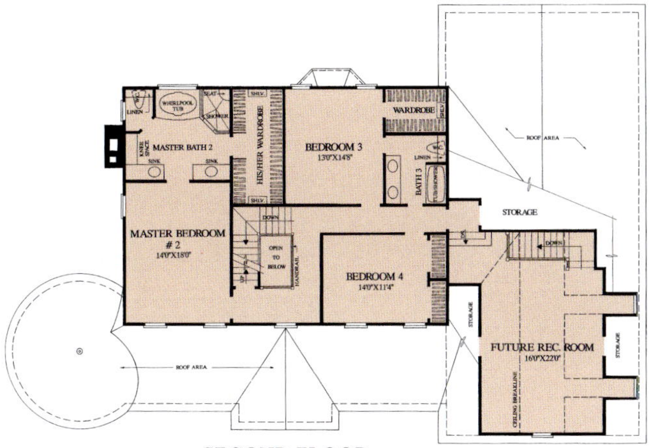

SEARCH ONLINE @ EPLANS.COM

MASTER SUITES

A WIDE VERANDA WITH A CHARMING GAZEBO welcomes family and friends to this classic Victorian design. A bay window brightens the living room, which opens to the octagonal sunroom. A butler's pantry connects the kitchen and dining room, and a breakfast area provides space for quiet family meals. The family room includes a fireplace and built-in entertainment center. Upstairs, the master bedroom includes a fireplace, a spacious bayed sitting area, and a luxurious bath. Three additional bedrooms, one with a window seat and private bath, also reside on the second floor.

plan # HPK0300094

STYLE: COUNTRY COTTAGE
FIRST FLOOR: 1,480 SQ. FT.
SECOND FLOOR: 1,651 SQ. FT.
TOTAL: 3,131 SQ. FT.
BEDROOMS: 4
BATHROOMS: 3½
WIDTH: 67' – 5"
DEPTH: 61' – 5"
FOUNDATION: CRAWLSPACE

SEARCH ONLINE @ EPLANS.COM

FIRST FLOOR

SECOND FLOOR

MASTER SUITES

YOU'LL NEVER FIND A MORE INVITING HOME THAN this!

With a true wraparound porch, bright interior, and special features, you'll love to call this beautiful design home. Three French-door entrances open to a great layout; from the formal foyer, a showcase kitchen is on the left, joined by an airy dining room. Continue to the family room, warmed by a hearth. The master suite is located on this level, adorned with a dazzling bath, walk-in closet, and porch access. Rounding out the first floor is a three-car garage with plenty of storage space. Upstairs, three bedrooms, one of which could be a secondary master suite, share a loft sitting area with a fireplace and access to the upper-level porch.

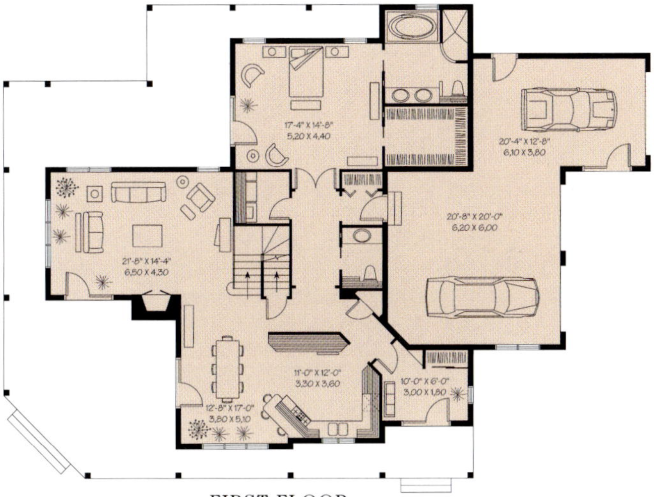

plan # HPK0300095

STYLE: FARMHOUSE
FIRST FLOOR: 1,654 SQ. FT.
SECOND FLOOR: 1,338 SQ. FT.
TOTAL: 2,992 SQ. FT.
BEDROOMS: 4
BATHROOMS: 3½
WIDTH: 72' - 0"
DEPTH: 52' - 0"
FOUNDATION: BASEMENT

SEARCH ONLINE @ EPLANS.COM

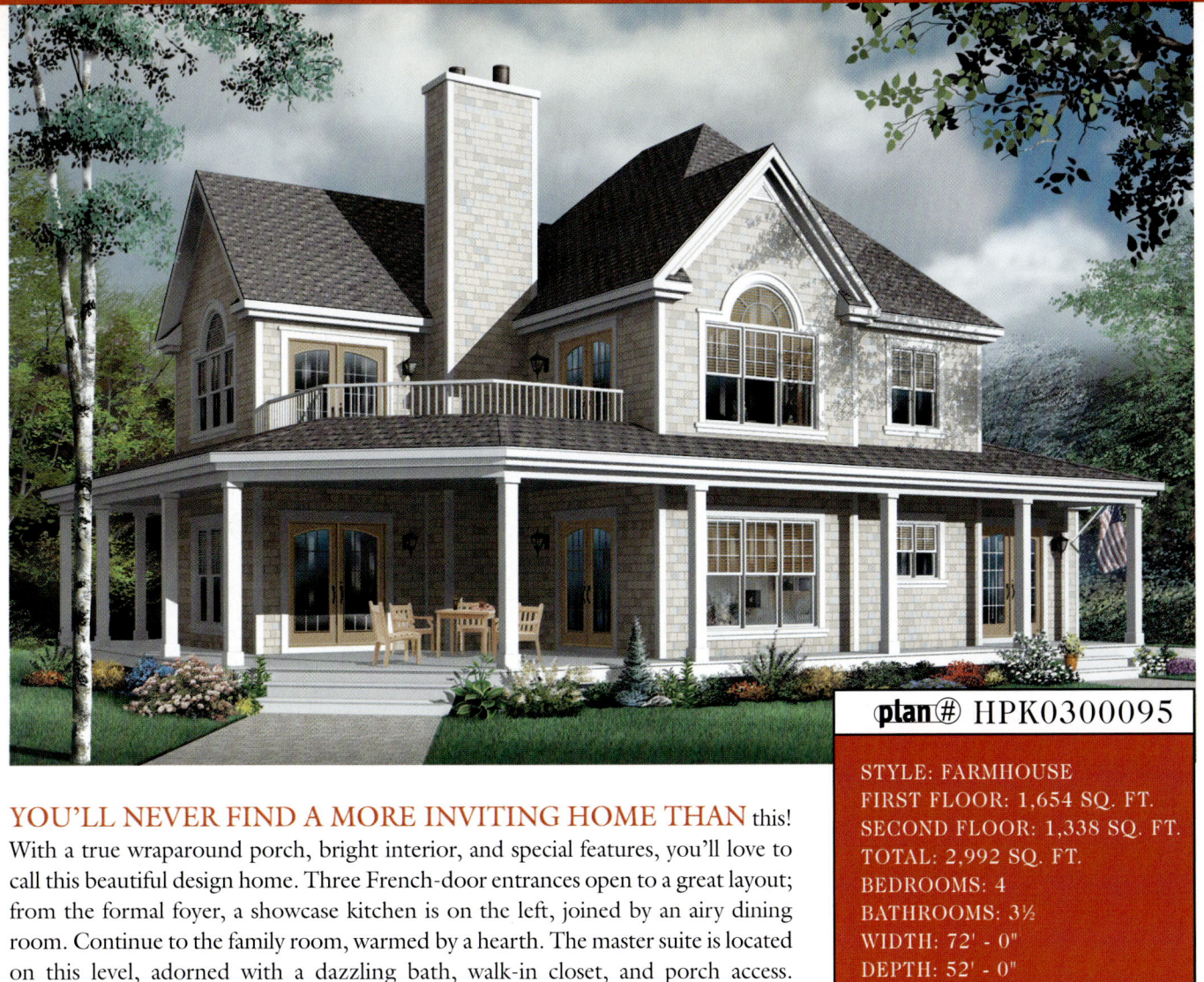

FIRST FLOOR

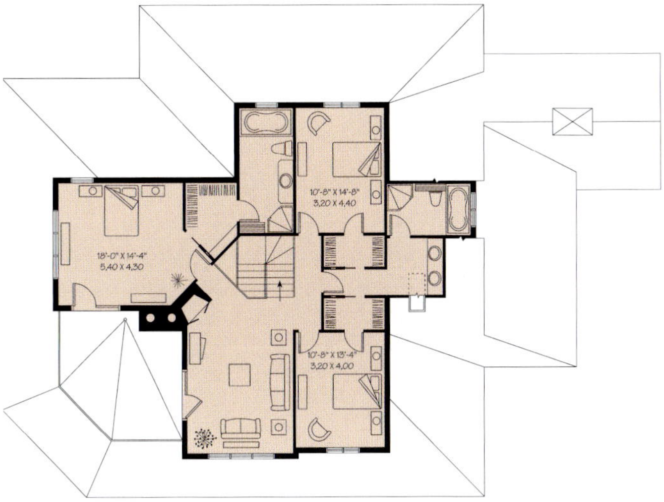

SECOND FLOOR

MASTER SUITES

plan# HPK0300096

STYLE: VICTORIAN
FIRST FLOOR: 1,044 SQ. FT.
SECOND FLOOR: 894 SQ. FT.
TOTAL: 1,938 SQ. FT.
BONUS SPACE: 228 SQ. FT.
BEDROOMS: 3
BATHROOMS: 2½
WIDTH: 58' - 0"
DEPTH: 43' - 6"
FOUNDATION: BASEMENT

SEARCH ONLINE @ EPLANS.COM

THIS CHARMING COUNTRY TRADITIONAL HOME provides a well-lit home office, harbored in a beautiful bay with three windows. The second-floor bay brightens the master bath, which has a double-bowl vanity, a step-up tub, and a dressing area. The living and dining rooms share a two-sided fireplace. The gourmet kitchen has a cooktop island counter and enjoys outdoor views through sliding glass doors in the breakfast area. A sizable bonus room above the two-car garage can be developed into hobby space or a recreation room.

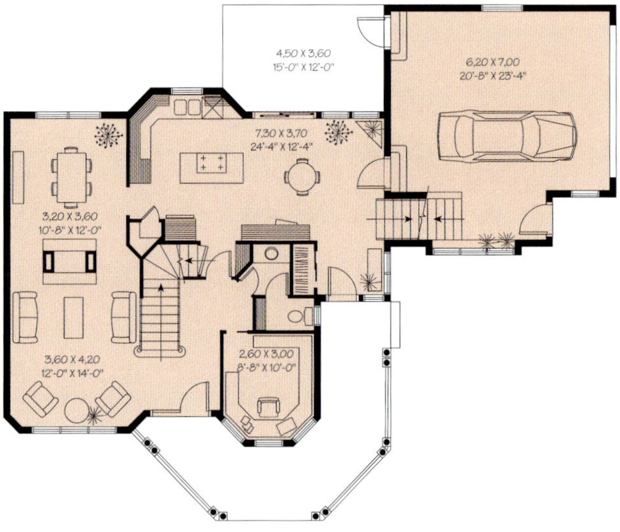

FIRST FLOOR

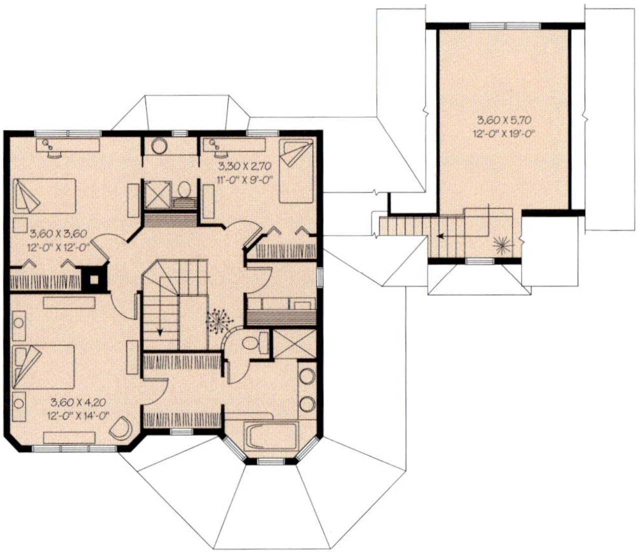

SECOND FLOOR

ORDER BLUEPRINTS 24 HOURS, 7 DAYS A WEEK, AT 1-800-521-6797

ROOMS FOR LIVING   123

MASTER SUITES

PHOTO COURTESY OF DESIGN BASICS, INC

plan# HPK0300097

STYLE: TRADITIONAL
FIRST FLOOR: 905 SQ. FT.
SECOND FLOOR: 863 SQ. FT.
TOTAL: 1,768 SQ. FT.
BEDROOMS: 3
BATHROOMS: 2½
WIDTH: 40' - 8"
DEPTH: 46' - 0"

SEARCH ONLINE @ EPLANS.COM

MULTIPLE GABLES AND DIFFERENT WINDOW treatments create an interesting exterior on this plan. A covered porch and Victorian accents create a classical exterior. Double doors to the entry open to a spacious great room and an elegant dining room. In the gourmet kitchen, features include an island snack bar and a large pantry—French doors lead to the breakfast area. Cathedral ceilings in the master suite and dressing area add an exquisite touch; additional enticing features here include a window seat, two walk-in closets, and a skylit bath. A vaulted ceiling in Bedroom 2 accents a window seat and an arched transom window.

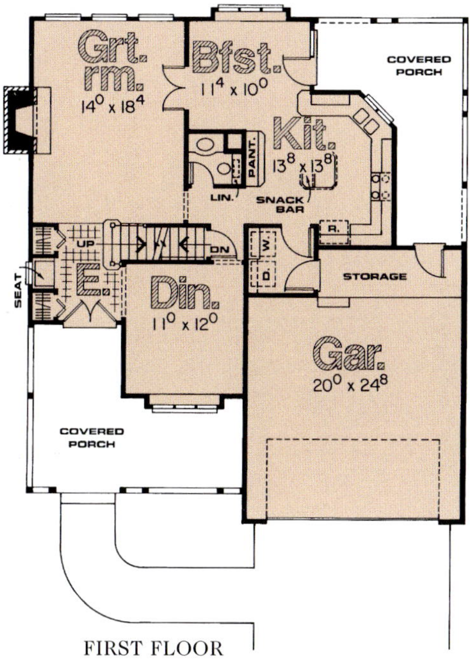

FIRST FLOOR

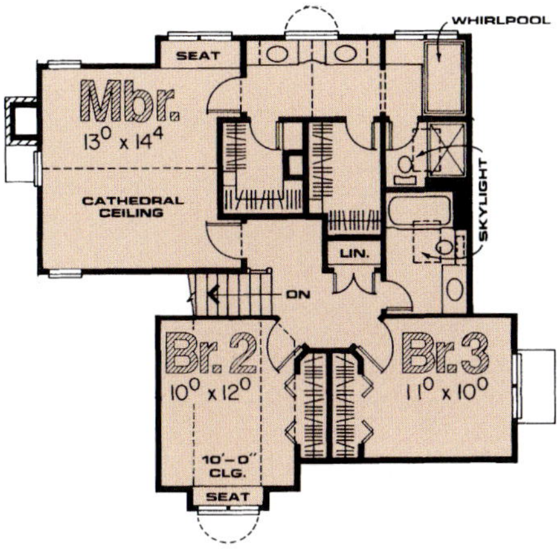

Grt. rm. 14⁰ x 18⁴
Bfst. 11⁴ x 10⁰
Kit. 13⁸ x 13⁸
Din. 11⁰ x 12⁰
Gar. 20⁰ x 24⁸
COVERED PORCH
SNACK BAR
STORAGE
LIN.
PANT.
UP
DN

SECOND FLOOR

Mbr. 13⁰ x 14⁴
CATHEDRAL CEILING
WHIRLPOOL
SEAT
SKYLIGHT
LIN.
DN
Br. 2 10⁰ x 12⁰
10'-0" CLG.
SEAT
Br. 3 11⁰ x 10⁰

124   ROOMS FOR LIVING   ORDER BLUEPRINTS 24 HOURS, 7 DAYS A WEEK, AT 1-800-521-6797

MASTER SUITES

© 2001 Donald A. Gardner, Inc.

plan # HPK0300098

STYLE: TRADITIONAL
FIRST FLOOR: 2,194 SQ. FT.
SECOND FLOOR: 973 SQ. FT.
TOTAL: 3,167 SQ. FT.
BONUS SPACE: 281 SQ. FT.
BEDROOMS: 4
BATHROOMS: 3½
WIDTH: 71' - 11"
DEPTH: 54' - 4"

SEARCH ONLINE @ EPLANS.COM

THIS UPDATED FARMHOUSE HAS BEEN GIVEN additional custom-styled features. Twin gables, sidelights, and an arched entryway accent the facade, and decorative ceiling treatments, bay windows, and French doors adorn the interior. From an abundance of counter space and large walk-in pantry to the built-ins and storage areas, this design makes the most of space. Supported by columns, a curved balcony overlooks the stunning two-story great room. The powder room is easily accessible from the common rooms, and angled corners soften the dining room.

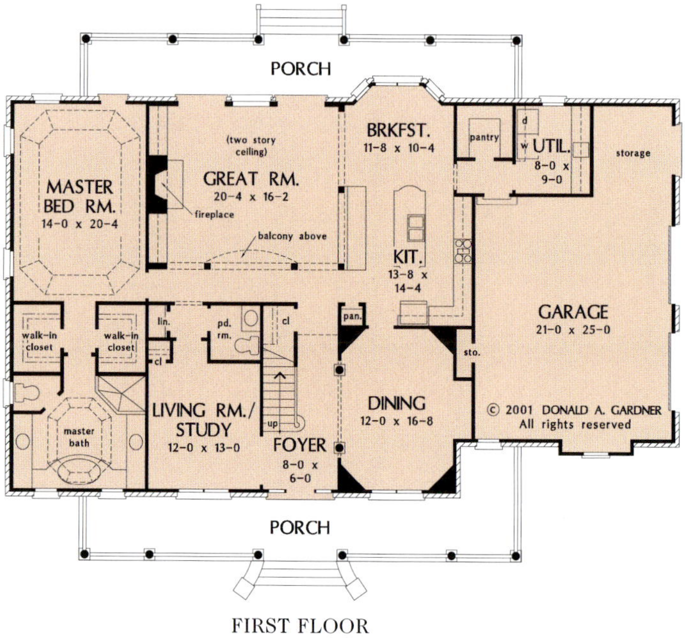

FIRST FLOOR

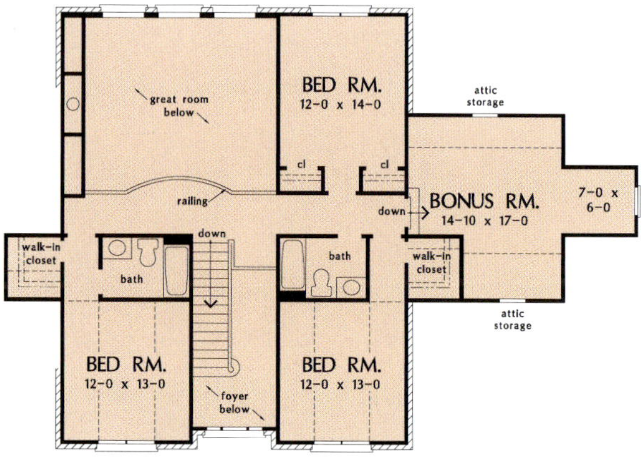

SECOND FLOOR

ORDER BLUEPRINTS 24 HOURS, 7 DAYS A WEEK, AT 1-800-521-6797

ROOMS FOR LIVING   125

MASTER SUITES

A WRAPAROUND COVERED PORCH AT THE FRONT AND sides of this house and an open deck at the back provide plenty of outside living area. The spacious great room features a fireplace, cathedral ceiling, and clerestory with an arched window. The island kitchen offers an attached skylit breakfast room complete with a bay window. The first-floor master bedroom contains a generous closet and a master bath with a garden tub, double-bowl vanity, and shower. The second floor sports two bedrooms and a full bath with a double-bowl vanity. An elegant balcony overlooks the great room.

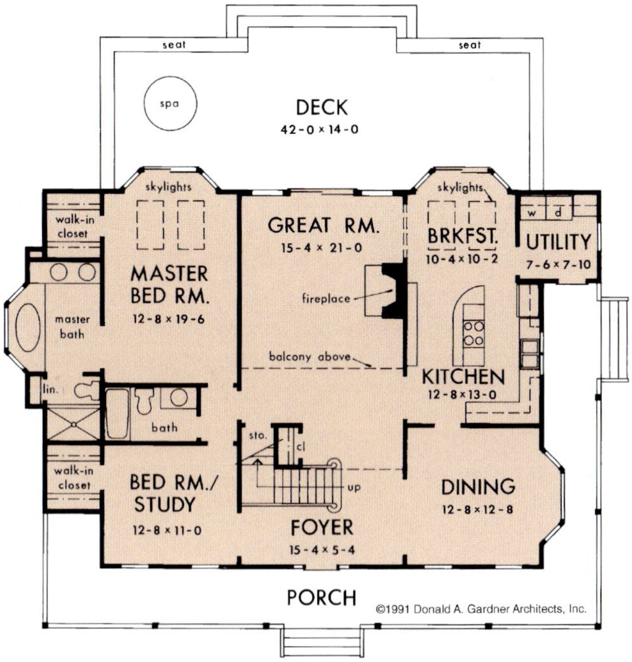

plan# HPK0300099

STYLE: FARMHOUSE
FIRST FLOOR: 1,756 SQ. FT.
SECOND FLOOR: 565 SQ. FT.
TOTAL: 2,321 SQ. FT.
BEDROOMS: 4
BATHROOMS: 3
WIDTH: 56' - 8"
DEPTH: 42' - 4"

SEARCH ONLINE @ EPLANS.COM

FIRST FLOOR

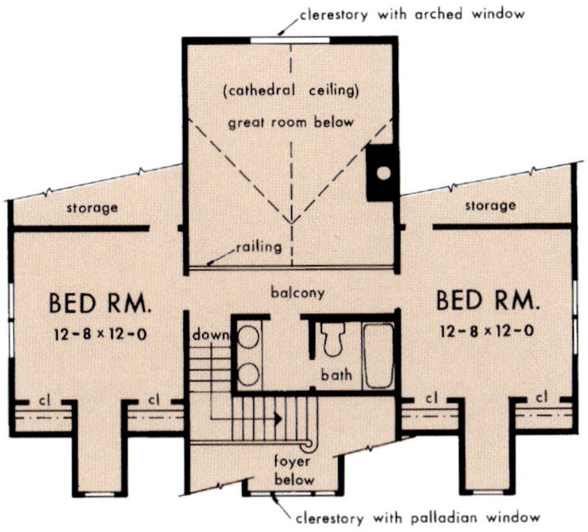

SECOND FLOOR

126   ROOMS FOR LIVING   ORDER BLUEPRINTS 24 HOURS, 7 DAYS A WEEK, AT 1-800-521-6797

MASTER SUITES

plan# HPK0300100

STYLE: COUNTRY COTTAGE
FIRST FLOOR: 2,891 SQ. FT.
SECOND FLOOR: 1,336 SQ. FT.
TOTAL: 4,227 SQ. FT.
BONUS SPACE: 380 SQ. FT.
BEDROOMS: 4
BATHROOMS: 3½ + ½
WIDTH: 90' - 8"
DEPTH: 56' - 4"
FOUNDATION: CRAWLSPACE,
BASEMENT

SEARCH ONLINE @ EPLANS.COM

THIS SOUTHERN COASTAL COTTAGE RADIATES CHARM

and elegance. Step inside from the covered porch and discover a floor plan with practicality and architectural interest. The foyer has a raised ceiling and is partially open to above. The library and great room offer fireplaces and built-in shelves; the great room also provides rear-porch access. The kitchen, featuring an island with a separate sink, is adjacent to the breakfast room and a study with a built-in desk. On the far right, the master bedroom will amaze, with a sumptuous bath and enormous walk-in closet. Three upstairs bedrooms share a loft and recreation room. Convenient storage opportunities make organization easy.

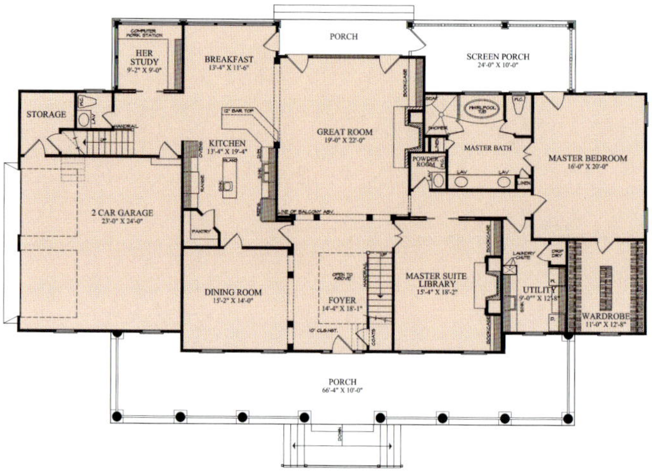

FIRST FLOOR

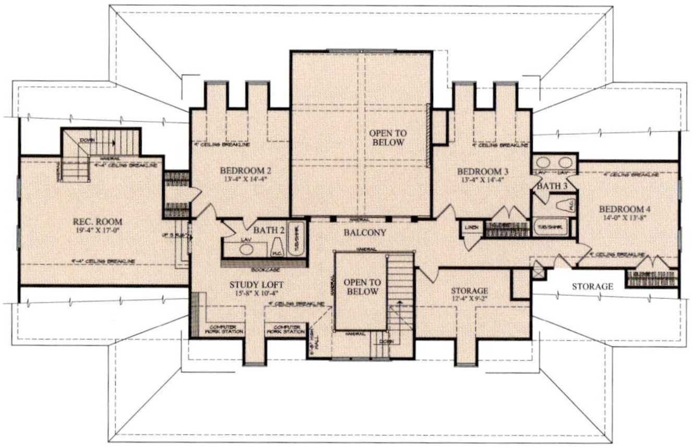

SECOND FLOOR

ORDER BLUEPRINTS 24 HOURS, 7 DAYS A WEEK, AT 1-800-521-6797

ROOMS FOR LIVING   127

MASTER SUITES

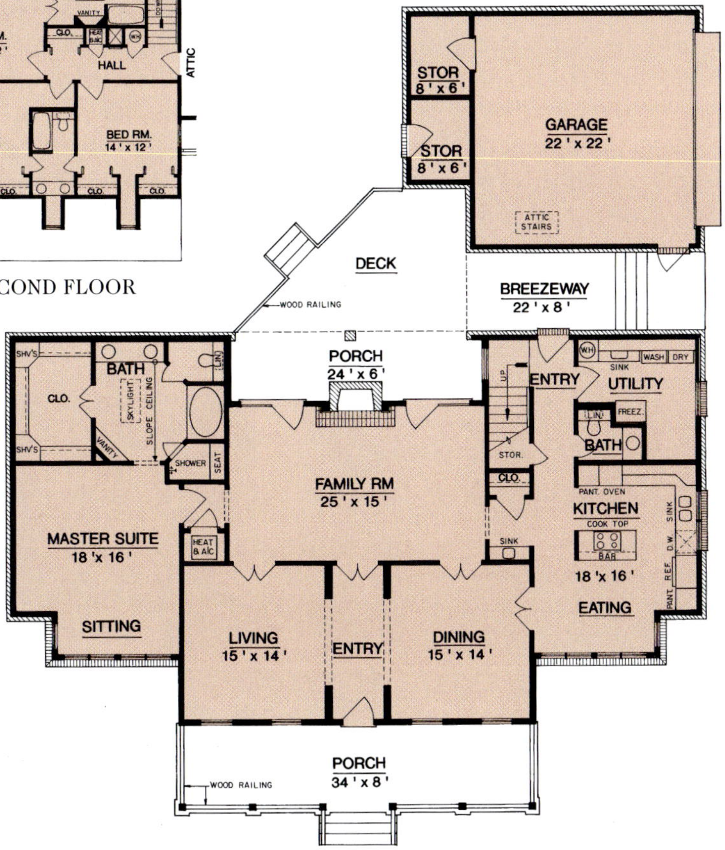

plan# HPK0300101

STYLE: FARMHOUSE
FIRST FLOOR: 2,008 SQ. FT.
SECOND FLOOR: 1,027 SQ. FT.
TOTAL: 3,035 SQ. FT.
BEDROOMS: 4
BATHROOMS: 3½
WIDTH: 66' - 0"
DEPTH: 74' - 0"
FOUNDATION: BASEMENT,
CRAWLSPACE, SLAB

SEARCH ONLINE @ EPLANS.COM

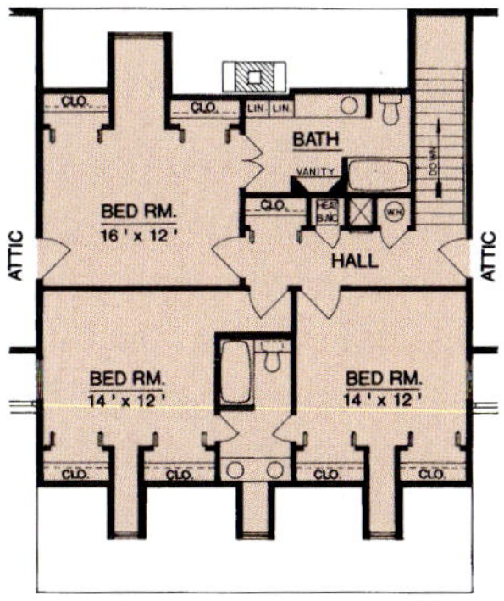

A PORCH WITH WOOD

railings borders the facade of this plan, lending a farmhouse or country feel. The family room includes a fireplace and French doors to the porch, which open further to the deck area. The master bedroom is filled with luxuries from the walk-in closet with shelves, the full bath with a skylight, sloped ceiling, and vanity to the shower with a convenient seat. Three additional bedrooms upstairs share two full baths between them. A breezeway, placed between the garage and the house, leads easily to the deck area. Extras include a large utility room, pantry, half-bath downstairs, and two storage areas.

SECOND FLOOR

FIRST FLOOR

128   ROOMS FOR LIVING   ORDER BLUEPRINTS 24 HOURS, 7 DAYS A WEEK, AT 1-800-521-6797

MASTER SUITES

plan# HPK0300102

STYLE: FARMHOUSE
FIRST FLOOR: 1,765 SQ. FT.
SECOND FLOOR: 595 SQ. FT.
TOTAL: 2,360 SQ. FT.
BEDROOMS: 3
BATHROOMS: 2½
WIDTH: 68' - 0"
DEPTH: 74' - 0"
FOUNDATION: BASEMENT, SLAB, CRAWLSPACE

SEARCH ONLINE @ EPLANS.COM

DORMER WINDOWS AND A COVERED FRONT PORCH lend a Southern country flavor to the exterior of this fine home. The interior is well planned and spacious. The living areas are open to one another and comprise a formal dining room, a family room with a sloped ceiling and fireplace, and a kitchen with an eating area. A huge pantry offers convenience to the kitchen. The master suite features a sitting area and large garden bath. The second floor holds two family bedrooms and a full bath. The balcony overlooks the family room below.

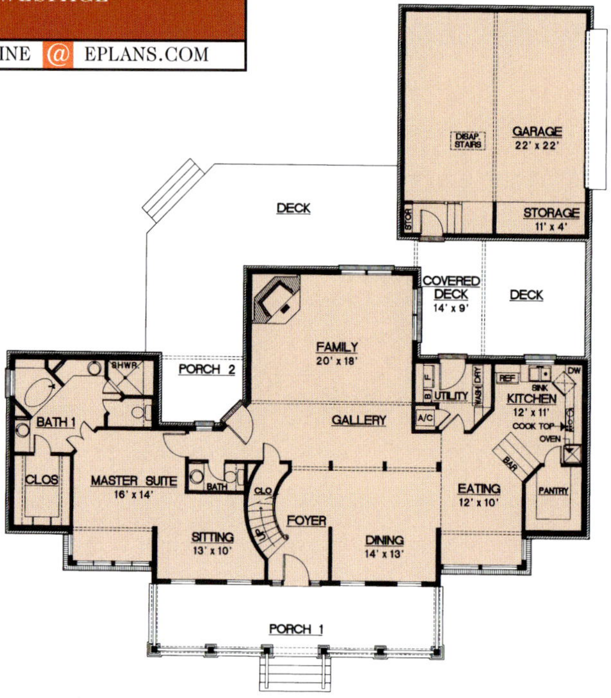

FIRST FLOOR

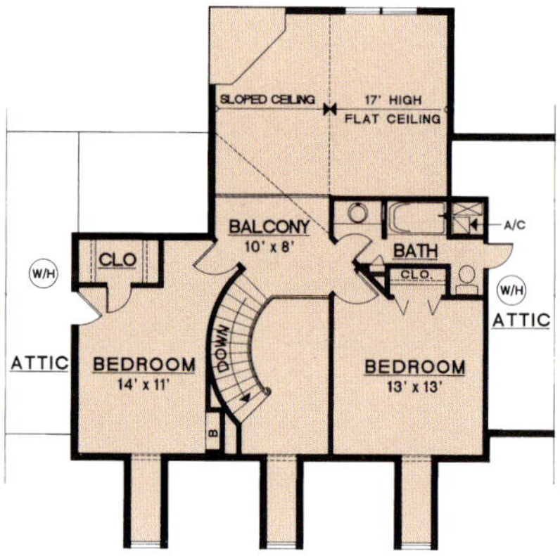

SECOND FLOOR

ORDER BLUEPRINTS 24 HOURS, 7 DAYS A WEEK, AT 1-800-521-6797

ROOMS FOR LIVING 129

MASTER SUITES

AN ARCHED ENTRY, SHUTTERS, AND A BRICK FACADE

highlight the exterior of this two-story modern Colonial home. Living and dining rooms at the front of the plan accommodate formal occasions. The rear of the plan is designed for informal gatherings, such as the generous family room, which includes a warming fireplace and bayed conversation area. The bright breakfast area is open to an efficient U-shaped kitchen with a snack bar. Bright windows and French doors add appeal to the living room. Upstairs, a U-shaped balcony hall overlooks the entry below and connects four bedrooms, including a master suite. This retreat features a private sitting room, two walk-in closets, a compartmented bath, separate vanities, and a window-brightened whirlpool tub.

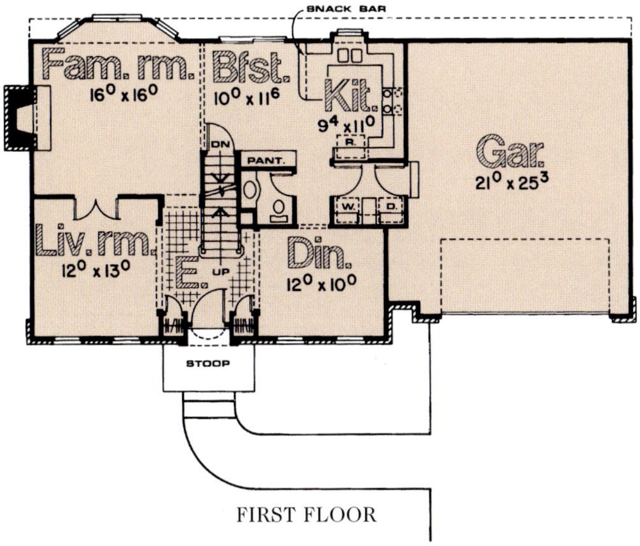

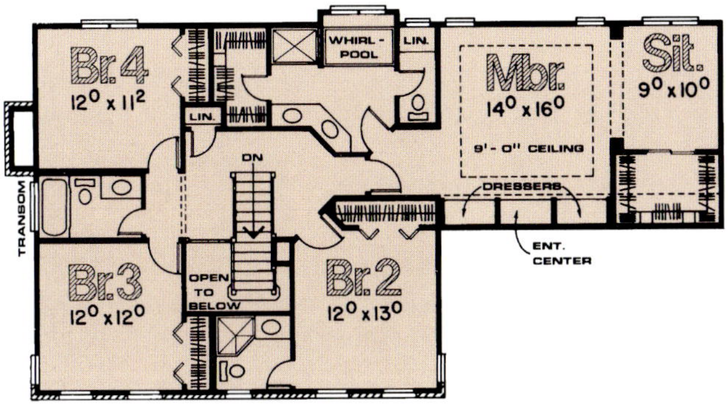

---

plan # HPK0300103

STYLE: COLONIAL
FIRST FLOOR: 1,000 SQ. FT.
SECOND FLOOR: 1,345 SQ. FT.
TOTAL: 2,345 SQ. FT.
BEDROOMS: 4
BATHROOMS: 3½
WIDTH: 57' - 4"
DEPTH: 30' - 0"

SEARCH ONLINE @ EPLANS.COM

PHOTO BY: DESIGN BASICS, INC.

MASTER SUITES

HERE IS A BEAUTIFUL EXAMPLE OF CLASSICAL REVIVAL

architecture complete with shuttered, jack-arch windows and a column-supported pediment over the entry. Inside, the foyer opens to the living room and leads to the family room at the rear. Here a panoramic view is complemented by an impressive fireplace framed by built-ins. To the left, the efficient island kitchen is situated between the sunny breakfast nook and the formal dining room. The right side of the plan holds two bedrooms and the lavish master suite.

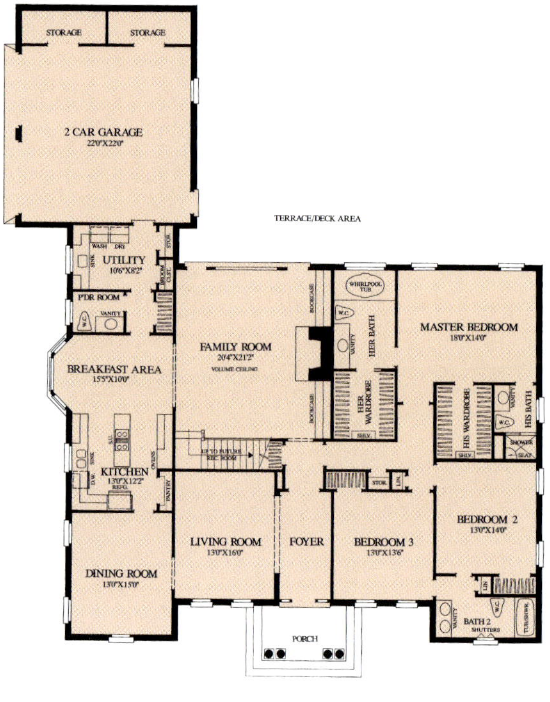

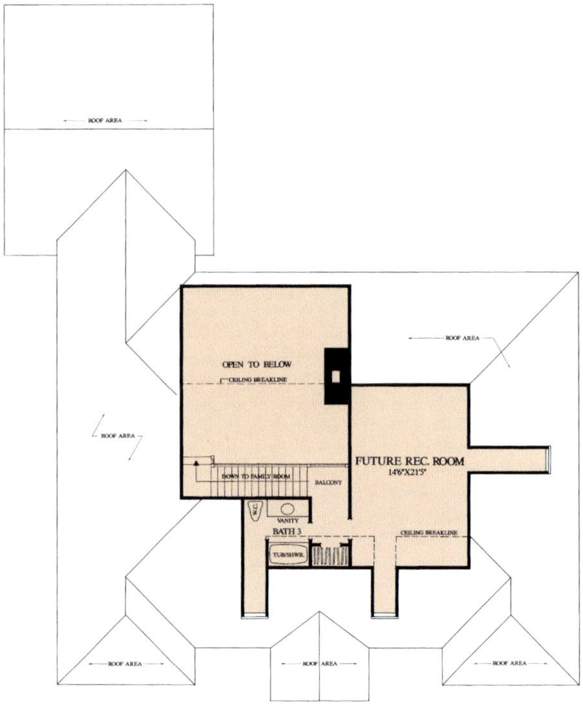

plan # HPK0300104

STYLE: GEORGIAN
SQUARE FOOTAGE: 2,869
BONUS SPACE: 541 SQ. FT.
BEDROOMS: 3
BATHROOMS: 2½
WIDTH: 68' - 6"
DEPTH: 79' - 8"
FOUNDATION: CRAWLSPACE

SEARCH ONLINE @ EPLANS.COM

MASTER SUITES

plan # HPK0300105

STYLE: TRADITIONAL
SQUARE FOOTAGE: 2,276
BEDROOMS: 3
BATHROOMS: 2½
WIDTH: 72' - 0"
DEPTH: 56' - 0"

SEARCH ONLINE @ EPLANS.COM

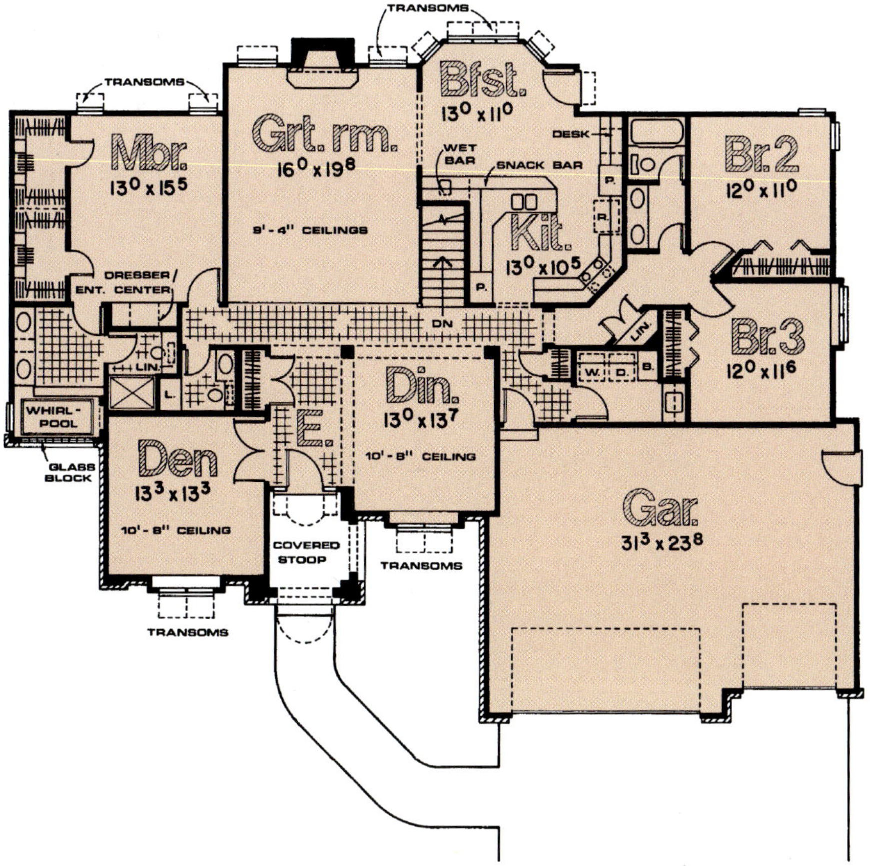

DRAMA AND HARMONY are expressed in this plan by utilizing a variety of elegant exterior materials. The great room with a window-framed fireplace is conveniently located next to the eat-in kitchen with a bayed breakfast area. Two secluded secondary bedrooms enjoy easy access to a compartmented bath with twin vanities. His and Hers closets and a built-in armoire grace the master suite where a private bath features glass blocks over the whirlpool tub, double sinks, and an extra linen storage cabinet.

MASTER SUITES

plan# HPK0300106

STYLE: TRADITIONAL
SQUARE FOOTAGE: 1,710
BEDROOMS: 3
BATHROOMS: 2
WIDTH: 53' - 4"
DEPTH: 54' - 10"

SEARCH ONLINE @ EPLANS.COM

COMFORT AWAITS YOU IN THIS APPEALING RANCH home. Inside, a formal dining room features elegant ceiling details. The volume great room is designed for daily family gatherings with a raised-hearth fireplace flanked by sparkling windows. Outdoor access and a lazy Susan are thoughtful details designed into the kitchen and bowed dinette. For added flexibility, two secondary bedrooms can be easily converted to a sunroom with French doors, and an optional den. The secluded master suite is enhanced by a boxed ceiling and deluxe skylit dressing room.

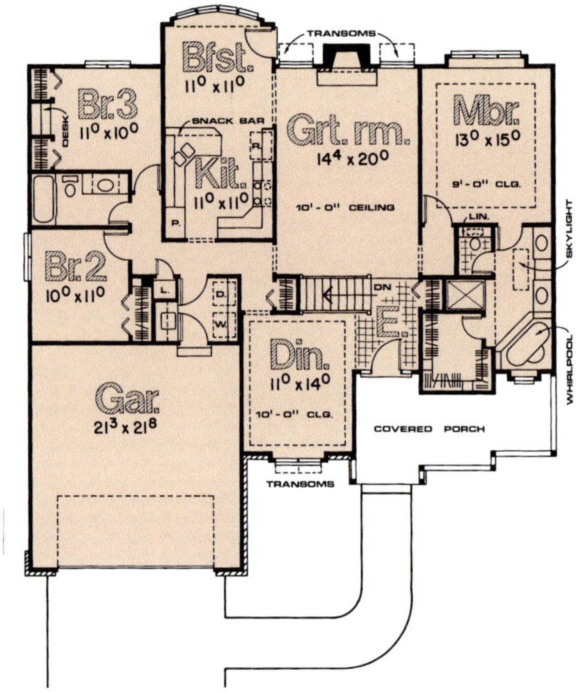

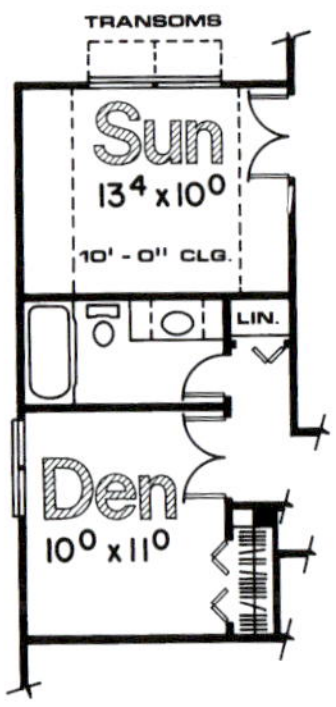

ALTERNATE LAYOUT

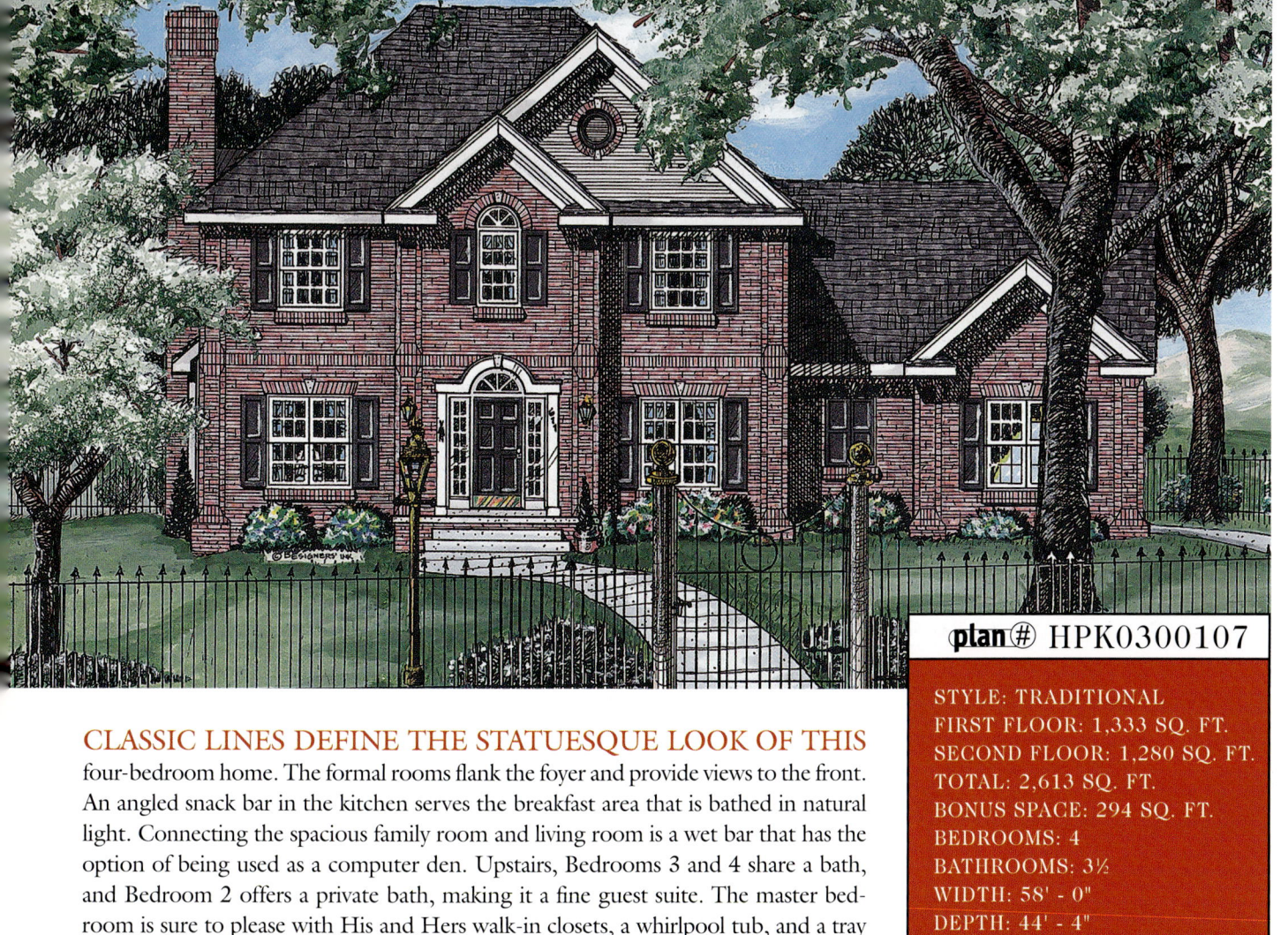

MASTER SUITES

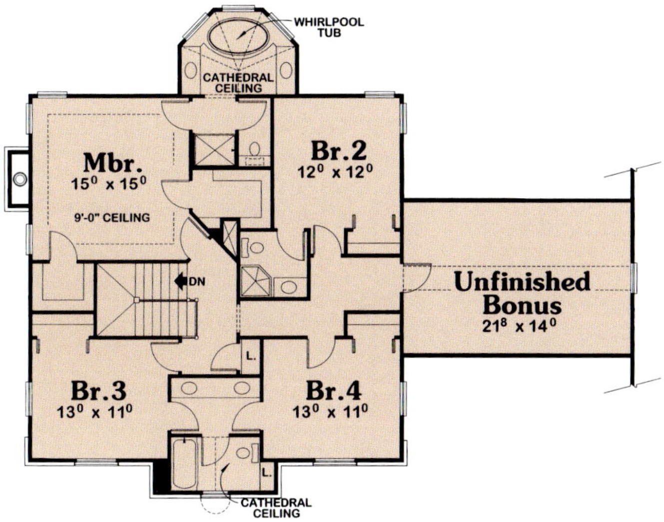

plan # HPK0300107

STYLE: TRADITIONAL
FIRST FLOOR: 1,333 SQ. FT.
SECOND FLOOR: 1,280 SQ. FT.
TOTAL: 2,613 SQ. FT.
BONUS SPACE: 294 SQ. FT.
BEDROOMS: 4
BATHROOMS: 3½
WIDTH: 58' - 0"
DEPTH: 44' - 4"

SEARCH ONLINE @ EPLANS.COM

CLASSIC LINES DEFINE THE STATUESQUE LOOK OF THIS

four-bedroom home. The formal rooms flank the foyer and provide views to the front. An angled snack bar in the kitchen serves the breakfast area that is bathed in natural light. Connecting the spacious family room and living room is a wet bar that has the option of being used as a computer den. Upstairs, Bedrooms 3 and 4 share a bath, and Bedroom 2 offers a private bath, making it a fine guest suite. The master bedroom is sure to please with His and Hers walk-in closets, a whirlpool tub, and a tray ceiling. Completing this level is a large bonus room available for future expansion.

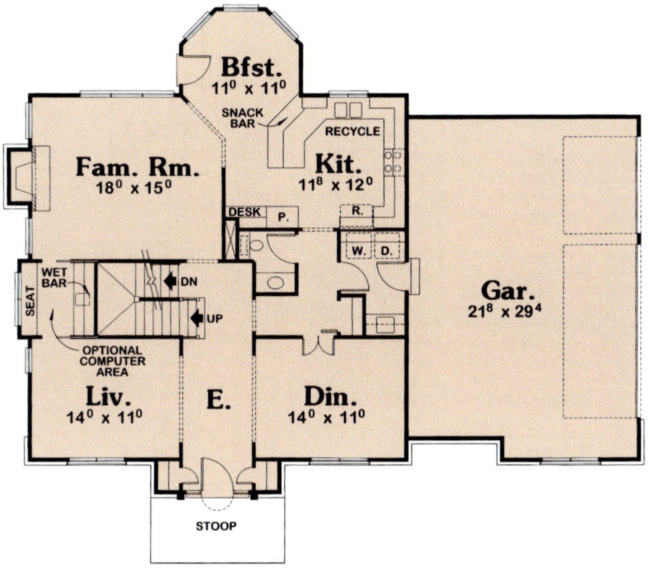

MASTER SUITES

plan # HPK0300108

STYLE: TRADITIONAL
FIRST FLOOR: 2,454 SQ. FT.
SECOND FLOOR: 986 SQ. FT.
TOTAL: 3,440 SQ. FT.
BEDROOMS: 4
BATHROOMS: 3½
WIDTH: 73' - 4"
DEPTH: 59' - 4"

SEARCH ONLINE @ EPLANS.COM

THIS TRADITIONAL DESIGN FITS WELL INTO A countryside setting and boasts an abundance of amenities. Inside, the great room and hearth room offer fireplaces. The kitchen features a snack bar and walk-in pantry. The master suite provides a sitting area, whirlpool bath, and walk-in closet. A den off the foyer easily converts to a library or home office. Upstairs, each of three secondary bedrooms provides a walk-in closet.

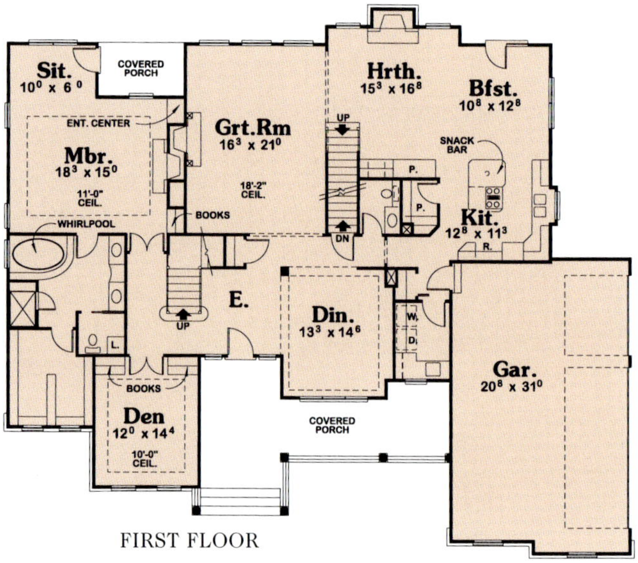

FIRST FLOOR

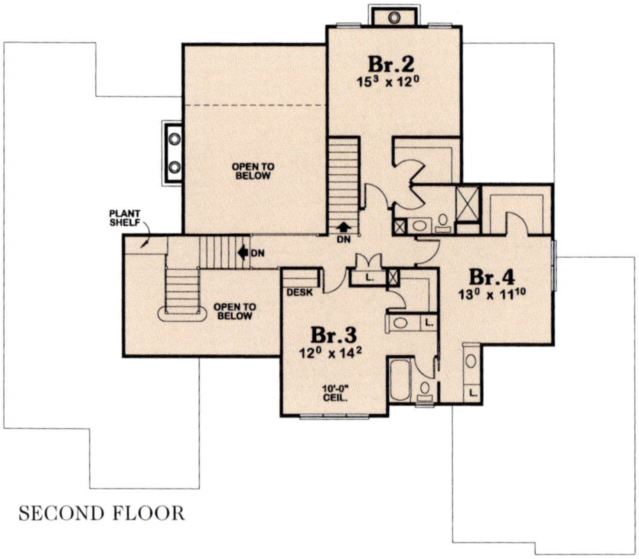

SECOND FLOOR

ORDER BLUEPRINTS 24 HOURS, 7 DAYS A WEEK, AT 1-800-521-6797

ROOMS FOR LIVING   135

MASTER SUITES

Plan# HPK0300109

STYLE: CONTEMPORARY
MAIN FLOOR: 3,990 SQ. FT.
LOWER LEVEL: 2,669 SQ. FT.
TOTAL: 6,659 SQ. FT.
BEDROOMS: 4
BATHROOMS: 4½
WIDTH: 99' - 6"
DEPTH: 84' - 2"
FOUNDATION: BASEMENT

SEARCH ONLINE @ EPLANS.COM

THE EXTRAORDINARY CHARM OF THIS HANDSOME home, with its brick-and-stone facade, is best exemplified by the exciting master suite. Not only does it have a gigantic walk-in closet, twin vanities, shower, and oversize garden tub, it enjoys an exercise room, easy access to a library, and a private entry to the rear deck. A guest suite is also found on the main floor, and two more bedrooms share the lower level with a spacious recreation room and entertainment center. The great room and dining area are especially designed for memorable social gatherings.

LOWER LEVEL

MAIN FLOOR

MASTER SUITES

plan # HPK0300110

STYLE: TRADITIONAL
FIRST FLOOR: 2,813 SQ. FT.
SECOND FLOOR: 1,091 SQ. FT.
TOTAL: 3,904 SQ. FT.
BEDROOMS: 4
BATHROOMS: 3½
WIDTH: 85' - 5"
DEPTH: 74' - 8"

SEARCH ONLINE @ EPLANS.COM

KEYSTONE LINTELS AND AN ARCHED TRANSOM OVER

the entry spell classic design for this four-bedroom home. The tiled foyer offers entry to any room you choose, whether it's the secluded den with its built-in bookshelves, the formal dining room, the formal living room with its fireplace, or the spacious rear family room and kitchen area with a sunny breakfast nook. The first-floor master suite features a sitting room with bookshelves, two walk-in closets, and a private bath with a corner whirlpool tub. Upstairs, two family bedrooms share a bath and enjoy separate vanities. A third family bedroom features its own full bath and a built-in window seat in a box-bay window.

MASTER SUITES

© 2001 Donald A. Gardner, Inc.

STONE AND HORIZONTAL SIDING GIVE A DEFINITE country flavor to this two-story home. The front study makes an ideal guest room with the adjoining powder room. The formal dining room is accented with decorative columns that define its perimeter. The great room boasts a fireplace, built-ins, and a magnificent view of the backyard beyond one of two rear porches. The master suite boasts two walk-in closets and a private bath. Two bedrooms share a full bath on the second floor.

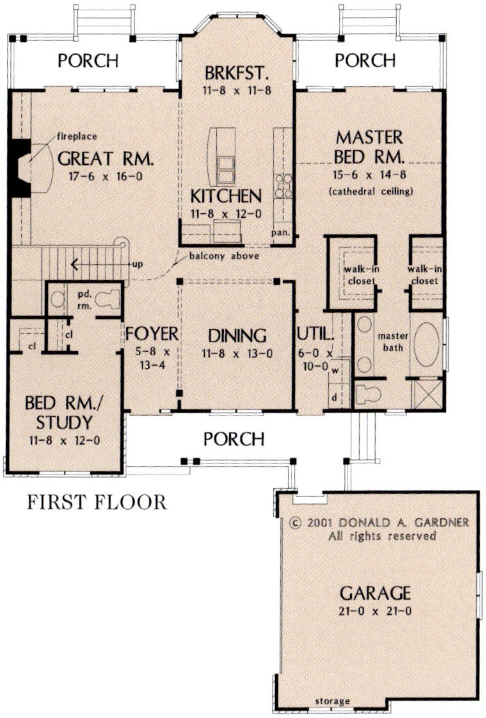

plan# HPK0300111

STYLE: CRAFTSMAN
FIRST FLOOR: 1,707 SQ. FT.
SECOND FLOOR: 514 SQ. FT.
TOTAL: 2,221 SQ. FT.
BONUS SPACE: 211 SQ. FT.
BEDROOMS: 4
BATHROOMS: 2½
WIDTH: 50' - 0"
DEPTH: 71' - 8"

SEARCH ONLINE @ EPLANS.COM

FIRST FLOOR

© 2001 DONALD A. GARDNER
All rights reserved

SECOND FLOOR

138   ROOMS FOR LIVING   ORDER BLUEPRINTS 24 HOURS, 7 DAYS A WEEK, AT 1-800-521-6797

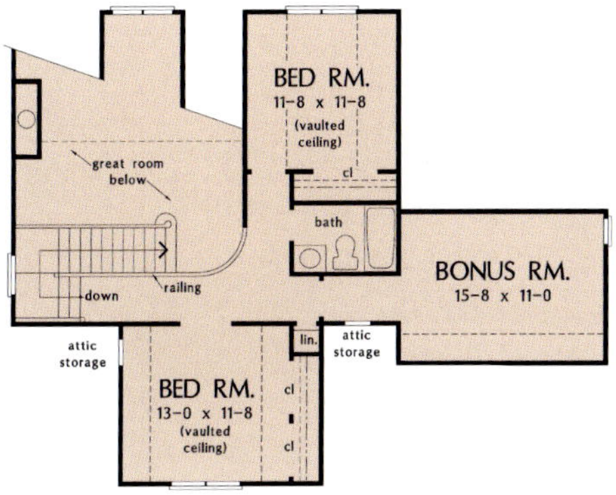

MASTER SUITES

plan # HPK0300112

STYLE: CRAFTSMAN
SQUARE FOOTAGE: 2,017
BONUS SPACE: 319 SQ. FT.
BEDROOMS: 3
BATHROOMS: 2½
WIDTH: 54' - 0"
DEPTH: 74' - 0"

SEARCH ONLINE @ EPLANS.COM

THIS BEAUTIFUL ARTS and Crafts cottage combines stone and siding to create stunning curb appeal. A pair of columns and an arch make a dramatic entrance to an open floor plan. A tray ceiling crowns the great room that features built-in cabinetry, French-door access to the rear porch, a fireplace, and a convenient pass-through to the kitchen. The dining room and breakfast nook are surrounded by windows and open space for an airy feeling. The master suite, located in the quiet wing, includes a sitting area, porch access, twin walk-ins, and a master bath. Note the optional study/bedroom and flexible bonus room.

© 2002 DONALD A. GARDNER
All rights reserved

MASTER SUITES

A EUROPEAN FEEL IS SHOWN ON THE FACADE OF this exciting two-story home and hints at the exquisite grace of the interior. The sensational view at the foyer includes high windows across the rear wall, a fireplace, open stairs with rich wood trim, and volume ceilings. The formal dining room offers dimension to the entry and is conveniently located for serving from the kitchen. The spacious breakfast room, wraparound bar in the kitchen, and open hearth room offer a cozy gathering place for family members. The deluxe master bedroom suite boasts an 11-foot ceiling, a sitting area, and a garden bath. The second-floor balcony leads to a bedroom suite with a private bath and two additional bedrooms with large closets and private access to a shared bath.

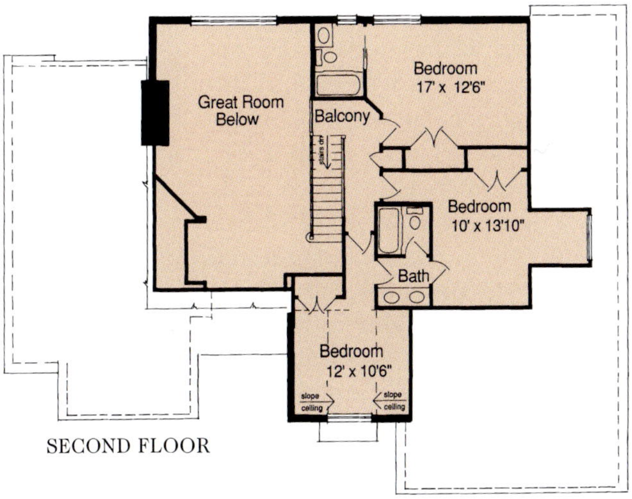

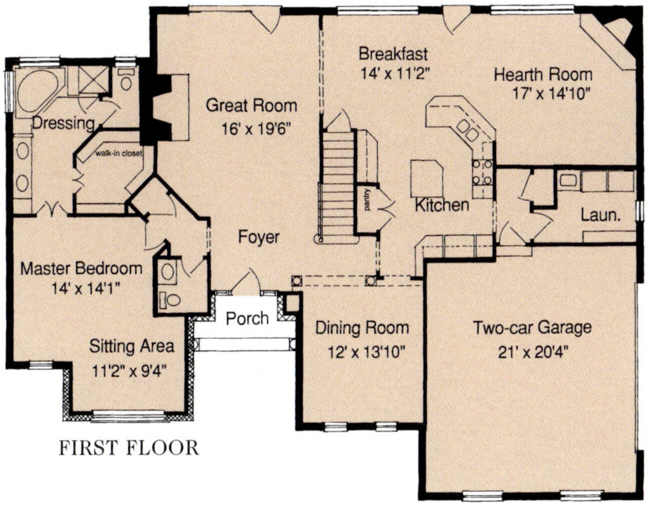

plan # HPK0300113

STYLE: TRANSITIONAL
FIRST FLOOR: 1,915 SQ. FT.
SECOND FLOOR: 823 SQ. FT.
TOTAL: 2,738 SQ. FT.
BEDROOMS: 4
BATHROOMS: 3½
WIDTH: 63' - 4"
DEPTH: 48' - 0"
FOUNDATION: BASEMENT

SEARCH ONLINE @ EPLANS.COM

MASTER SUITES

STONE ACCENTS AND A CHARMING TURRET ENHANCE

the exterior of this spacious plan. A beamed ceiling highlights the great room, which shares a two-sided fireplace with the foyer; another fireplace can be found in the hearth room, which overlooks a covered rear porch and deck area. A resplendent master suite, with easy access to the laundry area, sits to the right of the plan and boasts a private sitting bay, a dual-vanity dressing area, and a large walk-in closet. The lower level includes media, billiards, and exercise rooms, two bedrooms, and a gathering area that opens to a patio.

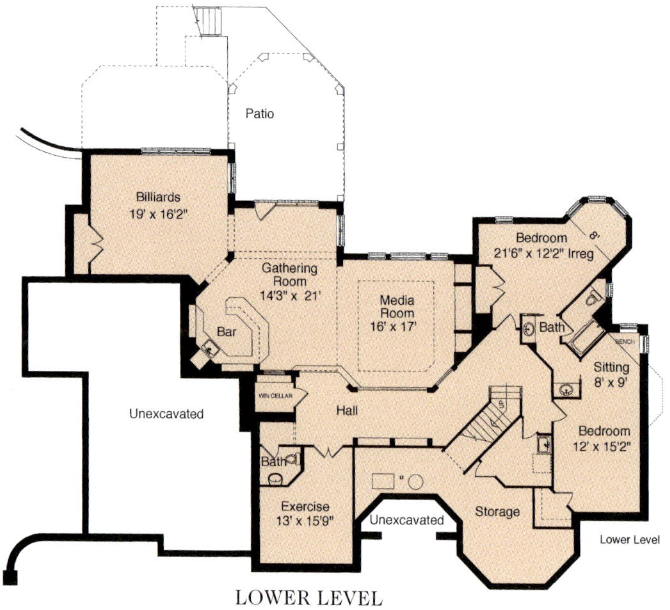

plan # HPK0300114

STYLE: EUROPEAN COTTAGE
MAIN LEVEL: 2,961 SQ. FT.
LOWER LEVEL: 2,416 SQ. FT.
TOTAL: 5,377 SQ. FT.
BEDROOMS: 3
BATHROOMS: 2½ + ½
WIDTH: 89' - 0"
DEPTH: 59' - 2"
FOUNDATION: BASEMENT

SEARCH ONLINE @ EPLANS.COM

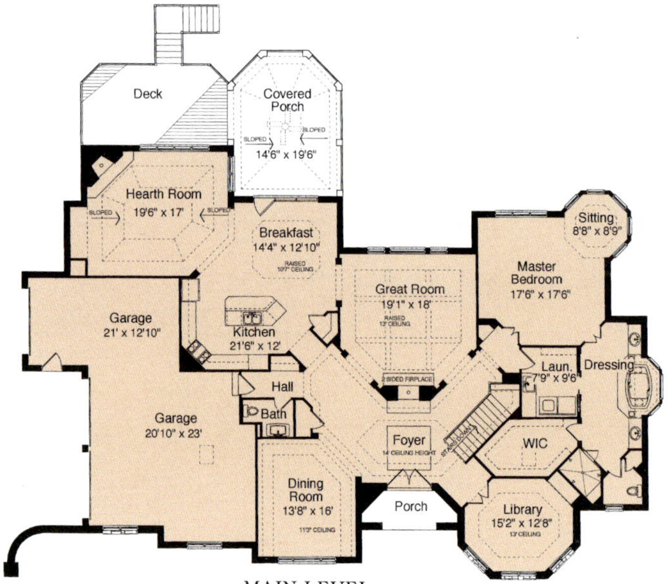

MASTER SUITES

plan# HPK0300115

STYLE: TRADITIONAL
SQUARE FOOTAGE: 2,538
BEDROOMS: 3
BATHROOMS: 2½
WIDTH: 68' - 8"
DEPTH: 64' - 8"

SEARCH ONLINE @ EPLANS.COM

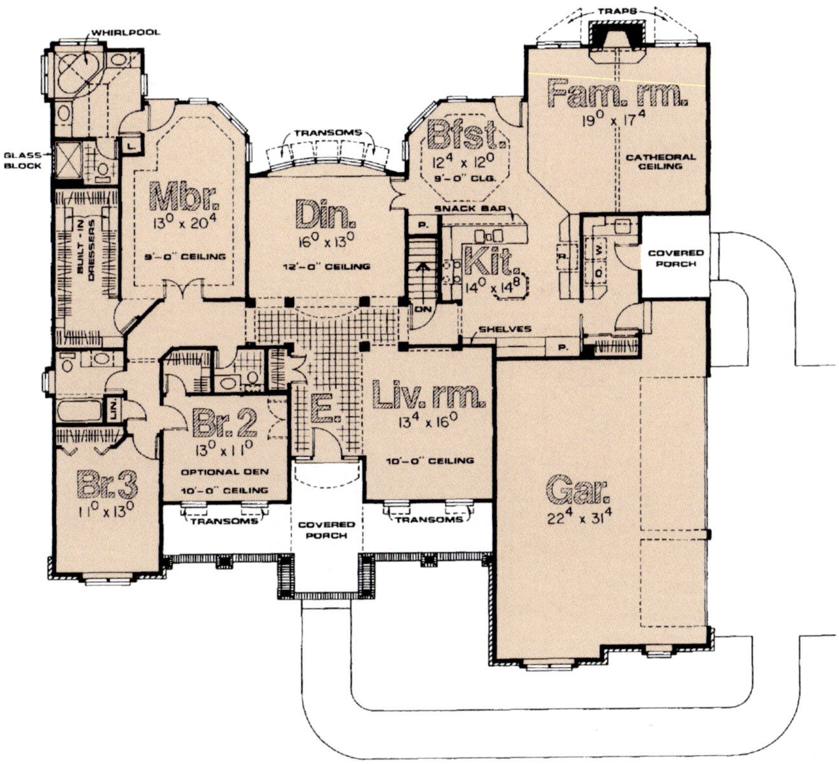

THE GRAND FRONT PORCH

gives this home unique style and majestic curb appeal. Inside, the entry centers on the stately dining room with its bowed window. Both the living room and the second bedroom—which can be converted into a den—have 10-foot ceilings. The island kitchen features abundant storage space, a lazy Susan, and a snack bar. A sun-filled breakfast area opens to the large family room with its cathedral ceiling and central fireplace. The private bedroom wing offers two secondary bedrooms and a luxurious master suite featuring a spacious walk-in closet with built-in dressers, and private access to the backyard. The master bath includes a vaulted ceiling, a corner whirlpool, and His and Hers vanities.

MASTER SUITES

plan # HPK030001

STYLE: EUROPEAN COTTAGE
FIRST FLOOR: 2,144 SQ. FT.
SECOND FLOOR: 920 SQ. FT.
TOTAL: 3,064 SQ. FT.
BONUS SPACE: 212 SQ. FT.
BEDROOMS: 4
BATHROOMS: 3½
WIDTH: 59' - 0"
DEPTH: 79' - 3"
FOUNDATION: CRAWLSPACE, SLAB

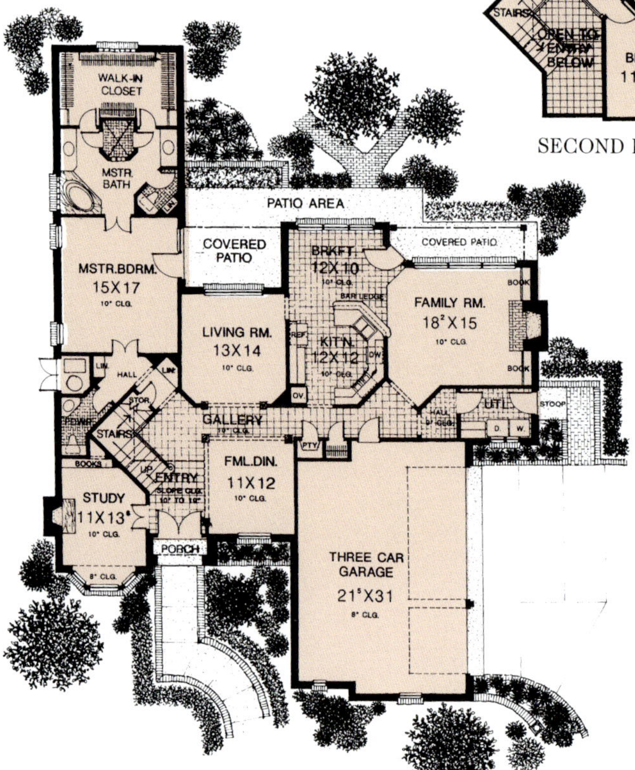

SEARCH ONLINE @ EPLANS.COM

FIELDSTONE, STUCCO, AND brick give this cottage harmony in variety. The foyer opens to a private study with bay windows and fireplace. The formal dining room is just down the hall and opens through column accents to the living room. The kitchen serves both the formal and casual spaces. The family room is as cozy with a fireplace and rear-window display. The master suite is really a work of luxury and features His and Hers walk-in closet entrances, vanities, and compartmented toilet. The second level houses three additional bedrooms, two full baths, and bonus space.

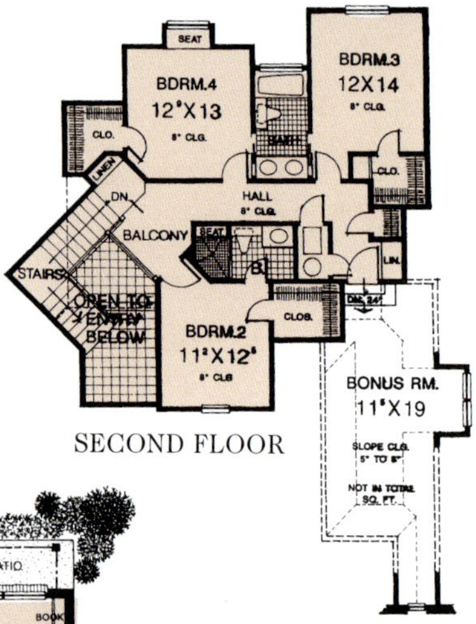

MASTER SUITES

THIS ENCHANTED CHATEAU SINGS OF REFINED

European luxury. A formal dining room and study flank the entry. The master bedroom is a sumptuous retreat with a bayed sitting area, pampering bath, and two walk-in closets. A massive stone fireplace warms the great room. Casual areas include the kitchen, breakfast, and recreation rooms. Three additional bedrooms are located upstairs.

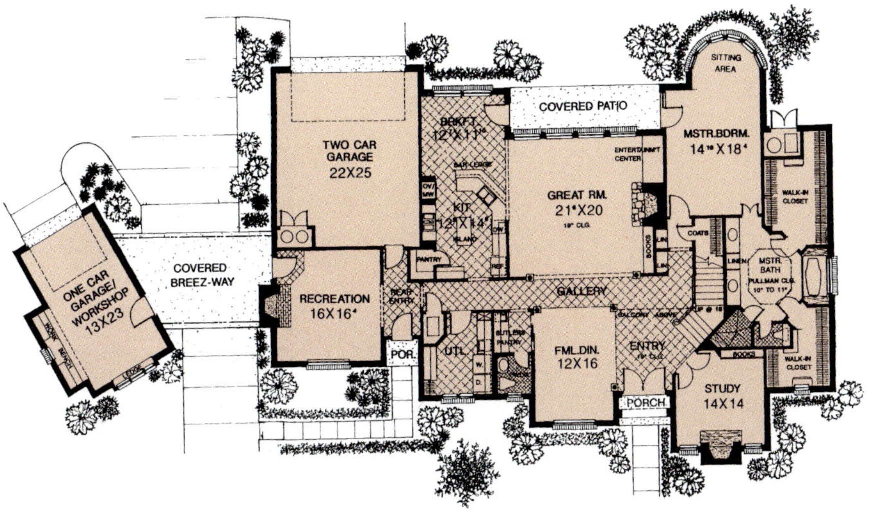

plan# HPK0300117

STYLE: EUROPEAN COTTAGE
FIRST FLOOR: 2,995 SQ. FT.
SECOND FLOOR: 1,102 SQ. FT.
TOTAL: 4,097 SQ. FT.
BEDROOMS: 4
BATHROOMS: 3½
WIDTH: 120' - 6"
DEPTH: 58' - 8"
FOUNDATION: SLAB

SEARCH ONLINE @ EPLANS.COM

FIRST FLOOR

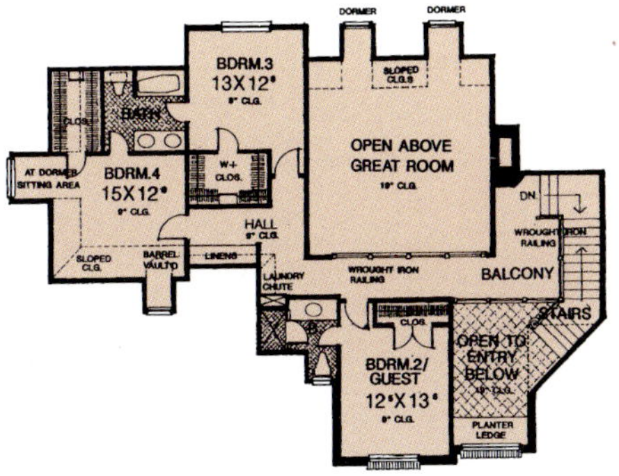

SECOND FLOOR

MASTER SUITES

plan # HPK0300118

STYLE: EUROPEAN COTTAGE
FIRST FLOOR: 4,958 SQ. FT.
SECOND FLOOR: 1,727 SQ. FT.
TOTAL: 6,685 SQ. FT.
BEDROOMS: 5
BATHROOMS: 5½
WIDTH: 120' - 9"
DEPTH: 114' - 7"
FOUNDATION: SLAB

SEARCH ONLINE @ EPLANS.COM

HIPPED ROOFLINES, STEEP GABLES, ARCH-TOPPED windows, and graceful balconies are just some of the evident charms of this wonderful mansion. Inside, the foyer is flanked by a formal dining room and a study/library. Directly ahead is the elegant curved staircase, beyond which awaits the formal living room with a fireplace and a wall of windows. The amazing kitchen easily accesses the sunny breakfast room and the formal dining room, as well as the nearby family room. A guest suite offers seclusion and features a bayed sitting area and a fireplace. The first-floor master suite is lavish with its amenities, which include an exercise room, a bayed sitting area, a fireplace, a huge walk-in closet, and a sumptuous bath. Upstairs, three bedrooms—each with a private bath and walk-in closet—share access to a recreation room with a deck.

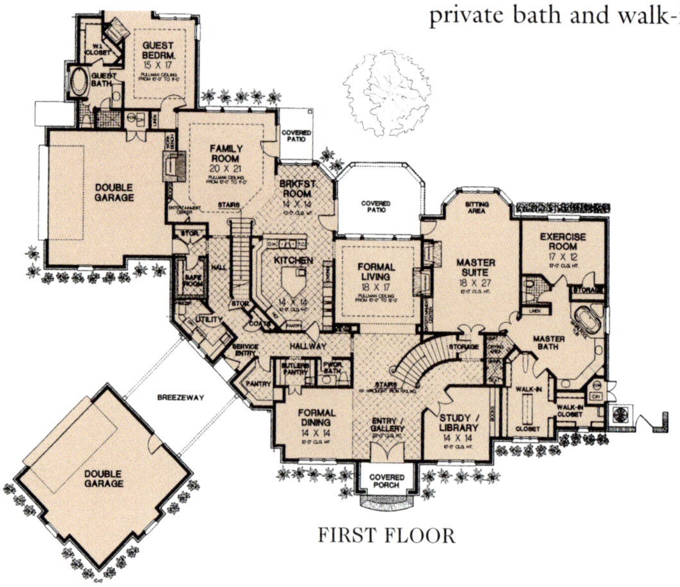

FIRST FLOOR

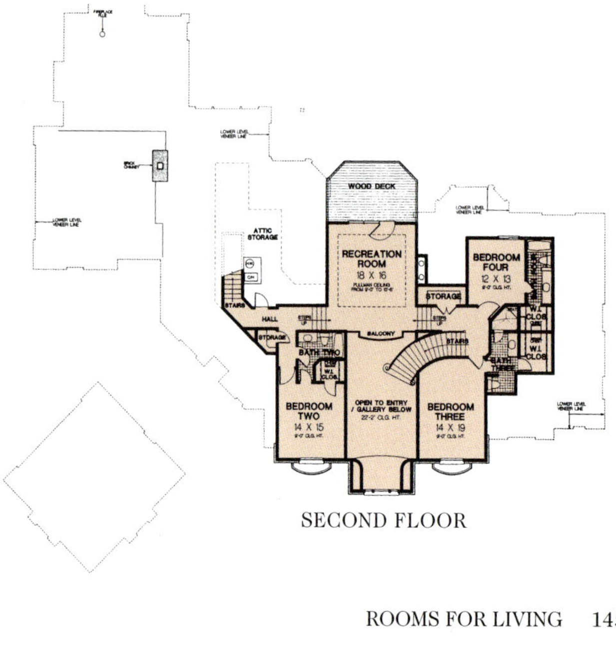

SECOND FLOOR

MASTER SUITES

STUCCO CORNER QUOINS, MULTIPLE GABLES, AND

graceful columns all combine to give this European manor plenty of appeal. Inside, a gallery entry presents a formal dining room on the right, defined by elegant columns, while the formal living room awaits just ahead. The highly efficient kitchen features a worktop island, pantry, and a serving bar to the nearby octagonal breakfast area. The family room offers a built-in entertainment center, a fireplace, and its own covered patio. The left side of the first floor is dedicated to the master suite. Here, the homeowner is pampered with an octagonal study, huge walk-in closet, lavish bath, and a very convenient nursery. The second floor contains two family bedrooms, each with a walk-in closet, and a media area with built-in bookshelves.

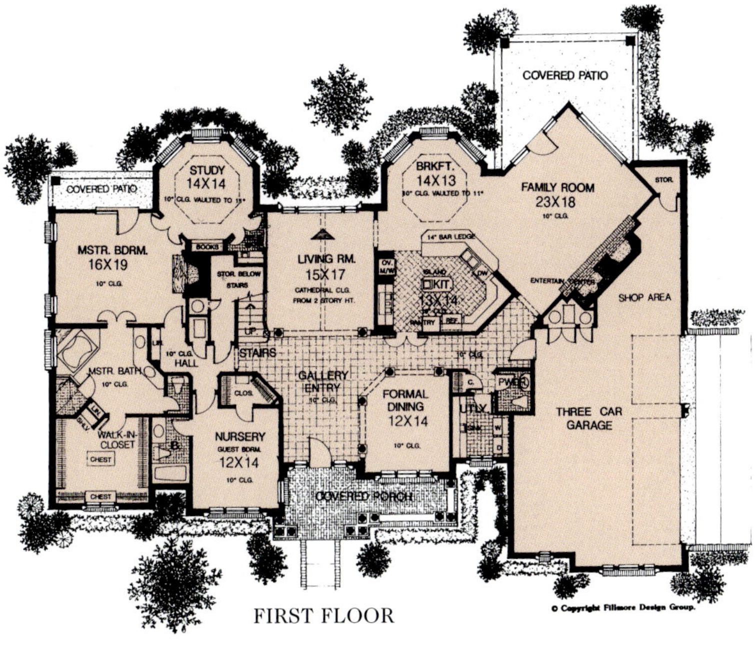

plan # HPK0300119

STYLE: FRENCH
FIRST FLOOR: 3,168 SQ. FT.
SECOND FLOOR: 998 SQ. FT.
TOTAL: 4,166 SQ. FT.
BONUS SPACE: 210 SQ. FT.
BEDROOMS: 4
BATHROOMS: 3½
WIDTH: 90' - 0"
DEPTH: 63' - 5"
FOUNDATION: SLAB, BASEMENT, CRAWLSPACE

SEARCH ONLINE @ EPLANS.COM

FIRST FLOOR

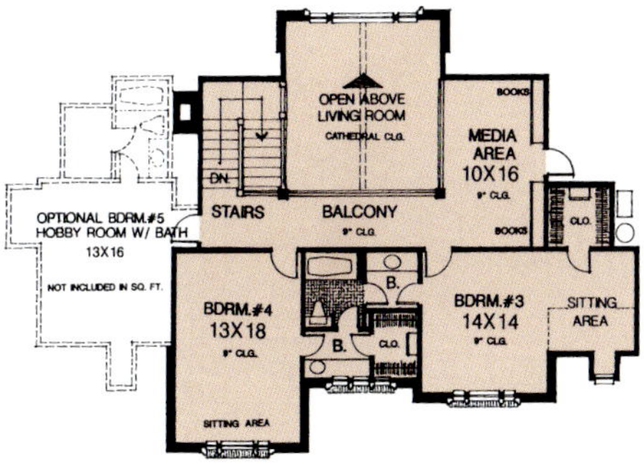

SECOND FLOOR

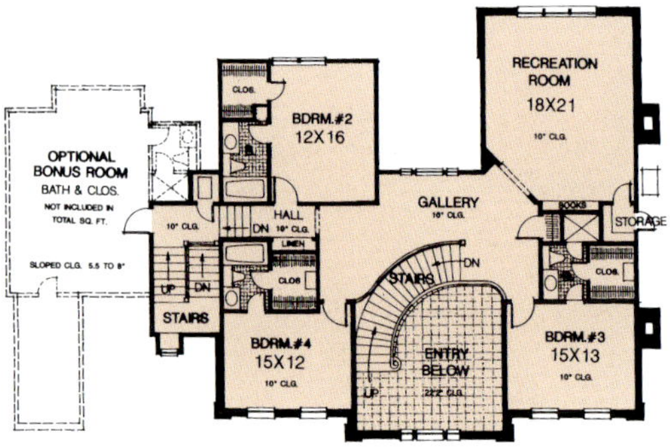

MASTER SUITES

plan # HPK0300120

STYLE: GEORGIAN
FIRST FLOOR: 3,599 SQ. FT.
SECOND FLOOR: 1,621 SQ. FT.
TOTAL: 5,220 SQ. FT.
BONUS SPACE: 537 SQ. FT.
BEDROOMS: 4
BATHROOMS: 5½
WIDTH: 108' – 10"
DEPTH: 53' – 10"
FOUNDATION: SLAB, BASEMENT

SEARCH ONLINE @ EPLANS.COM

A GRAND FAÇADE DETAILED WITH BRICK CORNER quoins, stucco flourishes, arched windows, and an elegant entrance presents this home. A spacious foyer is accented by curving stairs and flanked by a formal living room and a formal dining room. For cozy times, a through-fireplace is located between a large family room and a quiet study. The master bedroom is designed to pamper, with two walk-in closets, a two-sided fireplace, a bayed sitting area, and a lavish private bath. Upstairs, three secondary bedrooms each have private baths and walk-in closets. Also on this level is a spacious recreation room, perfect for a game room or children's playroom.

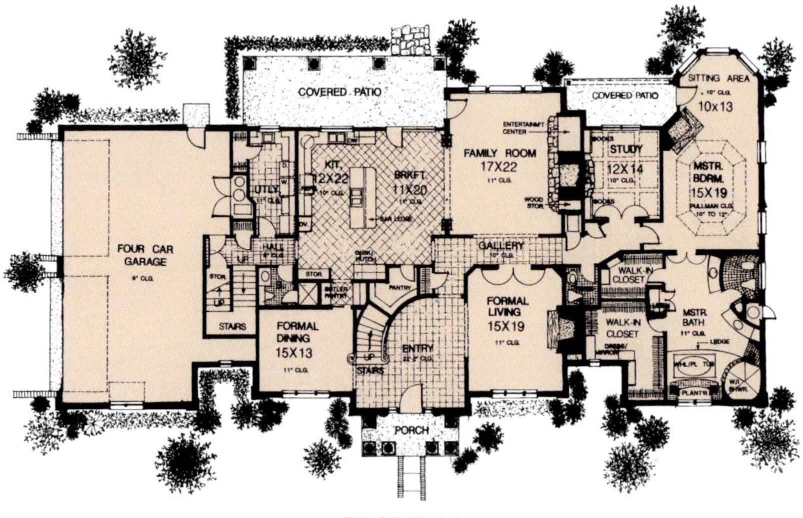

148 ROOMS FOR LIVING   ORDER BLUEPRINTS 24 HOURS, 7 DAYS A WEEK, AT 1-800-521-6797

MASTER SUITES

THIS STUNNING CONTEMPORARY COTTAGE HAS A heart of gold, with plenty of windows to bring in a wealth of natural light. Open planning allows the first-floor living and dining room to share the wide views of the outdoors. Glass doors frame the fireplace and open to the deck. A second-floor mezzanine enjoys an overlook to the living area and leads to a generous master suite with a walk-in closet, private bath, and a sitting area.

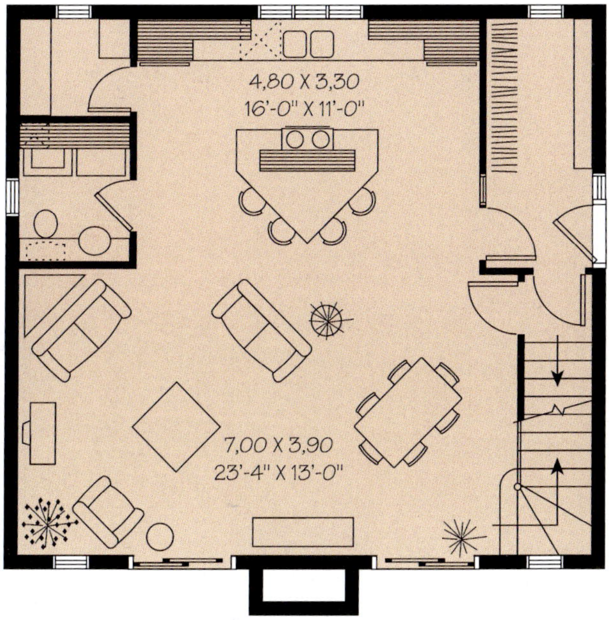

plan # HPK0300121

STYLE: COUNTRY COTTAGE
FIRST FLOOR: 728 SQ. FT.
SECOND FLOOR: 420 SQ. FT.
TOTAL: 1,148 SQ. FT.
BEDROOMS: 1
BATHROOMS: 1½
WIDTH: 28' - 0"
DEPTH: 26' - 0"
FOUNDATION: BASEMENT

SEARCH ONLINE @ EPLANS.COM

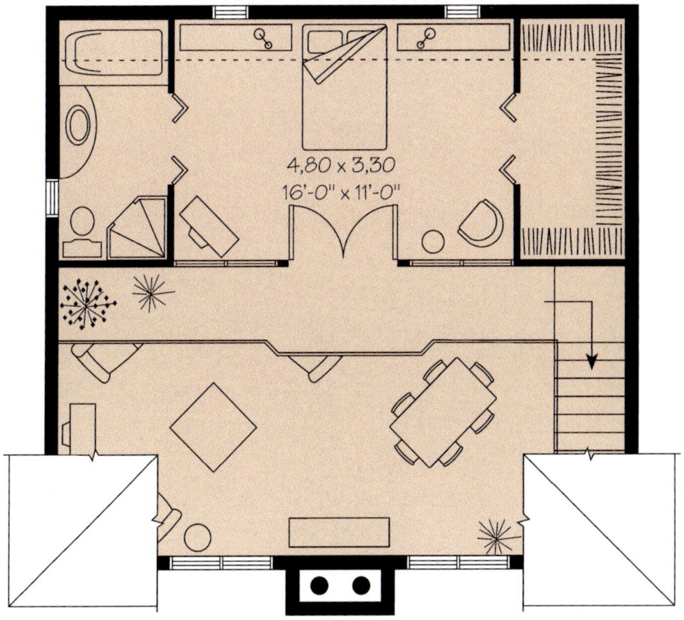

FIRST FLOOR
7.00 × 3.90
23'-4" × 13'-0"
4.80 × 3.30
16'-0" × 11'-0"

SECOND FLOOR
4.80 × 3.30
16'-0" × 11'-0"

THE GATEWAY TO YOUR NEW HOME

Looking for more plans? Got questions?
Try our one-stop home plans resource—eplans.com.

We'll help you streamline the plan selection process, so your dreams can become reality faster than you ever imagined. From choosing your home plan and ideal location to finding an experienced contractor, eplans.com will guide you every step of the way.

Mix and match! Explore! At eplans.com you can combine all your top criteria to find your perfect match. Search for your ideal home plan by any or all of the following:

> Number of bedrooms or baths,
> Total square feet,
> House style, and
> Cost.

With over 10,000 plans, the options are endless. Colonial, ranch, country, and Victorian are just a few of the house styles offered. Keep in mind your essential lifestyle features—whether to include a porch, fireplace, bonus room or main floor laundry room. And the garage—how many cars must it accommodate, if any? By filling out the preference page on eplans.com, we'll help you narrow your search.

At eplans.com we'll make the building process a snap to understand. At the click of a button you'll find a complete building guide. And our eplan task planner will create a construction calendar just for you. Here you'll find links to tips and other valuable information to help you every step of the way—from choosing a site to moving day.

For your added convenience, our home plans experts are available for live, one-on-one chats at eplans.com. Building a home may seem like a complicated project, but it doesn't have to be—particularly if you'll let us help you from start to finish.

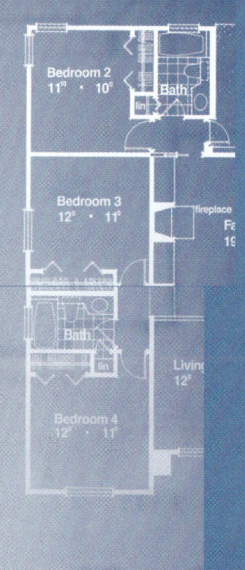

eplans.com

hanley▲wood HomePlanners

On sale now at your local bookseller! eplans.com

500 House Plans
From 1,000 to 6,300 square feet

Encyclopedia of Home Designs Third Edition
500 House Plans From 1,000 to 6,300 Square Feet

An excellent resource for every homebuyer, this completely revised showcase features over 500 best-selling designs in an easy-to-use format. These ready-to-build designs are packed with amenities giving you more value for your building dollar. Complete construction blueprints are available for every home.
$9.95

Encyclopedia of Home Designs
HOME PLANNERS

650 Home Plans
From Cottages to Mansions

The perfect home starts with the perfect plan. *650 Home Plans* offers a wide range of sizes and styles to fit any budget and lifestyle, from the most respected names in architectural and residential design the nation has to offer.
$8.95

1001 All-Time Best-Selling Home Plans
HomePlanners Biggest and Best Collection Ever

Over 1,000 hot home designs in our best collection ever. Detailed descriptions and easy-to-read floorplans give you a clear concept of the strengths and design features of each home. Styles range from bungalows to luxurious estates.
$12.95

1001 ALL TIME BEST SELLING HOME PLANS
HOME PLANNERS BIGGEST & BEST COLLECTION EVER

650 HOME PLANS
From Cottages To Mansions
HOME PLANNERS

Look for These Other Exciting House Plans Books from HomePlanners!

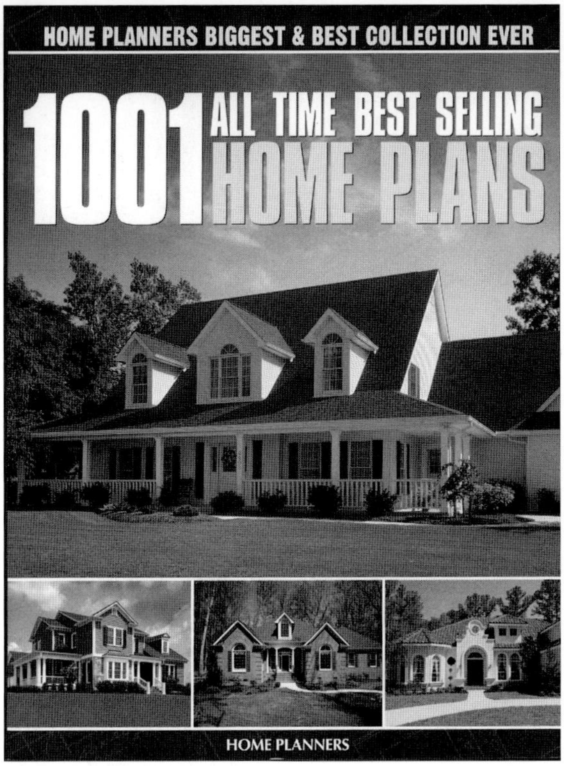

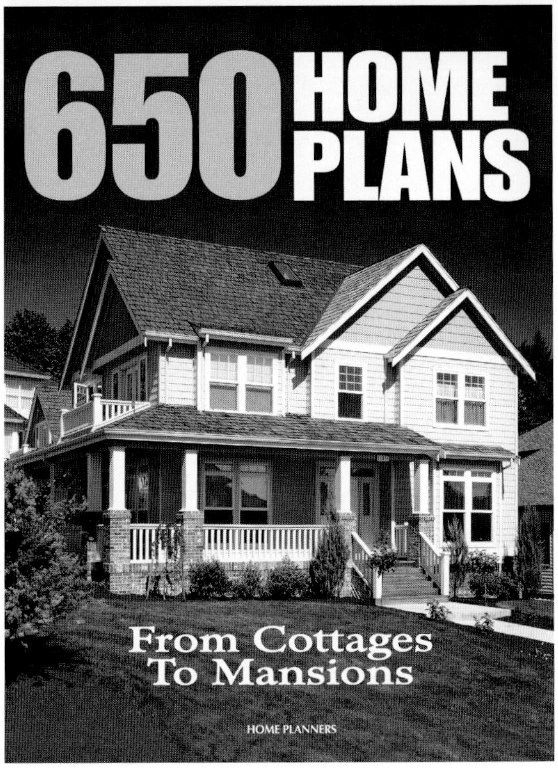

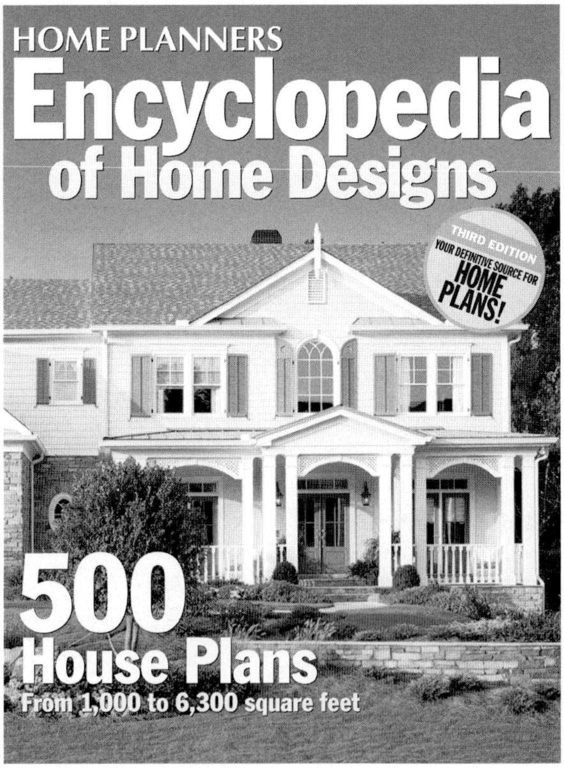

Build Or Remodel Your Dream Home

With HomePlanners Books & Blueprints

Choose Any of These Books— 10% Off the Regular Price

Hanley Wood brings you more choices from leading home plan designers than any other source. Our relationships with leading architects and designers give you access to the best home plans and a more comprehensive selection of home styles.

BOOK SALE!
ALL BOOKS 10% OFF REGULAR PRICE

FINE LIVING
Home Designs with Luxury Amenities
$17.95 NOW ONLY $16.15
ITEM: FL

CONTEMPORARY HOME PLANS
Sleek designs for modern lifestyles
$10.95 NOW ONLY $9.85
ITEM: CM2

AMERICAN DREAM HOMES
A collection of luxury designs
$19.95 NOW ONLY $17.95
ITEM: SOD2

ESTATE DREAM HOMES
Designs of unsurpassed grandeur
$16.95 NOW ONLY $15.25
ITEM: EDH3

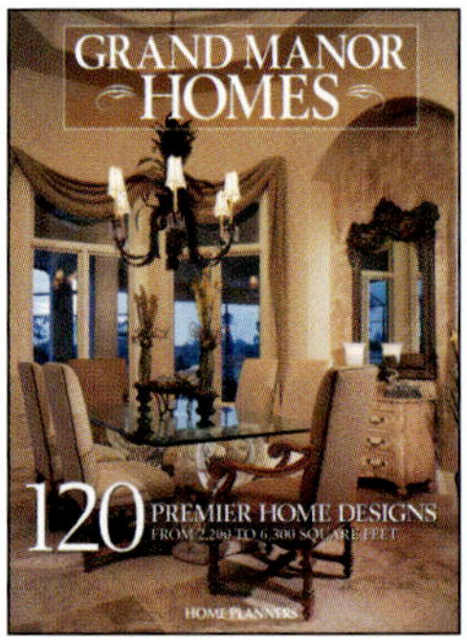

GRAND MANOR HOMES
Premier designs from Country to European
$17.95 NOW ONLY $16.15
ITEM: GMH

LUXURY DREAM HOMES
170 lavish designs
$12.95 NOW ONLY $11.65
ITEM: LD3

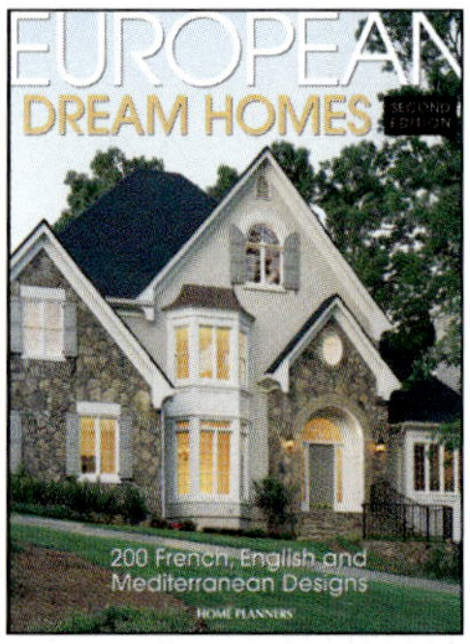

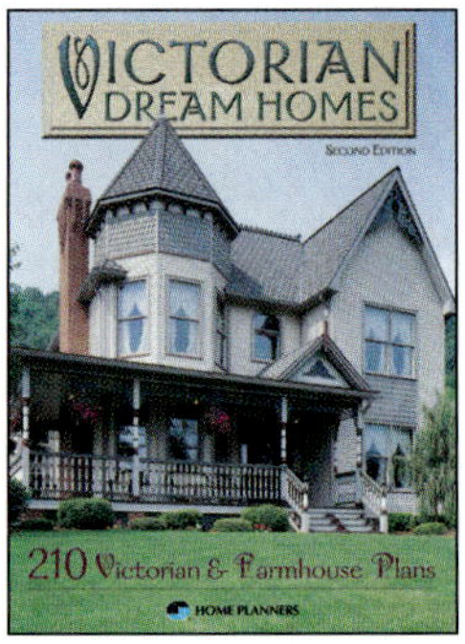

VICTORIAN DREAM HOMES
Victorian and Farmhouse plans
$15.95 NOW ONLY $14.35
ITEM: VDH2

EUROPEAN DREAM HOMES
French, English and Mediterranean designs
$15.95 NOW ONLY $14.35
ITEM: EUR2

OUR BEST PRICES EVER!

RFL04   **To Order Call 800.322.6797 or visit www.eplans.com**

hanley wood
HomePlanners

COPYRIGHT DOS & DON'TS

Blueprints for residential construction (or working drawings, as they are often called in the industry) are copyrighted intellectual property, protected under the terms of United States Copyright Law and, therefore, cannot be copied legally for use in building. However, we've made it easy for you to get what you need to build your home, without violating copyright law. Following are some guidelines to help you obtain the right number of copies for your chosen blueprint design.

COPYRIGHT DO

■ Do purchase enough copies of the blueprints to satisfy building requirements. As a rule for a home or project plan, you will need a set for yourself, two or three for your builder and subcontractors, two for the local building department, and one to three for your mortgage lender. You may want to check with your local building department or your builder to see how many they need before you purchase. You may need to buy eight to 10 sets; note that some areas of the country require purchase of vellums (also called reproducibles) instead of blueprints. Vellums can be written on and changed more easily than blueprints. Also, remember, plans are only good for one-time construction.

■ Do consider reverse blueprints if you want to flop the plan. Lettering and numbering will appear backward, but the reversed sets will help you and your builder better visualize the design.

■ Do take advantage of multiple-set discounts at the time you place your order. Usually, purchasing additional sets after you receive your initial order is not as cost-effective.

■ Do take advantage of vellums. Though they are a little more expensive, they can be changed, copied, and used for one-time construction of a home. You will receive a copyright release letter with your vellums that will allow you to have them copied.

■ Do talk with one of our professional service representatives before placing your order. They can give you great advice about what packages are available for your chosen design and what will work best for your particular situation.

COPYRIGHT DON'T

■ Don't think you should purchase only one set of blueprints for a building project. One is fine if you want to study the plan closely, but will not be enough for actual building.

■ Don't expect your builder or a copy center to make copies of standard blueprints. They cannot legally—most copy centers are aware of this.

■ Don't purchase standard blueprints if you know you'll want to make changes to the plans; vellums are a better value.

■ Don't use blueprints or vellums more than one time. Additional fees apply if you want to build more than one time from a set of drawings. ■

HANLEY WOOD HOMEPLANNERS ADVANTAGE
SELECTION! CONVENIENCE! SERVICE!

hanley ▲ wood
HomePlanners

ORDERING IS EASY

HANLEY WOOD HOMEPLANNERS HAS EVERYTHING YOU NEED to build the home of your dreams, and with more than 50 years of experience in the industry, we make it as easy as possible for you to reach those goals. Just follow the steps on these pages and you'll receive a high-quality, ready-to-build set of home blueprints, plus everything else you need to make your home-building effort a success.

WHERE TO BEGIN?
1. CHOOSE YOUR PLAN

■ Browsing magazines, books, and eplans.com can be an exciting and rewarding part of the home-building process. As you search, make a list of the things you want in your dream home—everything from number of bedrooms and baths to details like fireplaces or a home office.

■ Take the time to consider your lot and your neighborhood, and how the home you choose will fit with both. And think about the future—how might your needs change if you plan to live in this house for five, 10, or 20 years?

■ With thousands of plans available, chances are that you'll have no trouble discovering your dream home. If you find something that's almost perfect, our Customization Program can help make it exactly what you want.

■ Most important, be sure to enjoy the process of picking out your new home!

WHAT YOU'LL GET WITH YOUR ORDER

Each designer's blueprint set is unique, but they all provide everything you'll need to build your home. Here are some standard elements you can expect to find in your plans:

I. FRONT PERSPECTIVE
This artist's sketch of the exterior of the house gives you an idea of how the house will look when built and landscaped.

2. FOUNDATION PLANS
This sheet shows the foundation layout including support walls, excavated and unexcavated areas, if any, and foundation notes. If your plan features slab construction rather than a basement, the plan shows footings and details for a monolithic slab. This page, or another in the set, may include a sample plot plan for locating your house on a building site.

3. DETAILED FLOOR PLANS
These plans show the layout of each floor of the house. Rooms and interior spaces are carefully dimensioned and keys are given for cross-section details provided later in the plans. The positions of electrical outlets and switches are shown.

4. HOUSE CROSS-SECTIONS
Large-scale views show sections or cutaways of the foundation, interior walls, exterior walls, floors, stairways, and roof details. Additional cross-sections may show important changes in floor, ceiling, or roof heights, or the relationship of one level to another. Extremely valuable during construction, these sections show exactly how the various parts of the house fit together.

5. INTERIOR ELEVATIONS
These elevations, or drawings, show the design and placement of kitchen and bathroom cabinets, laundry areas, fireplaces, bookcases, and other built-ins. Little extras, such as mantelpiece and wainscoting drawings, plus molding sections, provide details that give your home that custom touch.

6. EXTERIOR ELEVATIONS
Every blueprint set comes with drawings of the front exterior, and may include the rear and sides of your house as well. These drawings give necessary notes on exterior materials and finishes. Particular attention is given to cornice detail, brick, and stone accents or other finish items that make your home unique.

ROOMS FOR LIVING   153

hanley▲wood
HomePlanners

ORDERING IS EASY

HANLEY WOOD HOMEPLANNERS ADVANTAGE
ORDER 24 HOURS!
1-800-521-6797

GETTING DOWN TO BUSINESS
2. PRICE YOUR PLAN

BLUEPRINT PRICE SCHEDULE

PRICE TIERS	1-SET STUDY PACKAGE	4-SET BUILDING PACKAGE	8-SET BUILDING PACKAGE	1-SET REPRODUCIBLE*
P1	$20	$50	$90	$140
P2	$40	$70	$110	$160
P3	$70	$100	$140	$190
P4	$100	$130	$170	$220
P5	$140	$170	$210	$270
P6	$180	$210	$250	$310
A1	$440	$490	$540	$660
A2	$480	$530	$580	$720
A3	$530	$590	$650	$800
A4	$575	$645	$705	$870
C1	$625	$695	$755	$935
C2	$670	$740	$800	$1000
C3	$715	$790	$855	$1075
C4	$765	$840	$905	$1150
L1	$870	$965	$1050	$1300
L2	$945	$1040	$1125	$1420
L3	$1050	$1150	$1240	$1575
L4	$1155	$1260	$1355	$1735
SQ1				.35/SQ. FT.

PRICES SUBJECT TO CHANGE

* REQUIRES A FAX NUMBER

plan ⊕
READY TO ORDER

Once you've found your plan, get your plan number and turn to the following pages to find its price tier. Use the corresponding code and the Blueprint Price Schedule above to determine your price for a variety of blueprint packages.

Keep in mind that you'll need multiple sets to fulfill building requirements, and only reproducible sets may be altered or duplicated.

To the right you'll find prices for additional and reverse blueprint sets. Also note in the following pages whether your home has a corresponding Deck or Landscape Plan, and whether you can order our Quote One® cost-to-build information or a Materials List for your plan.

IT'S EASY TO ORDER
JUST VISIT
EPLANS.COM OR CALL
TOLL-FREE
1-800-521-6797

PRICE SCHEDULE FOR ADDITIONAL OPTIONS

OPTIONS FOR PLANS IN TIERS P1-P6	COSTS
ADDITIONAL IDENTICAL BLUEPRINTS FOR "P1-P6" PLANS	$10 PER SET
REVERSE BLUEPRINTS (MIRROR IMAGE) FOR "P1-P6" PLANS	$10 FEE PER ORDER
1 SET OF DECK CONSTRUCTION DETAILS	$14.95 EACH
DECK CONSTRUCTION PACKAGE (INCLUDES 1 SET OF "P1-P6" PLANS, PLUS 1 SET STANDARD DECK CONSTRUCTION DETAILS)	ADD $10 TO BUILDING PACKAGE PRICE

OPTIONS FOR PLANS IN TIERS A1-SQ1	COSTS
ADDITIONAL IDENTICAL BLUEPRINTS IN SAME ORDER FOR "A1-L4" PLANS	$50 PER SET
REVERSE BLUEPRINTS (MIRROR IMAGE) WITH 4- OR 8-SET ORDER FOR "A1-L4" PLANS	$50 FEE PER ORDER
SPECIFICATION OUTLINES	$10 EACH
MATERIALS LISTS FOR "A1-C3" PLANS	$70 EACH
MATERIALS LISTS FOR "C4-SQ1" PLANS	$70 EACH

IMPORTANT EXTRAS	COSTS
ELECTRICAL, PLUMBING, CONSTRUCTION, AND MECHANICAL DETAIL SETS	$14.95 EACH; ANY TWO $22.95; ANY THREE $29.95; ALL FOUR $39.95
HOME FURNITURE PLANNER	$15.95 EACH
REAR ELEVATION	$10 EACH
QUOTE ONE® SUMMARY COST REPORT	$29.95
QUOTE ONE® DETAILED COST ESTIMATE (FOR MORE DETAILS ABOUT QUOTE ONE®, SEE STEP 3.)	$60

IMPORTANT NOTE

■ THE 1-SET STUDY PACKAGE IS MARKED "NOT FOR CONSTRUCTION."

Source Key
HPK03

154   ROOMS FOR LIVING

hanley▲wood HomePlanners
ORDERING IS EASY

PLAN #	PRICE TIER	PAGE	MATERIALS LIST	QUOTE ONE®	DECK	DECK PRICE	LANDSCAPE	LANDSCAPE PRICE	REGIONS
HPK0300001	SQ1	17							
HPK0300002	SQ1	44							
HPK0300003	L1	37							
HPK0300004	L1	79							
HPK0300005	SQ1	119							
HPK0300006	SQ1	14							
HPK0300007	C3	10	Y						
HPK0300008	C3	12	Y						
HPK0300009	SQ1	15							
HPK0300010	SQ1	16	Y	Y					
HPK0300011	SQ1	18	Y	Y			OLA001	P3	123568
HPK0300012	SQ1	19					OLA014	P4	12345678
HPK0300013	SQ1	20	Y						
HPK0300014	SQ1	21							
HPK0300015	C1	22	Y						
HPK0300016	C4	23					OLA004	P3	123568
HPK0300017	L3	24							
HPK0300018	C4	25							
HPK0300019	SQ1	26	Y	Y			OLA008	P4	1234568
HPK0300020	SQ1	27							
HPK0300021	SQ1	28	Y						
HPK0300022	A4	29							
HPK0300023	SQ1	30	Y						
HPK0300024	L2	31	Y						
HPK0300025	C1	32	Y	Y					
HPK0300026	C3	33							
HPK0300027	C4	34							
HPK0300028	C4	35							
HPK0300029	C1	36	Y						
HPK0300030	L2	38							
HPK0300031	L1	39							
HPK0300032	C3	40							
HPK0300033	C4	41							
HPK0300034	L2	42							
HPK0300035	C4	43							
HPK0300036	C3	45							
HPK0300037	C4	46							
HPK0300038	L2	47							
HPK0300039	C1	48	Y						
HPK0300040	A4	49							
HPK0300041	C1	50							
HPK0300042	A4	51	Y						
HPK0300043	C1	52							
HPK0300044	C3	53							
HPK0300045	SQ1	60	Y						
HPK0300046	SQ1	62							
HPK0300047	L1	64	Y	Y					
HPK0300048	C2	65	Y						
HPK0300049	SQ1	66	Y						
HPK0300050	SQ1	67	Y						
HPK0300051	C1	68	Y						
HPK0300052	C3	69							
HPK0300053	SQ1	70							
HPK0300054	C2	71	Y						
HPK0300055	SQ1	72							
HPK0300056	C3	73	Y	Y					
HPK0300057	SQ1	74							
HPK0300058	SQ1	75							
HPK0300059	C2	76							
HPK0300060	L1	77							
HPK0300061	L2	78							
HPK0300062	L1	80							
HPK0300063	C4	81							
HPK0300064	C2	82							
HPK0300065	C2	83	Y						
HPK0300066	C4	84							
HPK0300067	SQ1	85	Y						
HPK0300068	C2	86	Y						
HPK0300069	C2	87	Y	Y					
HPK0300070	SQ1	88	Y						
HPK0300071	C2	89	Y	Y					
HPK0300072	C1	90							
HPK0300073	C4	91							
HPK0300074	SQ1	92	Y	Y					
HPK0300075	L1	93	Y						
HPK0300076	C3	94							
HPK0300077	SQ1	95							
HPK0300078	C3	96							

ROOMS FOR LIVING 155

hanley▲wood HomePlanners
ORDERING IS EASY

PLAN #	PRICE TIER	PAGE	MATERIALS LIST	QUOTE ONE®	DECK	DECK PRICE	LANDSCAPE	LANDSCAPE PRICE	REGIONS
HPK0300079	C1	97							
HPK0300080	A4	98	Y		ODA013	P2	OLA001	P3	123568
HPK0300081	C2	99	Y	Y					
HPK0300082	C3	100							
HPK0300083	C2	101							
HPK0300084	SQ1	108	Y						
HPK0300085	SQ1	110							
HPK0300086	SQ1	112	Y				OLA008	P4	1234568
HPK0300087	C2	113					OLA004	P3	123568
HPK0300088	L1	114							
HPK0300089	C3	115							
HPK0300090	C1	116	Y						
HPK0300091	L2	117							
HPK0300092	A4	118	Y						
HPK0300093	C4	120							
HPK0300094	C4	121							
HPK0300095	C2	122	Y						
HPK0300096	C1	123	Y						
HPK0300097	A3	124	Y						
HPK0300098	C3	125	Y						
HPK0300099	C1	126	Y						
HPK0300100	L2	127							
HPK0300101	SQ1	128	Y						
HPK0300102	A4	129	Y						
HPK0300103	C1	130	Y						
HPK0300104	C3	131							
HPK0300105	A4	132	Y						
HPK0300106	A3	133	Y						
HPK0300107	C1	134	Y						
HPK0300108	C4	135	Y						
HPK0300109	SQ1	136							
HPK0300110	SQ1	137	Y						
HPK0300111	C1	138	Y						
HPK0300112	C1	139	Y						
HPK0300113	C1	140	Y						
HPK0300114	SQ1	141							
HPK0300115	C1	142	Y						
HPK0300116	C2	143							
HPK0300117	SQ1	144							
HPK0300118	SQ1	145							
HPK0300119	C4	146							
HPK0300120	SQ1	147							
HPK0300121	A3	148	Y						

PHOTO CREDITS

Page 4: Mark Samu
Page 6: Mark Samu
Page 7: Tony Giammarino
Page 8: Photo Courtesy of: William E. Poole Designs, Inc. - Islands of Beaufort, SC
Page 9: Peter Loppacher
Page 54: Mark Samu
Page 56: Sam Gray
Page 57: Mark Samu (top); Ivy D. Moriber (bottom)
Page 58: Mark Samu
Page 59: Courtesy of Living Concepts (top); Mark Samu (bottom)
Page 102: Sam Gray
Page 104: Mark Samu
Page 105: Sam Gray
Page 106: ©Laurence Taylor Photography
Page 107: Sam Gray

hanley▲wood
HomePlanners

ORDERING IS EASY

ORDER ONLINE AT EPLANS.COM

MORE TOOLS FOR SUCCESS
3. GET GREAT EXTRAS

WE OFFER A VARIETY OF USEFUL TOOLS THAT CAN HELP YOU THROUGH EVERY STEP OF THE home-building process. From our Materials List to our Customization Program, these items let you put our experience to work for you to ensure that you get exactly what you want out of your dream house.

MATERIALS LIST

For many of the designs in our portfolio, we offer a customized list of materials that helps you plan and estimate the cost of your new home. The Materials List outlines the quantity, type, and size of materials needed to build your house (with the exception of mechanical system items). Included are framing lumber, windows and doors, kitchen and bath cabinetry, rough and finished hardware, and much more. This handy list helps you or your builder cost out materials and serves as a reference sheet when you're compiling bids.

SPECIFICATION OUTLINE

This valuable 16-page document can play an important role in the construction of your house. Fill it in with your builder, and you'll have a step-by-step chronicle of 166 stages or items crucial to the building process. It provides a comprehensive review of the construction process and helps you choose materials.

QUOTE ONE®

The Quote One® system, which helps estimate the cost of building select designs in your zip code, is available in two parts: the Summary Cost Report and the Material Cost Report.

The Summary Cost Report, the first element in the package, breaks down the cost of your home into various categories based on building materials, labor, and installation, and includes three grades of construction: Budget, Standard, and Custom. Make even more informed decisions about your project with the second element of our package, the Material Cost Report. The material and installation cost is shown for each of more than 1,000 line items provided in the standard-grade Materials List, which is included with this tool. Additional space is included for estimates from contractors and subcontractors, such as for mechanical materials, which are not included in our packages.

If you are interested in a plan that does not indicate the availability of Quote One®, please call and ask our sales representatives, who can verify the status for you.

CUSTOMIZATION PROGRAM

If the plan you love needs something changed to make it perfect, our customization experts will ensure that you get nothing less than your dream home. Purchase a reproducible set of plans for the home you choose, and we'll send you our easy-to-use customization request form via e-mail or fax. For just $50, our customization experts will provide an estimate for your requested revisions, and once it's approved, that charge will be applied to your changes. You'll receive either five sets or a reproducible master of your modified design and any other options you select.

BUILDING BASICS

If you want to know more about building techniques—and deal more confidently with your subcontractors—we offer four useful detail sheets. These sheets provide non-plan-specific general information, but are excellent tools that will add to your understanding of Plumbing Details, Electrical Details, Construction Details, and Mechanical Details. These fact-filled sheets will help answer many of your building questions, and help you learn what questions to ask your builder and subcontractors.

ROOMS FOR LIVING 157

hanley▲wood
HomePlanners
ORDERING IS EASY

HANLEY WOOD HOMEPLANNERS ADVANTAGE
ORDER 24 HOURS!
1-800-521-6797

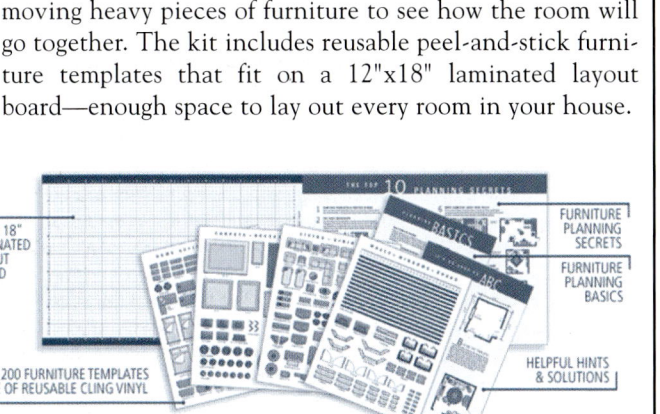

HANDS-ON HOME FURNITURE PLANNER

Effectively plan the space in your home using our Hands-On Home Furniture Planner. It's fun and easy—no more moving heavy pieces of furniture to see how the room will go together. The kit includes reusable peel-and-stick furniture templates that fit on a 12"x18" laminated layout board—enough space to lay out every room in your house.

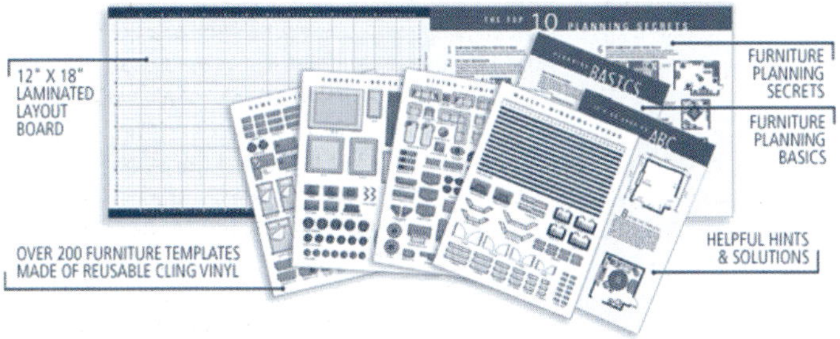

12" X 18" LAMINATED LAYOUT BOARD

THE TOP 10 PLANNING SECRETS

BASICS

ARC

FURNITURE PLANNING SECRETS

FURNITURE PLANNING BASICS

HELPFUL HINTS & SOLUTIONS

OVER 200 FURNITURE TEMPLATES MADE OF REUSABLE CLING VINYL

DECK BLUEPRINT PACKAGE

Many of the homes in this book can be enhanced with a professionally designed Home Planners Deck Plan. Those plans marked with a **D** have a corresponding deck plan, sold separately, which includes a Deck Plan Frontal Sheet, Deck Framing and Floor Plans, Deck Elevations, and a Deck Materials List. A Standard Deck Details Package, also available, provides all the how-to information necessary for building any deck. Get both the Deck Plan and the Standard Deck Details Package for one low price in our Complete Deck Building Package.

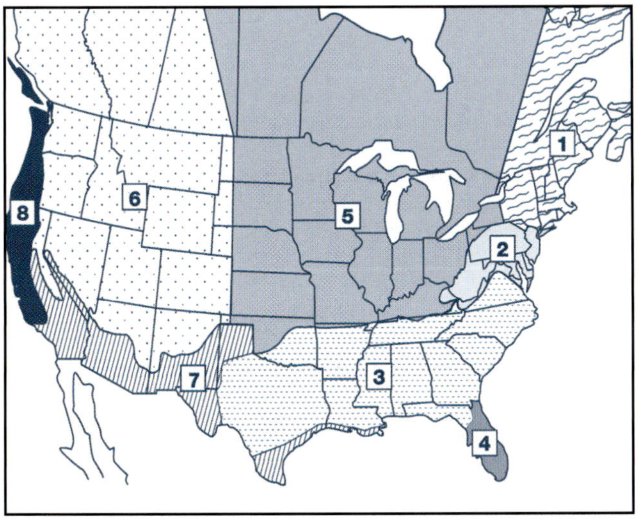

LANDSCAPE BLUEPRINT PACKAGE

Homes marked with an **L** in this book have a front-yard Landscape Plan that is complementary in design to the house plan. These comprehensive Landscape Blueprint Packages include a Frontal Sheet, Plan View, Regionalized Plant & Materials List, a sheet on Planting and Maintaining Your Landscape, Zone Maps, and a Plant Size and Description Guide. Each set of blueprints is a full 18" x 24" with clear, complete instructions in easy-to-read type.

Our Landscape Plans are available with a Plant & Materials List adapted by horticultural experts to eight regions of the country. Please specify from the following regions when ordering your plan:

Region 1: Northeast
Region 2: Mid-Atlantic
Region 3: Deep South
Region 4: Florida & Gulf Coast
Region 5: Midwest
Region 6: Rocky Mountains
Region 7: Southern California & Desert Southwest
Region 8: Northern California & Pacific Northwest

158   ROOMS FOR LIVING

hanley▲wood HomePlanners
ORDERING IS EASY

WHAT YOU NEED TO KNOW
4. BEFORE YOU ORDER

OUR EXCHANGE POLICY

With the exception of reproducible plan orders, we will exchange your entire first order for an equal or greater number of blueprints within our plan collection within **90 days** of the original order. The entire content of your original order must be returned before an exchange will be processed. Please call our customer service department at 1-888-690-1116 for your return authorization number and shipping instructions. If the returned blueprints look used, redlined, or copied, we will not honor your exchange. Fees for exchanging your blueprints are as follows: 20% of the amount of the original order, plus the difference in cost if exchanging for a design in a higher price bracket or less the difference in cost if exchanging for a design in a lower price bracket. (Reproducible blueprints are not exchangeable or refundable.) Please call for current postage and handling prices. Shipping and handling charges are not refundable.

ABOUT REPRODUCIBLES

Reproducibles (often called "vellums") are the most convenient way to order your blueprints. In any building process, you will need multiple copies of your blueprints for your builder, subcontractors, lenders, and the local building department. In addition, you may want or need to make changes to the original design. Such changes should be made only by a licensed architect or engineer. When you purchase reproducibles, you will receive a copyright release letter that allows you to have them altered and copied. You will want to purchase a reproducible plan if you plan to make any changes, whether by using our convenient Customization Program or going to a local architect.

ABOUT REVERSE BLUEPRINTS

Although lettering and dimensions will appear backward, reverses will be a useful aid if you decide to flop the plan. See Price Schedule and Plans Index for pricing.

ARCHITECTURAL AND ENGINEERING SEALS

Some cities and states now require that a licensed architect or engineer review and "seal" a blueprint, or officially approve it, prior to construction. Prior to application for a building permit or the start of actual construction, we strongly advise that you consult your local building official who can tell you if such a review is required.

ABOUT THE DESIGNS

The architects and designers whose work appears in this publication are among America's leading residential designers. Each plan was designed to meet the requirements of a nationally recognized model building code in effect at the time and place the plan was drawn. Because national building codes change from time to time, plans may not fully comply with any such code at the time they are sold to a customer. In addition, building officials may not accept these plans as final construction documents of record as the plans may need to be modified and additional drawings and details added to suit local conditions and requirements. Purchasers should consult a licensed architect or engineer, and their local building official, before starting any construction related to these plans.

LOCAL BUILDING CODES AND ZONING REQUIREMENTS

At the time of creation, these plans are drawn to specifications published by the Building Officials and Code Administrators (BOCA) International, Inc.; the Southern Building Code Congress International, (SBCCI) Inc.; the International Conference of Building Officials (ICBO); or the Council of American Building Officials (CABO). These plans are designed to meet or exceed national building standards. Because of the great differences in geography and climate throughout the United States and Canada, each state, county, and municipality has its own building codes, zone requirements, ordinances, and building regulations. Your plan may need to be modified to comply with local requirements. In addition, you may need to obtain permits or inspections from local governments before and in the course of construction. We authorize the use of the blueprints on the express condition that you consult a local licensed architect or engineer of your choice prior to beginning construction and strictly comply with all local building codes, zoning requirements, and other applicable laws, regulations, ordinances, and requirements. Notice: Plans for homes to be built in Nevada must be redrawn by a Nevada-registered professional. Consult your building official for more information on this subject.

TERMS AND CONDITIONS

These designs are protected under the terms of United States Copyright Law and may not be copied or reproduced in any way, by any means, unless you have purchased reproducibles which clearly indicate your right to copy or reproduce. We authorize the use of your chosen design as an aid in the construction of one single- or multi-family home only. You may not use this design to build a second or multiple dwellings without purchasing another blueprint or blueprints or paying additional design fees.

HOW MANY BLUEPRINTS DO YOU NEED?

Although a four-set building package may satisfy many states, cities, and counties, some plans may require certain changes. For your convenience, we have developed a reproducible plan, which allows you to take advantage of our Customization Program, or to have a local professional modify and make up to 10 copies of your revised plan. As our plans are all copyright protected, with your purchase of the reproducible, we will supply you with a copyright release letter. The number of copies you may need: 1 for owner, 3 for builder, 2 for local building department, and 1-3 sets for your mortgage lender.

DISCLAIMER

The designers we work with have put substantial care and effort into the creation of their blueprints. However, because we cannot provide on-site consultation, supervision, and control over actual construction, and because of the great variance in local building requirements, building practices, and soil, seismic, weather, and other conditions, **WE MAKE NO WARRANTY OF ANY KIND, EXPRESS OR IMPLIED, WITH RESPECT TO THE CONTENT OR USE OF THE BLUEPRINTS, INCLUDING BUT NOT LIMITED TO ANY WARRANTY OF MERCHANTABILITY OR OF FITNESS FOR A PARTICULAR PURPOSE. ITEMS, PRICES, TERMS, AND CONDITIONS ARE SUBJECT TO CHANGE WITHOUT NOTICE.**

IT'S EASY TO ORDER JUST VISIT EPLANS.COM OR CALL TOLL-FREE 1-800-521-6797

OPEN 24 HOURS, 7 DAYS A WEEK

If we receive your order by 3:00 p.m. EST, Monday-Friday, we'll process it and ship within two business days. When ordering by phone, please have your credit card or check information ready.

CANADIAN CUSTOMERS

Order Toll Free 1-877-223-6389

ONLINE ORDERING

Go to: www.eplans.com

After you have received your order, call our customer service experts at 1-888-690-1116 if you have any questions.

ROOMS FOR LIVING 159

Build Or Remodel Your Dream Home

With HomePlanners Books & Blueprints

Choose Any of These Books— 10% Off the Regular Price

Hanley Wood brings you more choices from leading home plan designers than any other source. Our relationships with leading architects and designers give you access to the best home plans and a more comprehensive selection of home styles.

BOOK SALE!
ALL BOOKS 10% OFF REGULAR PRICE

OUR BEST PRICES EVER!

NEW!
WATERFRONT HOMES
$10.95   NOW ONLY $9.85
ITEM: WF2

ARTS & CRAFTS HOME PLANS
$14.95   NOW ONLY $13.50
ITEM: AC

CRAFTSMAN COLLECTION
$12.95   NOW ONLY $11.65
ITEM: CC

EVERY THING YOU MUST KNOW IN BUILDING YOUR COUNTRY HOME
$14.95   NOW ONLY $13.50
ITEM: BYC

FARMHOUSE & COUNTRY PLANS
$10.95   NOW ONLY $9.85
ITEM: FCP

SOUTHWEST INSPIRATION
$14.95   NOW ONLY $13.50
ITEM: SI

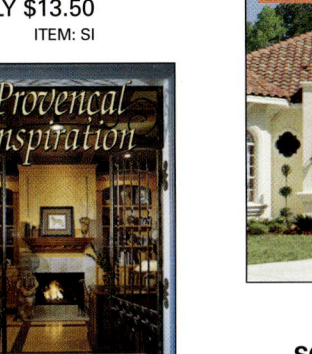

PROVENCAL INSPIRATION
$14.95   NOW ONLY $13.50
ITEM: PN

SUN COUNTRY
$9.95   NOW ON

SOUTHERN COUNTRY HOME PLANS
$10.95   NOW ONLY $9.85
ITEM: SC

MEDITERRANEAN INSPIRATION
$14.95   NOW ONLY $13.50
ITEM: MED

RFL04   **To Order Call 800.322.6797 or visit www.eplans.com**

hanley

Hom